AGRIBUSINESS
AND
INNOVATION
SYSTEMS IN AFRICA

AGRIBUSINESS AND INNOVATION SYSTEMS IN AFRICA

Kurt Larsen, Ronald Kim, and Florian Theus, Editors

A publication sponsored by the World Bank Institute and
Agriculture and Rural Development

THE WORLD BANK
Washington, D.C.

ISBN: 978-0-8213-7944-8
eISBN: 978-0-8213-7945-5
DOI: 10.1596/978-0-8213-7944-8

Library of Congress Cataloging-in-Publication Data

Larsen, Kurt, 1957-
 Agribusiness and innovation systems in Africa / Kurt Larsen, Ronald Kim, and Florian Theus.
  p. cm.
 Includes bibliographical references and index.
 ISBN 978-0-8213-7944-8 — ISBN 978-0-8213-7945-5 (electronic)
 1. Agriculture—Economic aspects—Africa. 2. Agricultural industries—Africa. 3. Agricultural innovations—Africa. 4. Agriculture and state. 5. Food supply—Economic aspects—Africa. I. Kim, Ronald, 1964- II. Theus, Florian, 1980- III. Title.
 HD9017.A2L37 2009
 338.1096—dc22

                                                                    2009014237

Cover photo: Richard Lord
Cover design: Patricia Hord

CONTENTS

BOXES, FIGURES, AND TABLES

Boxes

Figures

Tables

PREFACE

In May 2008, the World Bank Institute (WBI), in collaboration with the Danish Government, Global Development Network, Economic and Social Research Foundation, and other World Bank units, organized a conference in Tanzania on agricultural innovation in Africa. The conference was designed to facilitate learning on key policies, practices, and actors that help enable innovation and technology development in agriculture, with a special focus on agribusiness. The result was to inform various stakeholders on crucial agricultural innovation and technology development issues, and to discuss concrete achievements in these areas with an eye toward replicating and scaling up success in Sub-Saharan Africa (SSA).

To stimulate discussion at the conference, two sets of inputs were prepared in advance: commissioned analytical reports on policies and incentives for fostering innovation within the agricultural sector of the six African countries studied; and innovative case studies of successful technology projects related to agriculture that have been implemented within the six countries.

The objective of the country reports on Ghana, Kenya, Tanzania, and Uganda is to shed light on the dynamics of agricultural innovation, and the impact of public policies and institutions on innovation and value chains, by focusing on agribusiness and by taking the agricultural innovation system concept as the overarching analytical framework.[1] They are based on qualitative interviews with agribusiness leaders with the goal of synthesizing the most vital factors and drivers for agribusiness innovation in SSA.[2] This publication will discuss the major findings of the country reports, link common themes, and distill lessons learned to inform governments, farmers' organizations, non-governmental organizations (NGOs), research institutes, and donors.

It is the hope of WBI and the Agriculture and Rural Development Department of the World Bank, the two sponsors of this publication, that agricultural policymakers, farmers, agribusiness leaders, NGOs, and researchers in other countries can learn from the experiences of these countries. Given the prominence of agriculture in stimulating growth and employment, understanding how to facilitate and promote innovation in rural areas is a critical first step in reshaping and improving the enabling policies, practices, and institutions.

NOTES

1. The commissioned country reports also included Mozambique and Rwanda originally. For the purpose of getting a broader picture, reference will be made to these two reports in some instances. The six country reports in their original versions are accessible at http://go.worldbank.org/MYRNMAD2H0.
2. For a more detailed description of the methodology and the questionnaire for the interviews, see the appendix.

George Owusu Essegbey is the Director of the Science and Technology Policy Research Institute (STEPRI) of the Council for Scientific and Industrial Research (CSIR) of Ghana. He has previously been involved in studies conducted by the World Bank and other international organizations. His research interests are innovation studies, science and technology policy, and enterprise development.

Peter Gillah is a Professor of Wood Utilization and the Dean of the Faculty of Forestry and Nature Conservation at Sokoine University of Agriculture (SUA). He previously worked as a District Forest Officer before joining SUA. He is actively involved in teaching, research, consultancy, and outreach activities. Peter has published extensively in the areas of wood utilization and forestry in general. He has participated in consultancy works in Tanzania and other nations.

Romanus Ishengoma is a Professor in the Department of Wood Utilization, Faculty of Forestry and Nature Conservation at Sokoine University of Agriculture (SUA) in Tanzania. He has been the Component Leader for Institutional Transformation and Capacity Building for PANTIL (Programme for Agricultural and Natural Resources Transformation for Improved Livelihoods) Programme at SUA since 2005. Romanus has published widely in forestry and nature conservation in general and wood utilization in particular. He is active in the regional bodies and networks, and he has participated in a number of national and international consultancy assignments.

Joseph Kere holds a M.Sc. degree in agricultural economics and is currently Deputy Country Representative for Famine Early Warning System Network (FEWS NET) for Kenya. He is also a Research Associate of Centre for African Bio-Entrepreneurship (CABE) Africa. Previously, Mr. Kere worked for the Ministry of Agriculture in the Agribusiness Department and has wider experience in agricultural marketing, including market research, market development, and market information management. His current research interests include markets and food security.

Paul Kibwika is a Senior Lecturer at the Department of Agricultural Extension/Education at Makerere University in Uganda. His research interests include learning for change, agricultural and rural innovation systems, local organizational development, and knowledge management.

Ronald Kim is a Senior Operations Officer with the Knowledge for Development Program at the World Bank Institute and works on learning activities, World Bank education projects, and research. Previously, Mr. Kim was a visiting lecturer, program officer, and director of recruitment at a nongovernmental organization that was part of the Open Society Institute specializing in higher education reform in Eastern Europe and Central Asia. His research interests include innovation policies, higher education, and information and communication technologies.

Florence Burungi Kyazze is a Lecturer at the Department of Agricultural Extension/Education at Makerere University in Uganda. Her research interest lies in agricultural market systems and value chains and in innovations in higher agricultural education.

Kurt Larsen is a Senior Education Specialist with the Knowledge for Development Program at the World Bank Institute. Mr. Larsen works on education and innovation issues in the knowledge economy, including technical assistance to developing countries in their transition towards knowledge-based economies and the delivery of training courses on the knowledge economy and postbasic education. He has more than 20 years' experience as an education and research specialist at the Organisation for Economic Co-operation and Development and in the Danish government. His research interests include higher education, innovation systems, knowledge management, and information and communication technologies in postsecondary education.

John Lynam is an Independent Consultant working on a number of issues in the agricultural sector in Africa. Previously, Mr. Lynam was at the Rockefeller Foundation serving as an agricultural specialist based in Nairobi for two decades. His research interests include agricultural innovation and productivity and the role of the private sector in agriculture.

Joseph Mpagalile is the Coordinator for the Technology Transfer Office and Senior Lecturer at Sokoine University of Agriculture in Tanzania. He worked in the Ministry of Agriculture, Food, and Cooperatives in Dar es Salaam. His main areas of interest include agricultural innovations, postharvest and value chain analysis, and use of renewable energy in agroprocessing.

Michael Philliph Musyoka holds a M.Sc. degree in Agricultural Economics and is currently a Young Professional in Kenya Institute for Public Policy Research and Analysis (KIPPRA). He is a Research Associate of CABE Africa. Mr. Musyoka worked as a research consultant/associate in KIPPRA and in Egerton University Tegemeo Institute for Agricultural Policy and Development. His interests are in quantitative policy analysis, on agricultural trade, poverty, demand analysis, and technology adoption.

Maria Gorretti Nassuna-Musoke is a Senior Lecturer in the Department of Veterinary Surgery and Reproduction at Makerere University in Uganda. Her research interest is in livestock farming systems and interactions between human and livestock systems.

Hannington Odame is Director of the Nairobi-based CABE Africa. He is in the final stages of completing his Ph.D. study on systems dynamics of biotechnology and smallholders in Kenyan agriculture at the Institute of Social Studies (ISS) at The Hague, the Netherlands. For more than 25 years, Mr. Odame has gained wide experience in agricultural knowledge sharing and learning. From systemic and institutional perspectives, he has undertaken policy research and capacity building consultancy assignments for international and local agencies in Kenya and other African countries.

Florian Theus is a Consultant with the K4D Program in WBI, working on issues of agricultural innovation in Africa and the role of education and skills for innovation. Previously, Mr. Theus worked in the Strategy Division of DaimlerChrysler in Beijing, in the Development and Cooperation Section of the European Commission Delegation to China, and CSIS in Washington, D.C. His research interests include innovation systems, agribusiness competitiveness, commodity value chain development, and alternative energy sources for developing countries.

ACKNOWLEDGMENTS

This publication is a joint effort between the World Bank Institute (WBI) and the Agriculture and Rural Development (ARD) Department of the World Bank. WBI and ARD have been collaborating on activities related to agricultural innovation, and the WBI-commissioned country reports incorporate the Agricultural Innovation Systems approach that ARD has actively helped develop and pursue. The book would not have been possible were it not for the generous support of a number of individuals and organizations.

We are deeply appreciative of the major financial support provided by the Danish International Development Agency (DANIDA) that helped us commission the original country reports and synthesis paper, as well as sponsor the conference on agricultural innovation in Tanzania in 2008, where the findings of the reports were presented. Special thanks go to Morten Elkjaer, who participated actively during the meetings organized to discuss the research project, and Hanne Carus for valuable input. We also thank Irish Aid for the additional financial resources it kindly provided.

We want to thank Eija Pehu and Riikka Rajalahti of ARD for their ongoing support and their willingness to provide feedback on previous drafts and issues related to the research project. Ms. Rajalahti was a peer reviewer along with David Spielman of the International Food Policy Research Institute (IFPRI) in Addis Ababa, Ethiopia, and we thank them for their thoughtful and useful comments. In addition, we want to express our thanks to Sue Canney Davison, Kwadwo Asenso-Okyere of IFPRI, and Adewale Adekunle of the Fund for Agricultural Research in Africa for their guidance, particularly during the initial discussions and meetings.

We wish to acknowledge the tremendous efforts of both Bill Saint and John Lynam who were instrumental in helping us design the overall research project, draft and finalize the questionnaire that underpins the country reports, and draft the synthesis chapter. They also offered valuable feedback and advice on individual reports and previous drafts.

We are also very grateful for the support of our colleagues in WBI, in particular Anuja Utz, the team leader in the Knowledge for Development Program who has pushed the innovation agenda within WBI as part of its Knowledge Economy work, and Bruno Laporte, Manager of the Human Development Group in WBI. Thanks also go to Jean-Eric Aubert and Justine White for their comments on individual chapters.

Finally, we would like to thank Anna Socrates for editing the publication and Mary Fisk and Stephen McGroarty for shepherding us through the publication process.

ABBREVIATIONS

AAK	Agrochemicals Association of Kenya
ABS-TCM	American Breeding Society Total Cattle Management
ADB	Agricultural Development Bank
AET	agricultural education and training
AFC	Agriculture Finance Corporation
AFPEC	Association of Fresh Produce Exporting Companies
AGI	Association of Ghana Industries
AGRA	Alliance for a Green Revolution in Africa
AI	artificial insemination
AIS	agricultural innovation system
AIWG	Avian Influenza Working Group
AKEFEMA	Association of Kenya Feeds Manufacturers
AKIS	agricultural knowledge and information systems
ALP	Agricultural and Livestock Policy
ARI	Agricultural Research Institute
ASAL	arid and semi-arid land
ASCO	Ayensu Starch Company
ASDS	Agricultural Sector Development Strategy
BMU	Beach Management Unit
CAADP	Comprehensive Africa Agriculture Development Program
CAIS	Central Artificial Insemination Services
CATIC	China Aero-Technology Import-Export Corporation
CGA	Cereal Grain Growers

COCOBOD	Ghana Cocoa Board
COVE	Corporate Village Enterprise
CPC	Cocoa Processing Company
CSR	corporate social responsibility
CSSVD	cocoa swollen shoot virus disease
CRI	Cocoa Research Institute
DANIDA	Danish International Development Agency
DDA	Dairy Development Authority
DFR	Department of Fisheries Resources
DVS	Department of Veterinary Services
EAGC	Eastern Africa Grain Council
EDIF	Enterprise Development Investment Fund
EMS	express mail service
EPA	Environmental Protection Agency
ERP	Economic Recovery Program
ERS-WEC	Economic Recovery Strategy for Wealth and Employment Creation
ESADA	Eastern and Southern African Dairy Association
EU	European Union
FAAP	Framework for African Agricultural Productivity
FAO	Food and Agriculture Organization
FASDEP	Food and Agricultural Sector Development Policy
FAUEX	Federation of Associations of Ugandan Exporters
FBO	farmer-based organization
FCI	Farm Concern International
FDB	Food and Drugs Board
FINSAP	Financial Sector Adjustment Program
FOCAL	Future Opportunities and Challenges in Agricultural Learning
GDP	gross domestic product
GEPC	Ghana Export Promotion Council
GNAPF	Ghana National Association of Poultry Farmers
GPRS	Growth and Poverty Reduction Strategy
GSB	Ghana Standards Board
HCDA	Horticulture Crops Development Authority
HORTEXA	Horticultural Exporters' Association
HPOU	Horticulture Promotion Organization of Uganda
ICT	information and communication technology
IFAD	International Fund for Agricultural Development
ILRI	International Livestock Research Institute
INDUTECH	Industry and Technology Fair
IPM	integrated pest management
ISF	International Seed Federation
GNAPF	Ghana National Association of Poultry Farmers
KAM	Kenya Association of Manufacturers

KARI	Kenya Agricultural Research Institute
KBA	Kenya Banking Association
KCC	Kenya Cooperative Creameries
KDB	Kenya Dairy Board
KEBS	Kenya Bureau of Standards
KEPHIS	Kenya Plant Health Inspectorate Service
KHDP	Kenya Horticulture Development Program
KMA	Kenya Millers Association
KMDP	Kenya Maize Development Program
KNUST	Kwame Nkrumah University of Science and Technology
KSC	Kenya Seed Company
MAAIF	Ministry of Agriculture, Animal Industry, and Fisheries
MAFC	Ministry of Agriculture, Food, and Cooperatives
MAP	marketing and agroprocessing
MFI	microfinance institution
MFPED	Ministry of Finance, Planning, and Economic Development
MOA	Ministry of Agriculture
MOFA	Ministry of Food and Agriculture
MTTI	Ministry of Tourism Trade and Industry
MVIWATA	Mtandao wa Vikundi vya Wakulima Tanzania (Tanzania Farmers Network)
NAADS	National Agricultural Advisory Services
NaFri	National Fisheries Research Institute
NALEP	National Agricultural and Livestock Extension Program
NARI	national agricultural research institute
NARO	National Agricultural Research Organization
NARS	national agricultural research systems
NBS	National Bureau of Standards
NCPB	National Cereals and Produce Board
NEMA	National Environmental Management Agency
NEMC	National Environment Management Council
NFAST	National Fund for Advancement of Science and Technology
NEPAD	New Partnership for African Development
NGO	nongovernmental organization
NLP	National Livestock Policy
NMB	National Microfinance Bank
NOGAMU	National Organic Movement of Uganda
NSGRP	National Strategy for Growth and Reduction of Poverty
NTE	nontraditional export
PANTIL	Program for Agricultural and Natural Resources Transformation for Improved Livelihoods
PBC	Produce Buying Company
PBFP	Property and Business Formalization Program
PDB	Poultry Development Board

PEAP	Poverty Eradication Action Plan
PEARL	Partnership for Enhancing Agriculture in Rwanda through Linkages
PMA	Plan for Modernization of Agriculture
PPP	public-private partnership
PRSP	Poverty Reduction Strategy Paper
PSI	Presidential Special Initiative
R&D	research and development
RALG	Regional Administration and Local Government
RNFE	Rural Non-Farm Economy
SACCO	savings and credit cooperative
SAP	Structural Adjustment Program
SDDP	Small-holder Dairy Development Program
SIDO	Small Industry Development Organization
SMEs	small and medium enterprises
SOE	state-owned enterprise
SRA	Strategy for Revitalizing Agriculture
SSA	Sub-Saharan Africa
STAK	Seed Trade Association of Kenya
SUA	Sokoine University of Agriculture
SUCICP	Sustainable Uptake of Cassava as an Industrial Commodity Project
TAFOPA	Tanzania Food Processors Association
TAMISEMI	Ministry of Regional Government and Local Governance
TAMPA	Tanzania Milk Processors Association
TAMPRODA	Tanzania Milk Producers Association
TARP	Tanzania Agricultural Research Project
TBS	Tanzania Bureau of Standards
TCCIA	Tanzania Chamber of Commerce, Industry, and Agriculture
TDB	Tanzania Dairy Board
TFDA	Tanzania Food and Drugs Administration
UDAMACO	Umutara Dairy Marketing Cooperative Union
UDSM	University of Dar es Salaam
UFPEA	Uganda Fish Processors and Exporters' Association
UHT	Ultra Heat Treated
WAMCO	West African Mills Company

PART I

Introduction and Main Messages

Ronald Kim, Kurt Larsen, and Florian Theus

"All of us yearn for practical solutions to address the major cause of our continental poverty—an agricultural sector that has languished, but is now poised to be so much more productive and dynamic. We know that the path to prosperity in Africa begins at the fields of African farmers who, unlike farmers almost anywhere else, do not produce enough food to nourish our families, communities, or the populations of our growing African cities."

—Kofi Annan, speech delivered at the launch of the Alliance for a Green
Revolution in Africa (AGRA), 2007[1]

AGRICULTURE AND DEVELOPMENT

The role of agriculture in sustainable development and poverty reduction for the vast majority of developing countries cannot be overemphasized. Forty-five percent of the developing world's population lives in households involved in agriculture—and 27 percent in smallholder households—and most depend on agriculture for their livelihoods. The agricultural sector generates on average 29 percent of gross domestic product (GDP), employs 65 percent of the labor force in agriculture-based countries, and is key to generating overall growth.[2]

The growth strategy for most developing countries should focus on agricultural revitalization for several reasons. Agriculture will provide the largest source of employment in many countries and will remain the lead economic sector of comparative advantage. Moreover, agricultural productivity growth is the primary driver of global poverty reduction, by directly raising farmers' incomes, as well as indirectly leading to the reduction of food prices. In fact, the potential of agricultural growth to reduce poverty is four times greater than the potential of growth from other economic sectors.

Accelerated agricultural growth is broadly transformative: growing farm incomes raise demand for industrial goods, lower food prices, and curb inflation, and overall growth increases the demand for unskilled workers. Rising agricultural productivity can also encourage broad entrepreneurial activities such as diversification into new products, the growth of rural service sectors, emergence of agro-processing industries, and expansion into new markets (Diao and others 2008).

The growing prominence of agriculture exists amid growing concerns about food security, exacerbated by the unprecedented rise in food and fuel prices. Although the situation has improved lately due to the global recession, world maize, wheat, and rice prices remain much higher than in the past. High food prices create daily hardship for more than 2 billion people and threaten to increase malnutrition, already an underlying cause of death for more than 3.5 million children a year. Between 130 million and 155 million people have fallen into poverty in 2007–08, and prices are expected to stay high through 2015 according to the World Bank.[3] Governments and donor communities must act decisively to avert the crisis. As World Bank President Robert Zoellick reminds us (World Bank 2008): "This is not a natural catastrophe. It is man-made and can be fixed by us."

Another reason for the growing awareness of agriculture's critical role is the development community's recognition that the agricultural sector has been ignored for many years. In Sub-Saharan Africa (SSA), where most crop yields have remained stagnant since the 1960s, efforts to bolster yields have been hampered by cuts in research projects and aid programs such as fertilizer distribution. The biggest cutbacks from international donors affected a range of projects from research on pests and crops to programs educating farmers in improved methods and technologies. Sustained annual agricultural productivity led to a reallocation of the focus and resources devoted to agriculture. "People felt that the world food crisis was solved, that food security was no longer an issue, and it really fell off the agenda," notes Robert S. Zeigler, the director general of the International Rice Research Institute.[4] After forgetting that food and therefore human survival are linked unequivocally to agriculture, the development community has "rediscovered" agriculture and is again making it a priority. Most donor governments and international organizations like the World Bank have increased funding dedicated to agriculture-related programs and better understand how to improve donor support to agriculture (World Bank 2007a).

THE SUB-SAHARAN AFRICAN CONTEXT AND FOCUS OF THE BOOK

On the one hand, nowhere is the potential for poverty reduction through the agricultural sector greater than in SSA. On the other hand, recently, nowhere has the food crisis been more damaging in its impact than in SSA—21 of 36 countries experiencing a food security crisis are in SSA, according to the Food and Agriculture Organization (FAO) of the United Nations. Africa is home to most of the world's agriculture-based countries, a region where 70 percent of the people live in rural areas and 90 percent of the rural population depends on agriculture as their main source of income (United Nations Economic Commission for Africa 2007).

Agriculture accounts for over 20 percent of GDP, 15 percent of exports, and about 60 percent of the labor force in the region. In comparison to other regions, productivity levels in SSA for many food products are extremely low and, as a consequence, SSA has not kept pace with a rapidly growing population, and food imports have grown since 1973 when SSA became a net food importer (World Bank 2007a). Higher agricultural productivity is thus a precondition for growth and development in most African countries, and increasing yields is a key to raising incomes and reducing poverty in rural areas. However, the previous two decades were marked by declining government attention to and decreasing donor support for the agricultural sector in SSA. In fact, within the donor community, official development assistance to agriculture in SSA dropped sharply between 1975 and 2005.[5]

Until it raises its agricultural productivity, SSA is unlikely to register significant developmental advances. Recognizing this reality, African governments adopted in 2002 a Comprehensive Africa Agriculture Development Program (CAADP) under the auspices of their New Partnership for African Development (NEPAD). The program states that larger investments in agricultural research, extension, and education systems are required to achieve the targeted increase in agricultural output of 6 percent a year over the next 20 years. In March 2005, the Commission for Africa argued that greater attention should be paid to the economic growth agenda in Africa and recommended higher investments in human resource capacities linked to agriculture, science, and technology, and in tertiary education. Shortly thereafter, participants at a G-8 meeting affirmed this report and committed their governments to provide significant additional funding in support of the report's objectives. In 2006 NEPAD issued a *Framework for African Agricultural Productivity* (FAAP) as a guideline to member states for attaining the goal of 6 percent annual increases in agricultural production. Because of these developments, many of the political and financial elements necessary for a concerted effort to improve African agricultural productivity are being put into place.

In SSA, innovation in agriculture is a powerful means to address relatively low production and add value. Higher agricultural productivity is a precondition for growth and development, and higher yields are a way to raise incomes and reduce poverty, particularly in rural areas, either directly through enhanced smallholder incomes or indirectly through increased employment and wages. Understanding how innovation takes place and developing policies and institutions that facilitate enhanced innovation are thus central to the process of agricultural development on the African continent. But if innovation is central to enhancing agricultural productivity and growth, a number of challenging questions arise: What are effective ways to innovate? How is innovation promoted? What are the roles of the private sector, researchers, and the government? Which policies help or hinder innovation?

This book attempts to address these questions and challenges, by examining how agricultural innovation arises in four African countries—Ghana, Kenya, Tanzania, and Uganda—through agribusiness, public policies, and specific value chains for food staples, high value products, and livestock.[6] Determinants of innovation are not viewed individually but within the context of a complex agricultural innovation system (AIS) involving many actors and interactions. The country reports are based on qualitative interviews with agribusiness representatives about their experiences in this area.[7] The synthesis chapter preceding the country reports presents the main findings of the country reports, links common themes, and distills lessons learned.

A CHANGING LANDSCAPE

Another positive development for SSA and other regions has been a growing acknowledgment that agricultural development has changed over the past 25 years with new markets, innovations, and roles for the state, the private sector, and civil society. In the so-called new agriculture private entrepreneurs, including many smallholders, are linking producers to consumers and are finding new markets for staple food crops and export commodities. This vision of agriculture requires rethinking the roles of producers, the private sector, and the state. Production is done both by smallholders, who are often supported by organizations such as cooperatives, and by labor-intensive commercial farming, which sometimes offers a more productive and efficient model. The state's role, through enhanced capacity and new forms of governance, is to correct market failures, regulate competition, and engage strategically in public-private partnerships (World Bank 2007b).

The overall characteristics of the new agriculture are discussed extensively in the World Bank's *World Development Report 2008: Agriculture for Development*. They include the following (Saint 2007):

- **Increasing complexity:** Agriculturally based rural development must respond to greater demands: livelihoods for the rural poor, environmental sustainability, agribusiness development, uncertainties of global warming, and new cross-cutting issues such as food safety, biofuels, and ecotourism.
- **Networked knowledge:** Information and technology are no longer located in a single source such as a university or research center; thus innovation requires interactive collaboration among various possessors of knowledge, often located at widely dispersed sites.

- **Rapidly advancing technological frontiers:** The results of public and private research and development present fresh social and economic opportunities, but also raise new questions about a society's relationship with science and the governance of science. Issues range from intellectual property rights to the ethics of genetically modified crops.
- **Global links:** Local production and livelihoods are increasingly connected through international value chains to global preferences, trade standards, and phenomena such as climate change and animal disease outbreaks.
- **Competitive advantage linked to capacities for knowledge application:** Innovation capabilities based on accessing, adapting, and applying worldwide knowledge are becoming a main source of economic competitive advantage in the 21st century. As a result, country economies can no longer compete solely on the basis of natural resource endowments, cheap labor, or advantages associated with particular locations.
- **Increasing pace and nonlinearity of change:** This global economic network composed of diverse stakeholders, multiple partners, and shifting actors is accelerating the pace of change with unpredictable nonlinear consequences. Contributing to this dynamic are the more rapid transmission of ideas and the wider set of interactions that the Internet now facilitates among technologies, markets, and policies.

A number of examples illustrate how some SSA countries have sparked their economic performance through the adoption of approaches associated with the new agriculture, where mutually supporting, often knowledge-intensive innovations can assist a country's agricultural producers to move up the value chain in various markets. Some examples include cut flowers in Kenya, fish exports in Uganda, the dairy industry in Kenya, pineapple production in Ghana, coffee cultivation in Rwanda, and banana production in Uganda. The new agriculture offers a developing country the possibility to exploit its latecomer status to close the gap with developed countries in particular commodities or subsectors through the application of more knowledge-intensive and market-driven production technologies. Farmers and commercial producers may benefit especially if they can diversify their production into higher-value products, enter new markets, or take advantage of partnerships.

AGRICULTURAL INNOVATION SYSTEMS

Different approaches to promoting agricultural innovation have emerged since the 1980s. The period before the mid-1980s emphasized the creation of national agricultural research systems (NARS) to strengthen research at the national level and encourage technology transfer and invention. In the 1990s, this approach changed to the pluralistic agricultural knowledge and information systems, (AKIS), which emphasized greater client participation and financing, technology adoption and adaptation, and knowledge exchange mechanisms.

More recently, the AIS approach incorporates major agents such as universities, firms, and other organizations that can tap into the growing stock of global knowledge, assimilate and adapt knowledge to local needs, and create new technology and products. Borrowing some valuable ideas from the more general innovation systems approach, AIS recognizes that many types of innovation—related to technology, new organizations and partnerships, processes, products, and marketing—can take place at any time in different places within the overall system (see box 1.1 for a diagram of AIS). The role of strong and connecting institutions and actors is significant—promoting innovations in agriculture requires coordinated support to agricultural research, extension, and education, while fostering innovation partnerships and links along and beyond agricultural value chains, and enabling agricultural development. The new agriculture, with its increasingly complex agricultural markets, networked knowledge, and a competitive advantage linked to capacities for knowledge application, emphasizes institutions, coordination, and improved links between main actors of the innovation system.

Within the changing agricultural context, AIS emphasizes technology and knowledge generation and adoption rather than strengthening research systems and their outputs. At the same time, it looks at the totality and the whole range of actors and factors needed for innovation and growth and assumes that innovations derive from an interactive, dynamic process that increasingly relies on collective action and multiple knowledge sources at diverse scales. AIS builds on the premise that interactions within a sector are more inclusive because they leverage the collective resources of different actors, including the private sector, civil society, and farmers' associations. Building the innovative capacity of the diverse actors, including agricultural education and training systems, must be done in a coordinated and context-specific way. Eventually the objective of the AIS approach is to identify opportunities and binding constraints as the first step in designing more effective support and investments (adapted from Rajalahti 2008).

AGRIBUSINESS, VALUE CHAINS, AND PUBLIC POLICIES

In its most basic form, AIS is an interactive network of diverse actors. The interplay among value chains, public policies, and agribusiness is of special interest and importance in the country reports. With their focus on multidirectional links and key organizations and actors along the value chains of different agricultural subsectors, the reports reveal and analyze crucial aspects of AIS and determinants of innovation. The reports focus on the entire value chain rather than concentrating on one specific component, which has been the traditional approach to this kind of research (Berdegué, Biénabe, and Peppelenbos 2008). These value chains include the full range of activities from the initial production of a commodity to its end use, such as cultivation, storage, processing,

Box 1.1 A Conceptual Diagram of an Agricultural Innovation System

Informal institutions, practices, behaviors, and attitudes
Examples: Organizational culture; learning orientation; communication practices

Agricultural value chain actors and organizations

- Consumers
- Processing, distribution, wholesale, retail
- Agricultural producers (of various types)
- Input suppliers

Bridging institutions

- Political channels
- Stakeholder platforms
- **Agricultural extension system**
  public sector
  private sector
  civil society
- Cooperatives, contracts, and other arrangements

Agricultural research and education systems

- **Agricultural education system**
  primary/secondary
  post-secondary
  vocational/technical
- **Agricultural research system**
  public sector
  private sector
  civil society

General agricultural policies and investments

Links to political system

Agricultural innovation policies and investments

Links to science and technology policy

Links to international actors

Links to other economic sectors

Source: Spielman and Birner 2008; adapted from Arnold and Bell 2001.

distribution, and marketing. Value chains are gaining greater prominence in nearly every developing country and often represent one of the few options for local firms and suppliers to access larger markets and innovative technologies (UNCTAD 2007:20).

The AIS approach implies that innovations can arise at any point of the value chain as the result of mediated or coordinated interactions among different actors. Thus, the appearance of innovation does not necessarily depend on any specific government role or action. Nevertheless, because public policies directly influence the national competitiveness of firms and the health of value chains, the innovation system requires a comprehensive and complex set of pro-innovation agriculture, trade, science and technology, finance, and education policies. Well-crafted and coordinated public policies may facilitate, steer, and reinforce innovation by providing incentives and structures for individuals, companies, and institutions to innovate.

In addition, improving AIS in SSA benefits the commercial production of food staples, livestock, and high-value crops by smallholders and, where applicable, commercial farms. The successful commercial exploitation of new domestic and regional market opportunities and food security strategies in the quest for higher income and profits, increased production of better products, smallholder integration, and rural poverty reduction relies on the adaptive and innovative capacity of various actors in the agricultural landscape. Many new agricultural activities and products emerge when private entrepreneurs respond to new market opportunities. Farmers and commercial producers may benefit especially if they can diversify their production into higher value-added products and if they can expand their adaptive capacity to exploit those new market opportunities in both staple food and high value commodity subsectors. Accordingly, agribusiness is increasingly seen as the locus where innovation can have a widespread and profound economic and social impact.

Agribusiness provides the inputs, expertise, and services needed for farm production and the markets for farm products. It also provides employment and entrepreneurial opportunities in rural and urban areas and contributes to the growth of micro- and small enterprises though the establishment of market links. As the key interface between markets and rural households, agribusiness firms are the key actors involved in linking agriculture to industry (OECD 2007:112). Moreover, in many developing countries, agribusiness often fills the vacuum caused by the retreat of inefficient state-supported operations in delivering essential input and marketing services. Agribusiness also responds to opportunities growing out of the liberalization of economies and globalization of trade. Although the growth and development of agribusiness depend largely on private sector initiatives, public policies are essential in creating and facilitating an enabling environment.

In summary, the country reports detail interplay within AIS, involving commodity value chains, agribusiness, and public policies. By closely examining different actors and their interactions within the context of each country's specific circumstances, the book identifies main messages that are critical from a policy perspective. The following section articulates and elaborates upon these messages.

MAIN MESSAGES

In spite of their differences, the agribusiness innovation country studies of Ghana, Kenya, Tanzania, and Uganda share commonalities and point to some important conclusions and policy implications about agribusiness innovation, commodity value chains, and public policies. The country studies also analyze broader innovation processes within the agricultural sector while providing a more in-depth understanding of the drivers and constraints of innovation, particularly within agribusiness interactions and specific markets. What lessons can we distill from the main themes of the studies? What can policy makers, research institutes, donors, nongovernmental organizations (NGOs), farmers' organizations, and others learn about policies, institutions, and strategies that nurture innovation in the agricultural sector, especially related to agribusiness?

The main policy messages addressed in greater detail in chapter 1 are included here:

1. **Evolving domestic and regional markets offer new opportunities for agribusiness and farmers, including, potentially, staple food sectors; they complement opportunities in export markets and substitutes from imports as drivers for innovation.**

   The rise of new domestic and regional markets offers new opportunities for agribusiness and farmers to sell their products and raise incomes, supplementing or replacing production for export markets when the transaction, investment, and compliance costs are too high for participation. These markets display a remarkable degree of innovation; therefore innovation strategy should not focus solely on overseas export markets. Instead, programs and initiatives should focus on the evolving domestic and regional markets.

   The staple food sector has the potential for growth, innovation, and poverty reduction. The country studies point to the paradox that the relative gains from agricultural production for economic growth and poverty reduction are greatest in those subsectors such as staple food where value chains and marketing systems face the greatest challenges and where the state has to spend high resources for development. Policy makers face difficult choices in the allocation of scarce resources and the timing of further liberalization.

2. **Innovation in formal markets requires significant adaptation, coordination, and collaboration.**

   The country studies suggest increased innovation is underway in SSA value chains, as a reaction to export markets and evolving local and regional markets as well as a delayed response to the market liberalization of the

1990s. This adaptive process to both pull and push factors depends on the local economic context and the particular characteristics of the value chain.

The entire value chain is critical: The need to maintain grades and standards within the value chain, not only in export markets but also in evolving domestic and urban markets, drives innovation in agribusiness.

Coordination is a key to success: Quality assurance, driven by the search for competitive advantage within domestic markets or access to export markets, in turn requires coordination along the value chain, starting at the farm all the way through to the consumer. Moreover, coordination is necessary to assure continuity of supply, as well as efficiency in the assembly and bulking process of some commodities.

Organizational innovation has proliferated: Coordination has led to vertical integration and collective actions by agribusinesses, most often initiated and enacted at the agroprocessing stage of the value chain. These, in turn, precipitate organizational innovation, especially in markets with higher profit margins such as dairy, horticulture, or coffee. In those formal markets, outsourcing to smallholder farmers by large growers and exporters has become a viable option as smallholders become better organized and supported by private sector extension and input supply. Technical innovation is usually associated with complementary adaptive organizational innovation.

3. **Context-specific public sector programs and the prospect of higher profit margins are crucial to integrating smallholder farmers into more innovative formal markets.**

Most smallholder farmers, and particularly poor rural farmers, do not participate in the formal value chains discussed in the country studies. Rather, smallholders tend to be limited to informal markets for such commodities as raw milk, unrefined sunflower oil, or maize grain.

Although innovations are already taking place in these informal markets, they rarely lead to significant improvements in profits and incomes. From a public policy viewpoint, the question is how to strengthen innovation processes in these value chains so that they present a real opportunity for the rural poor to escape poverty and regular cycles of food insecurity. The challenge is how to integrate smallholder farmers into formal markets, especially in staple food subsectors. The public sector plays an important supporting role in making inputs affordable by lowering the transaction costs of market access and supporting producer organizations that will achieve economies of scale. The state also can provide and facilitate coordination in staple food markets, which in many cases have not yet been taken over by the private sector.

Context-specific programs and sufficient profit margins are critical. Failed initiatives in a variety of countries to open new markets by introducing new technology and adapting supply and organizational systems suggest that technology must be appropriate to the specific context. Further, push strategies and initiatives are only successful if markets offer sufficient profit margins for agribusiness. Similarly, sufficient profit margins in export and regional markets are drivers for innovation by the private sector and farmers. SSA, with insufficient infrastructure, long distances, and medium-term climate change effects, faces additional challenges in increasing the productivity of staple foods.

4. **The structure, quality, and dynamics of the agricultural innovation system drive agribusiness and the agricultural sector.**

   Successes in value chain innovation and agribusiness production depend critically on the whole AIS structure, and they are highly context specific. The value chain focus of the country studies provides a useful organizing principle for identifying the key actors in the production-to-consumption process. However, to understand the forces of innovation and the reasons behind lagging or leapfrogging agrarian economies, the country studies demonstrate that the AIS structure and dynamics, coupled with land and climatic characteristics, determine innovation and production outcomes. Neither potential profit margins in new markets nor the regulations for entering export markets were sufficient to transform a subsector into a productive, innovative, and competitive growth engine. Instead, the specific interplay of all actors and institutions, conditioned by industry characteristics, transport conditions, policies, and the enabling environment, determine the level of innovation and competitiveness that emerged.

   The most successful subsectors created synergies by combining market-based and knowledge-based interactions and strong links within and beyond the value chain. The context of a specific subsector determines whether a combined or independent public sector and agribusiness effort can best provide services and coordination, and transmit knowledge. Conversely, weak patterns of interaction among important actors create the most significant bottlenecks to innovation, including the ineffectual relationships between public research institutes and companies or between extension institutions and farmers.

5. **The state needs to build institutional capacity, align investment priorities with wider economic strategies, and provide more access to finance, particularly in rural areas, to create a functioning enabling environment for agribusiness innovation.**

   Policy formulation and investment priorities in the agricultural sector must be linked to wider agricultural and economic development strategies. The state can play a pivotal role in SSA in providing public goods to address market failures, especially in seed and staple food markets, when the private sector is unable to provide goods and services. The country studies suggest a number of areas where insufficient quality and capacity significantly weaken the whole AIS and the enabling environment, and therefore inhibit strategies to boost production and innovative capacity. Investment in transport, energy, and education infrastructure are among the most urgent priorities.

The state needs to build institutional capacity to provide a functioning enabling environment for agribusiness innovation. The AIS framework, according to the country reports, emphasizes the critical role of the enabling environment for innovation. The reports indicate, however, that the different actors in the innovation system rarely benefit. The lack of effective enforcement or implementation of standards and certification systems or other supportive governmental policies hinders agribusiness efforts to compete in export markets with higher profit margins.

In the absence of effective state implementation capacity, agribusiness establishes its own enabling environment. In some cases, primarily in high value commodity value chains where higher profit margins served as an incentive, the private sector proved to be remarkably innovative in its ability to create its own system of self-regulation and self-financing, sometimes facilitated by the state and/or NGOs.

The state should strive to close those gaps, and, in the event of scarce resources, legitimize and support private sector institutions for quality management and regulations enforcement. The country studies show as well that SSA needs drastic changes in public sector management and capabilities as well as agricultural research and educational institutions.

Another important aspect of the establishment of an enabling environment is that the private and public sectors need to provide more access to finance for agribusiness, particularly in rural areas. For agribusiness, limited access to finance coupled with an insufficient transport infrastructure and education system are the most common barriers to innovation. Innovative financial services provision in SSA lags behind innovation in other service areas. High risks, the uncertainty of collateral, and high transaction costs for smallholder farmers or community-based processors have limited the extension of financial services into rural areas. The country studies provide some examples of innovative financial instruments that overcome those challenges, such as the expansion of micro-credit banks and savings and credit cooperatives (SACCOs) into rural areas, as well as warehouse receipt systems and credit schemes offered by agribusiness organizations. Effective training programs for bank personnel to evaluate the risk and creditworthiness of clients must accompany innovative loan and credit schemes.

6. **To promote innovation, the public sector could further support interactions, collective action, and broader public-private partnership programs.**

Supporting and strengthening interactions and links: The country studies suggest that, from a public sector perspective, improvements in AIS policy design, governance, implementation, and the enabling environment will be most effective when combined with activities to strengthen innovation capacity. Success stories where synergies could be created by combining market-based and knowledge-based interactions and strong links within and beyond the value chain point to an innovation strategy that has to be holistic in nature and focus, in particular, on strengthening the interactions between key public, private, and civil society actors.

Scaling up of collective action and agribusiness organizations: Both formal markets and infrastructure in SSA put a premium on organizational innovation for agribusiness, especially in high value and cash crop subsectors, after the post–liberalization public sector retreated to play a more regulatory and facilitating role while agribusiness took over the value chain, leaving coordination to the processing industry, in some instances aided by NGOs. On both the processing and the production level, cooperatives and other organizations are pivotal for achieving critical mass, economies of scale, and credit scheme organization. The country studies stress further support to collective action organizations.

Public-private partnerships (PPPs) must be strengthened and extended beyond the traditional field of research and development (R&D): As the country studies suggest, the traditional view of public-private partnerships focusing mainly on R&D should be replaced by a broader notion of PPPs that extends to advisory, extension, and other support services. Partnerships are critical to ensure that agribusiness demands will be heard by the public sector, which often plays a supply function. In the absence of the public sector's capacity to perform finance, extension, training, and regulations enforcement functions on its own in SSA, PPPs may provide a possible solution. The country studies show collaborative government and private sector programs that successfully provided farmers and agribusiness with the necessary training, demonstration sites, information, technical capacity, and inputs to increase their adaptive innovative capacity and raise the volume and quality of their agricultural products.

NOTES

1. Text of the complete speech is available at the AGRA Web site at: http://www.agra alliance.org/.

2. Data from the *World Development Report* 2008 (World Bank 2007) and the World Bank Web site.

3. World Bank Web site 2009, http://www.worldbank.org/html/extdr/foodprices/.

4. Quoted in Bradsher and Martin (2008).

5. Although funding for agricultural research and development is perhaps the best investment that a country can make—the average internal rate of return for 700 agricultural research and development projects from developing countries was an impressive 43 percent—budgets for agricultural research and development declined in half of the countries of Africa over the past 20 years (World Bank 2007b: 14).

6. The commissioned country reports also included Mozambique and Rwanda in the original phase. To present a broader picture, occasional reference will be made to these two reports in some instances. The six original country reports are available at http://go.worldbank.org/MYRNMAD2H0.

7. For a more detailed description of the methodology and the questionnaire for the interviews see "Appendix: Survey Questionnaire."

REFERENCES

Arnold, Erik, and Martin Bell. 2001. *Some New Ideas about Research and Development.* Copenhagen: Science and Technology Policy Research/Technopolis.

Berdegué, Julio, Estelle Biénabe, and Lucian Peppelenbos. 2008. "Innovative Practice in Connecting Small-Scale Products with Dynamic Markets." Draft 2, Sustainable Markets Group, London.

Bradsher, Keith, and Andrew Martin. 2008 "World's Poor Pay Price as Crop Research Is Cut." *New York Times,* May 18.

Diao, Xinshen, Shenggen Fan, Derek Headey, Michael Johnson, Alejandro Nin Pratt, and Bingxin Yu. 2008. "Accelerating Africa's Food Production in Response to Rising Food Prices: Impacts and Requisite Actions." IFPRI Discussion Paper 825, International Food Policy Research Institute, Washington, DC.

OECD (Organisation for Economic Co-operation and Development). 2007. *Business for Development: Fostering the Private Sector.* Paris: OECD

Rajalahti, Riikka. 2008. "Agricultural Innovation Systems: Why this Approach." Concept Note prepared for the World Bank.

Saint, William. 2007. "How National Public Policies Encourage or Impede Agribusiness Innovation: Studies of Six African Countries." Concept Note prepared for the World Bank.

Spielman, David J., and Regina Birner. 2008. "How Innovative Is Your Agriculture? Using Innovation Indicators and Benchmarks to Strengthen National Agricultural Innovation Systems." ARD Discussion Paper 41, World Bank, Washington, DC.

UNCTAD (United Nations Conference on Trade and Development). 2007. *The Least Developed Countries Report 2007.* New York: United Nations.

United Nations Economic Commission for Africa. 2007. "Africa Review Report on Agriculture and Rural Development." United Nations Economic Commission for Africa, Addis Ababa.

World Bank. 2007a. *World Bank Assistance to Agriculture in Sub-Saharan Africa: An IEG Review.* Washington, DC: World Bank.

———. 2007b. *World Development Report 2008: Agriculture for Development.* Washington, DC: World Bank.

———. 2008. "Action, Resources, and Results Needed Now for Food Crisis, Zoellick Says." Press Release 2008/349/EXC, World Bank, Washington, DC, June 4.

CHAPTER ONE

Value Chains, Innovation, and Public Policies in African Agriculture: A Synthesis of Four Country Studies

John Lynam and Florian Theus

This synthesis chapter and the country studies[1] for Ghana, Kenya, Tanzania, and Uganda aim to illuminate the dynamics of innovation, including the impact of public policies and institutions on innovation and value chains, by focusing on the perceptions of agribusiness and by using the agriculture innovation system (AIS) concept as an analytical framework. The country reports were first prepared for the World Bank Institute conference on agricultural innovation in Dar es Salaam held on May 12–14, 2008, to kick-start action plans on national agricultural innovation systems. The country studies are based on qualitative interviews with agribusiness to discover the most vital factors and drivers for agribusiness innovation in Sub-Saharan Africa (SSA).[2] The synthesis chapter discusses the major findings of the country studies reports to inform governments, farmer organizations, nongovernmental organizations (NGOs), and donors of policies and practices for innovation promotion.

The Context of Agricultural Innovation in Sub-Saharan Africa

Two basic principles define innovation system theory, namely, that innovation is context specific and that innovation occurs within an interacting system of diverse actors, where value chains are a particularly important organizational form (Elliot 2008). The private sector in SSA increasingly drives innovation, although the public sector and NGOs support innovation through research on public goods, whereby market conditions, policies, and institutional arrangements provide the incentives and the competitive pressures to drive private sector investment.

Table 1.1 identifies four principal factors that—according to current innovation theory—provide the context for the types of innovations and pressures for innovation within the AIS framework for the six countries examined in the country studies.

Land/labor ratios. Innovation theory sees land-labor ratios (which are determined by population density within the agricultural sector) as a principal determinant of the pressures for and types of innovation. Innovation through relative factor prices is motivated by a search for the means to compensate for the most limiting factor. Thus, in land-scarce agricultural sectors such as Rwanda, agricultural producers seek to maximize returns from the land, whether through increasing yields or shifts to higher value crops. Land-extensive economies, such as Mozambique, develop the dual strategy of promoting large-scale operations while simultaneously trying to better integrate smallholders into the market economy. Smallholder innovation in land-extensive economies is particularly problematic given the lack of incentives to apply inputs, especially where transport infrastructure is limited.

Postconflict society. Half of the countries examined in the country studies are recovering from the effects of civil war in recent decades. The economies of postconflict societies can produce mixed effects on innovation. The risks of continued political instability are often too high to justify innovative investments. However, new political leadership—a factor in three of the countries

Table 1.1	Four Principal Contextual Factors for Innovations and Value Chains within Six Sub-Saharan African Countries					
Factor	Kenya	Tanzania	Uganda	Ghana	Mozambique	Rwanda
Land/labor ratios	Dense	Extensive	Medium	Medium	Extensive	Dense
Postconflict society	No	No	Yes	No	Yes	Yes
Landlocked geography	No	No	Yes	No	No	Yes
Open economy	Partial	Mostly	Open	Open	Mostly	Mostly

Source: Authors.

studied—often leads to a new economic openness, as entrenched economic interests have been eliminated in the conflict and rebuilding efforts can create an economic surge. Where good governance in a postconflict society coincides with relatively intensive agriculture, such as in Rwanda and Uganda, the environment can be favorable for innovation.

Landlocked geography and open markets. The other two factors—namely, whether the country is landlocked, with markets protected and isolated by higher transport costs, and whether the country pursues an open trade policy— determines what new economic opportunities international markets will provide and how much international competition domestic producers will face. Ghana, because of open geography and economic policy, faces the full pressures of international competition, especially in the major coastal cities that are in easy reach of U.S. and European exporters. The southern region of Mozambique faces similar competition, especially given Maputo's proximity to South African exporters. In contrast, high transport costs to ports insulate the urban markets (apart from Dar es Salaam) of the other countries from foreign competition.

These four factors create quite different market contexts within which innovation takes place across the various countries studied. In general, the prevailing economic market conditions determine the structure of value chains and influence the innovation system. In the early stages of structural transformation, agricultural sector growth (the stage of most SSA economies) rather than urban-led growth (the stage of most Asian economies) determines the potential for market expansion and competitive pressures that drive innovation. Drivers of innovation such as changes in relative factor prices, changing output markets, and competitive pressures to economize on input use (Haggblade, Reardon, and Hyman 2007) are generally associated with an expanding agricultural economy. During the study period, growth in agricultural gross domestic product (GDP) was relatively strong across the different countries. Moreover, as Haggblade, Reardon, and Hyman (2007) note, "technological change in the Rural Non-Farm Economy (RNFE) occurs most frequently in rapidly growing rural regions; growing local demand in the rural economy seems to increase opportunities for market growth and attracts new entrepreneurial activity and investment as well as demand for higher-value goods and services." Thus, even within a country, innovation strength is directly related to the strength of the rural economy, whether reinforced or constrained by marketing systems.

Preliminary Generalizations from the Country Reports

This chapter's synthesis identifies three preliminary generalizations arising from the country studies. First, whether the source of innovation is either from the public or private sector varies from stage to stage, within the value chain as well as across sectors. Technical change at the farm level in the four countries stems primarily from public sector research with farmer organizations and extension services as intermediaries—apart from horticulture and floriculture—although over the last decade, private seed companies have been developing their own research capacity. In contrast, technical change in nonfarm activities, especially agroprocessing, has primarily relied on the private sector, either through indigenous innovators or the adoption of techniques from foreign sources. Processing of local products, such as cassava flour or Rwandan banana beer, generally relies on relatively small-scale plants that have evolved from home processing efforts. Specialization has emerged within processing households through a range of indigenous innovations. Larger-scale processors, especially in horticulture and dairy, primarily borrow or adapt from foreign companies as the principal sources of innovation. The role of agroprocessing in generating innovation through the value chain will be discussed in greater detail.

Second, the process of market liberalization in the 1990s in SSA has had a mixed effect on agricultural innovation. The green revolution started in many countries before market liberalization, and has, to a significant degree, resulted from the introduction of improved varieties and technologies that used higher levels of inputs, with either increased availability in kind or better access to credit and extension services. The most significant impact of market liberalization is the public sector's relatively rapid withdrawal from marketing boards and state-supported (parastatal) processing companies where prices were controlled, often to the disadvantage of farmers—and the development of functional markets that provide sufficient incentives for private sector investment and innovation. The country studies suggest that the effects of the market liberalization process—completed in some countries to a greater degree than in others—has only relatively recently brought about significant investment and innovation in some commodity value chains. For example, the Ugandan fish industry has benefited from exposure to international markets through enhanced opportunities for innovation and the development of a competitive advantage in these markets. In contrast, intense competition has undercut further innovation in Ghana's cassava starch market. This synthesis chapter will further explore the market conditions that both drive and constrain innovation.

Third, African markets have quite different structural features across different value chains and in different economic contexts. These differences are created by the relative distribution of road and transport infrastructure, by the relative distance to principal urban or export markets, and by the relative efficiency in assembling commodity supplies and supply chain management and coordination.

With the emergence of urban supermarkets and the hotel industry in Uganda and elsewhere, supermarkets that serve the poorer peripheries (Weatherspoon and Reardon 2003) and local niche markets have developed to serve specific customer preferences and provide new opportunities for farmers, agribusiness, and value chain evolution. The spread of supermarkets in southern and eastern Africa beyond middle-class urban areas into smaller towns and less-affluent areas means the extension of supermarket procurement systems involving purchase consolidation, a shift to specialized wholesalers, and stringent quality and safety standards (Weatherspoon and Reardon 2003)—all challenges for small producers. Nevertheless, the evidence is still too inconclusive to project the scope of this trend—other studies indicate that supermarkets will not account for more than 10 to 20 percent of urban fresh fruit and vegetable markets (see, for example, Tschirley and others 2004). The traditional marketing system might continue to characterize African agricultural markets in the near future.

Lack of market integration is a key constraint in developing efficient value chains in the context of the high costs of "distance to market." The high costs of distance results in market fragmentation and reliance on local markets as outlets for marketable surpluses from smallholders, especially for staple food commodities. Figure 1.1 illustrates the differential evolution of value chains in terms of formal and informal market structures.

There is a high degree of vertical coordination in formal value chains, often without reliance on markets as the vehicle for organizing transactions. Informal value chains, on the other hand, are characterized by reliance on hierarchical market structures where small volumes are traded on a cash basis and aggregated through a significant number of transactions, resulting in high marketing margins and significant inefficiency (Fafchamps 2004). Thus innovations are more likely to be transmitted through the more vertically integrated value chains in an effective and equitable manner,[3] even though there is a countertrend to outsource production to smallholder farmers in those subsectors such as horticulture in Kenya that have become better organized and

Figure 1.1   Input and Output Market Structures Serving African Farmers

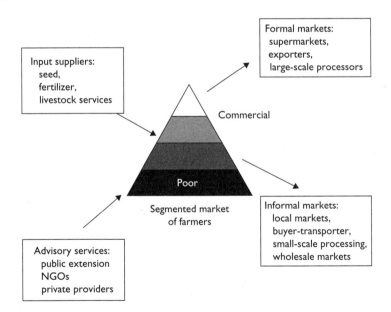

Source: Authors.

supported by private sector extension and input supply (Nyambo and Nyagah 2006). However, because formal markets tend to be private sector driven, farmers in more productive agricultural regions with more resources and better access to markets are more likely to participate in such value chains, while poorer farmers in more marginal areas have access to only informal markets. Market development and innovation that focus only on formal markets can result in quite inequitable growth.

AGRICULTURAL INNOVATION SYSTEMS IN SUB-SAHARAN AFRICA: THE VALUE CHAINS

The cassava and staple food value chains in Ghana and Tanzania and the coffee high-value chain in Rwanda, as well as the cocoa sector in Ghana, offer examples of innovation and coordination across an entire value chain.

Innovation and Coordination across a Value Chain: A Comparison of High-Value Cash Crop and Staple Food Value Chains

The cases of Ghana and Rwanda are similar in that they involve government facilitation of private sector innovation in the value chain, but there are also differences. Rwanda successfully adopted new techniques and organizational forms within the coffee subsector, whereas improvement of Ghana's cassava value chain is still emerging. Comparing the cases of Rwanda and Ghana supports the basic argument that successful innovation within a commodity subsector has a higher probability of success if the market structure has the characteristics of a formal marketing chain as described above. Success is more likely because margins tend to be higher in formal market chains, and coordination across the value chain is more easily implemented. The country studies generally show that although widespread innovation is much more difficult in the staple food sector, the potential impacts on rural poverty and smallholder growth dynamics are much greater in this subsector (Diao and others 2008). A theme of this book is that understanding innovation within the formal marketing chains will help inform potential innovation in the staple food sector to the benefit of smallholders.

High-value cash crop chain: The coffee value chain in Rwanda. Increased net margins are critical to successful development and innovation in any marketing chain in that net margins create incentives for entrepreneurship and investment. Table 1.2, comparing Rwandan coffee and Ghanaian cassava, illustrates how the structure of the market chain sets the constraints within which innovation takes place.[4] The key to Rwanda's success was capturing the increased returns from exporting high-value coffee to European and American markets, which pay a premium for quality products. The value added from maintaining quality through the value chain was the core organizing feature of the innovation process. However, maintaining quality required significant

Table 1.2   Factors within the Value Chain That Conditioned Innovation in Rwandan Coffee and Ghanaian Cassava

Conditioning factor	Rwanda—coffee	Ghana—cassava
Coordination mechanism	NGOs, reinforced by consortium of actors	Government program and a starch factory
Margin and investment Incentive	High-quality premium for export market	Competition in export and domestic markets
Raw material supplies	Supplies with increased farmer prices	Competition for roots with domestic food market
Grades and standards	Well-defined with appropriate certification	None
Processing scale	Medium-sized with potential for coverage	Large-scale with high assembly costs
Farmer technology	New varieties and management practices	High starch varieties but still below global market and unacceptable in local gari market
Farmer organization	Effective cooperatives	Ineffective farmer associations due to competition with gari market

Source: Authors.

coordination at all stages of the Rwandan coffee value chain from farmer to processing to exportation. This coordination was not provided through the vertical integration of a single firm—how most export horticulture is organized—but rather through the interventions of specialized NGOs supported by government and donors through the PEARL project.[5] The coordinating role of NGOs is apparent in other value chains studied in this book, particularly in the dairy sector.

The NGOs promoted a range of technical and organizational innovations, including new varieties and changes in harvest routines at farm level; timely bulking, sorting, and transport processes; aggregating floating, washing, and depulping functions in new wet processing stations; cupping to grade the coffee and control quality at the processing station; forming farmer cooperatives to develop financial and management skills; and developing links to premium coffee buyers in the United States and Europe.

A principal point in the Rwandan case is that no one innovation would achieve the quality objective; all were necessary. For example, NGOs had previously introduced a wet processing station, but it had little impact without the links throughout the rest of the value chain.

Moreover, changes in government policy were critical preconditions to the entry of the private sector. The Rwandan country study characterized the prior situation in the coffee market as follows: "almost 500,000 coffee producers, each one producing and processing [the commodity] differently, all selling to one buyer (Rwandex), without any incentive for higher quality" (Rukazam-buga 2008). The government withdrew from coffee marketing, allowing exporters to transact business abroad without controls. However, the government established a new entity, OCIR-CAFÉ, which was charged with "elaborating a national coffee policy, establishing quality standards and classification systems, and issuing certificates of origin and quality." The government facilitated credit lines through the banking system for the wet processing stations, which were owned by both private investors and cooperatives. The government thus moved from a managing role within the coffee sector to a facilitating role for private sector investment and quality assurance.

High-value cash crop chain: The cocoa value chain in Ghana. As a cash crop for an export market, the cocoa value chain in Ghana shares important characteristics with the coffee chain in Rwanda. Similar to coffee, the value added from maintaining quality through the cocoa value chain was the core organizing feature of the innovation process. The emphasis on maintaining sufficient quality to meet export requirements necessitated significant coordination from the farmer to the processing companies to export. In fact, farmers were an important link in the chain, because they not only cultivate and harvest the crop, they process and dry the cocoa for the buying companies. In contrast to Rwandan coffee, the state-established Ghana Cocoa Board (COCOBOD) provides the extensive support services that cocoa production requires, as well as the major coordination of the whole cocoa value chain. COCOBOD dominates the value chain by making input supplies available to farmers. Further various COCOBOD subdivisions, such as the Quality Control Division, the Seed Production Unit, and the Cocoa Research Institute have established links to farmers and provide extensive support (Essegbey 2009). As a consequence, considerable innovations at the primary production level improved agronomic practices that enhanced crop yields, monitored against disease, and improved seed quality.

Although the state still provides support services, facilitates disease control, and ensures quality, it has adopted a policy of deregulation for the cocoa industry. Until recently, the Produce Buying Company (PBC) of COCOBOD held a monopolistic market position for purchasing cocoa. After deregulation and the introduction of competition, several additional PBCs have evolved out of transportation or haulage companies that now also act as purchasing companies (Essegbey 2009). Deregulation has introduced an element of vertical integration in the value chain. Cocoa industry liberalization combined with COCOBOD's state-initiated coordination role has led to increased private sector involvement and more than doubled cocoa production from $500 million in 2002 to approximately $1,200 million in 2006 (Essegbey 2009). Predominantly smallholder farmers have realized much of these gains. Government initiatives that trigger phenomenal yield increases have important implications for farmers' income and Ghana's foreign exchange earnings. However, very little of these earnings came from processed cocoa production; the percentage of value addition in the cocoa processing area was only 20 percent of total production volume, and policy implementation has not kept up with growth and poverty reduction targets (Essegbey 2009).

Staple foods: The cassava value chains in Ghana and Tanzania. The cassava value chain in Ghana represents a policy focus on agroindustrial development of the most important staple food crop in the country (Essegbey 2009). The strategy for cassava production has three principal strains: facilitating innovation in cassava processing (the SUCICP project[6]), developing cassava into a new export product through the creation of a starch factory, and improving yields through the adoption of new varieties with support from the International Fund for Agricultural Development (IFAD).

Cassava differed from staple grain crops in that there was little previous government involvement in cassava markets—except indirectly through policies on direct substitutes—and the policies represented a relatively new government interest in cassava cultivation. Moreover, the strong domestic market for cassava led to the development of a cheap and convenient substitute, gari,[7] for urban markets. The domestic market was being served through many transactions through the value chain and a large number of participants at each stage operating on very thin margins. The technological and process-related manufacturing innovations in small-scale processing companies were coming from outside sources, particularly food research institutes collaborating with international partners (World Bank 2006a).

To a certain extent, the interventions in Ghanaian cassava, like those in Rwandan coffee or Ghanaian cocoa, focused on value addition in the marketing chain. The important differences were the low margins and lack of a coordinating mechanism throughout the cassava value chain. Cassava in Ghana is an example of an inappropriate government investment in agroprocessing to develop export markets when the economics did not justify intervention into the export market. The production of cassava for industrial starch processing came under the Presidential Special Initiative (PSI) on Cassava Starch, which organized the cassava farmers into an association and assisted with cultivating large acres. As in the case of the cocoa farmers, the PSI supplied production inputs and extension services to the farmers, and the farmers received a contractually guaranteed price for selling to the processing company. The addition of processing capacity to develop another market with a different price and cost structure complicated the value chain; this was not the case with cocoa and coffee. Further, Southeast Asian cassava starch was highly developed, strongly competitive, and closer to principal markets. For these reasons, cassava producer organizations were less effective, there were fewer incentives for farmers to adopt new technology, and the availability of raw materials varied with price fluctuations in the local gari market. Moreover, the plant location was not optimal, being too close to the Accra urban market and gari supplies. The necessary conditions for successful innovation across the value chain could not be put in place given the price structure and lack of market coordination.

Conversely, small-scale gari production and processing for the local markets increased. Gari processing innovation was determined by the (im)balance between potential efficiencies achieved by switching from hand to mechanical grating and pressing and by offsetting costs. Conditions favorable to efficiency— a shift from household processing to specialized processing units, the price of labor, the potential for economies of scale—were not offset by countervailing costs in root assembly and bulking. As with maize flour, improving the processing improved the quality, which increased potential incomes through urban market stratification. A few food companies began to refine and appropriately package gari for local markets. As with Rwandese coffee, price premiums for quality drove innovation. Haggblade and others (2007) focus on the potential innovation in the processing of traditional African foods such as cassava and locally brewed beer, where processing innovations originate either from the local private sector or the few public sector research institutes on food technology. A World Bank study (2006a) explored how to best facilitate this innovation process in Ghana and concluded that an interactive process between the private sector and public sector research institutes was the most effective. The World Bank's finding is corroborated in the Ghana country study, which examines the active role of the domestic Food Research Institute in transmitting knowledge and technologies. For example, the Food Research Institute has set up a model of an integrated processing plant to demonstrate processing technologies from cassava grinding to water removal and starch roasting. Some positive results are already visible even though the innovations have not yet been fully adopted (Essegbey 2009).

The cassava value chain in Tanzania, where cassava is the second most important staple food after maize, displays similar characteristics—lack of a predominant coordinating mechanism and weak organization within the value chain—to the Ghanaian cassava value chain. In contrast to Ghana's public sector support and organizational efforts to steer the industry toward starch production for export markets, Tanzania's innovations were mostly private sector driven, with little government support. As in the Ghanaian case, research institutes helped educate producers about processing technology management; the development of new cassava varieties and products, such as cassava chips and fortified flours; and assistance in acquiring better processing tools such as chippers, graters, and presses. Similar to Ghana, processing companies also shifted from manual to equipment-based processing technologies. Cassava producers also indirectly benefited from the government's effort to boost the livestock production and meat processing industries because it opened a new market for cassava as animal feed. The livestock market, in turn, encouraged small-scale cassava processing companies to develop new products and processing techniques, such as blending cassava with maize flour.

Although increased profit margins through new processing techniques and the development of the new animal feed market stimulated innovation, weak value chain organization and the lack of a predominant coordinating mechanism in Tanzania hindered more widespread innovation.

High-value Horticulture Value Chains and Innovation in Sub-Saharan Africa: Ugandan Vegetables, Especially Green Peppers, and Kenyan Tomatoes

The horticulture sector has become important for many Sub-Saharan countries. Horticulture is attractive to small farmers because vegetable crops yield higher and more regular returns and are more labor intensive (Sivakumar 2007), but horticulture requires more informed management. The example of Kenyan green beans demonstrates that the poverty rate among smallholder horticulture farmers is lower (28 percent, compared to more than 80 percent) than that among nonhorticulture farmers (World Bank 2006b). The income of horticultural farmers is 1.5 to 3.0 times higher than that of nonhorticulture farmers (World Bank 2006b). By the late 1990s, SSA's export of fresh produce was approximately equal to two-thirds of the export value of traditional agricultural commodities (Tyler 2006), and exports of fresh produce have grown since then.

Horticulture is characterized by high-income elasticity of demand—as people get richer, they eat more fresh produce, particularly more prepared, packaged, "added-value" produce (Tyler 2006; Musyoka and others 2006[8]). Kenyan tomatoes and Ugandan vegetables illustrate how new market demand has increased in recent years, both in the European export markets and in domestic markets. The development of new markets and market segmentation has altered and expanded value chains, fostered innovation, and demanded new coordination. The rise in supermarkets has rapidly transformed the African food retail sector in recent years. These new retail formats for fresh produce are displacing the more traditional small shops and public markets (Weatherspoon and Reardon 2003). Supermarkets are also starting to penetrate rural areas, a trend that has advanced furthest in Kenya, but is also visible in Tanzania and Uganda. Supermarkets are driving innovation, even though their percentage in the overall market system should not be overstated—supermarkets constitute only approximately 10 to 20 percent of the total urban fresh produce market (Tschirley and others 2004).

Vegetable value chains grapple with inherent limitations and challenges, even as they drive certain innovations. The country studies—Kenyan tomatoes and Ugandan green peppers—attempt to explain the current impediments to further innovation and growth. First, vegetable value chains need a higher capital outlay and require access to low-cost credit. Second, export markets require higher food safety and quality standards and greater crop management knowledge. Third, because of higher production costs and risks, producers require access to crop and weather insurance. Fourth, product perishability and extreme price volatility create higher market risks, requiring more access to better information and coordination along the processing and retailing stages of the value chain (Sivakumar 2007).

Quality inputs (seed, fertilizer, and chemicals) constitute the largest cost element in tomato production; consequently, innovations improving access to high-quality and affordable seeds and chemicals have been necessary for growth. Input companies have intensified their extension services, including the provision of credit, to farmers. The problem lies often more in the weak links between input companies and research institutes to develop inputs that best meet the needs of the producers. The challenge of product perishability has triggered two farm-level innovations in cooling and processing. The need for cooling facilities, especially in remote areas, led to the unsuccessful introduction of the charcoal cooler in Uganda; its high investment costs can only be recouped through higher export volume (Kibwika, Kyazze, and Nassuna-Musoke 2008). Innovations in farm-level processing have been more successful in increasing product diversity. In Kenya, the government policy of promoting common farmer interest groups has led to greater farm-level processing for agricultural commodities, including tomatoes. Large-scale processing companies have also broadened their product portfolio to include tomato paste and tomato sauce.

Most locally produced vegetable products, including almost 70 percent of tomatoes (Odame, Musyoka, and Kere 2008), serve local markets. The Uganda and Kenya country studies indicate a recent increase in this percentage for two reasons: First, producers divert more of their products to local markets when investments to meet stringent export regulations are not profitable, given the high cost of establishing sophisticated value chains. Second, the local demand for horticulture products is increasing in Africa, because of the rise of supermarkets and consumers with new preferences. Supermarket procurement systems for produce suppliers require intermediaries in wholesale supply markets that can meet supermarket supply needs (Weatherspoon and Reardon 2003). Increasingly, actors in the value chain benefit from investments and innovations in value-added operations such as processing, packaging, labeling, certification, and product diversification that respond to the segmentation of perishable vegetable markets.

Export standards for the European Union (EU) market, particularly in pesticide residue amounts, traceability requirements, and packaging and processing standards, have hastened the shift to more integrated value chains dominated by larger exporters. At the same time, there is a countertrend to outsource production to smallholder farmers by growers and exporters in those subsectors, such as horticulture in Kenya, that become better organized and supported by private sector extension and input supply (Nyambo and Nyagah 2006). Exporters with strong links to end markets and producers through contractual agreements and ownership play a significant coordinating role along integrated value chains, particularly in Kenya, but elsewhere as well. In Uganda, for example, exporters extend credit for inputs to farmers, and the loans are then recovered after the sale of their produce. Exporters also provide training and technical support to farmers by exporters (Kibwika, Kyazze, and Nassuna-Musoke 2008). In some instances, exporters themselves assume integrated producer and transporter roles across the value chain to overcome bottlenecks in financing, information, quality assurance, and risk management.

Exporters and producers have formed umbrella organizations to coordinate along the value chain to meet the increasing demands of export markets. The Horticulture Promotion Organization of Uganda (HPOU) coordinates among exporters, provides a forum for dialogue with the government, and assists agribusiness in lobbying efforts. Increasing market segmentation, however, fragments umbrella organizations into more specialized associations. In Uganda, for example, National Organic Movement of Uganda (NOGAMU), the organization for producers of organic products, coordinates and streamlines activities for emerging organic niche markets (Kibwika, Kyazze, and Nassuna-Musoke 2008).

In Kenya, no umbrella coordinating institution along the horticultural value chain exists. Coordination appears to be spontaneous and localized (Odame, Musyoka, and Kere 2008). Processing and retailing agribusinesses offer extension services to tomato growers to ensure a stable supply, and input suppliers coordinate producers. NGOs have room for local coordination at different stages of the value chain, in particular linking smallholder farmers and producers to the local tomato market.

Because of continued public-private dialogue, the Kenyan government has implemented regulatory changes, invested in education and skill development, and improved infrastructure to make the horticulture industry more competitive (Webber 2007). A public-private partnership between agricultural input suppliers and the Kenyan government through the Kenya Horticulture Development Program (KHDP) recently launched a greenhouse tomato farming program, including greenhouse kits and demonstration sites, to address the issues of seasonality and input intensity, improve marketing and production, and increase smallholder incomes (Odame, Musyoka, and Kere 2008). The initiative promotes a shift to a less labor-intensive, more cost-effective, and more environmentally sustainable method of farming that avoids crop protection chemicals. If this method is adopted on a larger scale in other sectors, it could lead to substantial leaps in production, output, and incomes. Experience and time will demonstrate whether potential production increases and cost reductions outweigh higher capital costs and irrigation facilities.

Government and public policy play an important role in increasing quality standards development and enforcement demanded by the export market, as well as increasing local supermarket consumers. Although the Kenyan government disengaged from overall coordination in agriculture after market liberalization, it remained involved with developing regulations and standards. The Horticulture Crops Development Authority (HCDA) of Kenya initially traded vegetables, but eventually switched to a more facilitative function; it now focuses solely on certification schemes (Webber 2007). Over the last decade, HCDA has developed a regulations scheme supported by enabling investments to make the horticulture sector more competitive.

Still, the Kenyan tomato industry and other SSA horticultural sectors require additional investment to serve export and high-end local markets, while competing with cheaper imports (Odame, Musyoka, and Kere 2008). Horticulture sectors elsewhere in SSA that are still developing regulation regimes and value chain organization face considerable challenges to become profitable. For example, in the vegetable industry in Uganda, stringent regulations led many smallholder farmers to drop out of the value chain, thereby adversely affecting other actors along the chain (Kibwika, Kyazze, and Nassuna-Musoke 2008). Evolving domestic market segmentation and agribusiness responses to the challenges of competition and profitability in horticulture include novel ways of organization and coordination, such as large growers and exporters outsourcing production to smallholders or more vertically integrated value chains.

Innovation in Fish and Livestock I: The Ugandan Fish Industry and the Ghanaian Poultry Industry

The livestock market is similar to horticulture in that development is driven by high income elasticity of demand and growing domestic markets. Livestock, like horticulture, suffers similar perishability problems and carries potential health risks for consumers, thus necessitating quality assurance systems. Unlike horticulture, however, the livestock export market is highly restricted, and the domestic market is affected by "cheap" imports. However, smaller-scale farmers in SSA may find it easier to intensify small livestock production than staple food or cereal production, as small livestock production is more able to access microfinance investment, thus overcoming the coordination problems in finance (Dorward, Kydd, and Poulton 2008). In contrast to horticulture, which often requires large-scale production to achieve critical mass and economies of scale to effectively compete in world markets, small-scale livestock production is better suited to subsistence agriculture and serves primarily domestic markets because it faces stiff competition from foreign large-scale producers. The lack of transportation infrastructure and problems in maintaining and enforcing quality standards have impeded growth and explain in part why SSA lags behind in livestock production.

In contrast to poultry and other livestock, the SSA fish industry, specifically in Uganda, has been growing in recent years. The Ugandan fish exporting industry, after the lifting of EU bans on all major African fish exporters, has capitalized on high European demand for Nile perch due to few substitutes in the market (Ducker and Webber 2007). The Ugandan fish industry is an example of how compliance with EU regulations can drive innovation and improvements in the value chain to make an industry competitive for export markets. Pressures on both the demand and supply sides of the market provided major

AGRIBUSINESS AND INNOVATION SYSTEMS IN AFRICA

incentives for actors throughout the value chain to face the problem of quality management. As Kiggundu (2006) concludes, "the Uganda fisheries case supports the observation that investment in technology change may not occur through invisible market forces. These forces were simply too weak to induce technological upgrading. Standards imposed on producers exerted strong pressure to upgrade and stimulated the emergence of an improved support system." The EU (which had an interest in a thriving Ugandan fish industry), the Ugandan government (which could pressure producers to adhere to standards), and finance sources (which came up with creative financing possibilities) provided assistance to enable technological and organizational innovation in the processing industry (Kiggundu 2006).

Effective operation of the fish value chain requires a quality assurance system for fish handling from the beginning of production to marketing. The Ugandan government has tried to streamline its fish regulatory and inspection systems through the Department of Fisheries Resources (DFR), which has formally become the sole authority for fish safety issues. However, DFR does not have the capacity to control fishermen at the production level or at remote landing sites (Kibwika, Kyazze, and Nassuna-Musoke 2008). Collective action organizations at the production and processing states fill in the gaps. The processing industry has a formal organization, the Uganda Fish Processors and Exporters' Association (UFPEA), to control fish quality, foster partnerships with government, and train quality managers. Further coordination is necessary because of competition between different exporters. The government's weak enforcement of fishermen and producers has led to the formation of community-driven committees at landing sites and Beach Management Units (BMUs) that register boats and equipment. Comanaged, power-sharing arrangements have shifted responsibilities from the national state to local communities. BMUs are now in charge of most of the regulatory activities on Lake Victoria and the landing sites (Kibwika, Kyazze, and Nassuna-Musoke 2008). Other parts of the value chain are still lacking substantial coordination. Traders and transporters lack collective action, and coordination is sporadic. To ease financial constraints, traders occasionally provide boats and fishing equipment to the fishermen, who contract to sell their catch to that particular trader, who then can provide a guaranteed volume to a processor.

The fish industry in Uganda has become one of the fastest growing nontraditional export sectors (Kibwika, Kyazze, and Nassuna-Musoke 2008), mainly due to technology adaptation and quality management, but fish production has also expanded because of new domestic and regional market opportunities. As in the case of horticulture products, the emergence and growth of supermarkets and hotels in Uganda has created local niche markets with specific customer preferences requiring some form of primary processing. With fishermen filleting the fish, processing and value addition starts at the landing site and is directly marketed to supermarkets and hotels (Kibwika, Kyazze, and Nassuna-Musoke 2008). Commercial fish ponds, which continue to exist, offer new market opportunities as well, with fish farmers selling the nutrient-rich pond water after the harvest to farmers who use it as fertilizer. This innovative use of pond water illustrates how new rising markets such as supermarkets and organic food drive innovations and alter value chains across agricultural sectors.

The spillover effects of new market growth especially benefit poor agricultural labor. Ugandan fish farmers at the production level benefit from value-addition and new markets. At the production and the processing level, fish farmers are developing residual by-products, such as fish pond water, and selling them to new markets. Processing companies have also developed new by-products, such as turning processed fat into affordable cooking oil, which is then sold locally to poor families. Both the supply and demand sides benefit as processing industries diversify their product portfolios and markets and local consumers have access to more affordable products. Further integration and efficiency of the value chain will depend on public investment in cold storage facilities at the processing level and in transportation infrastructure, as well as further enhancement of the production-level quality management. Moreover, although the export market has provided incentives for collective action around quality assurance, it has been far less effective in sustainable management of fish stocks at Lake Victoria.

In comparison, the preconditions for developing an export industry based on poultry and associated products such as cheap feed grains for the feed concentrate industry do not yet exist in Ghana's poultry subsector or elsewhere in SSA. Ghana also lacks sufficiently integrated and efficient value chains for domestic commercial markets. Most poultry production is small scale and channeled through traditional markets, where long-established marketing arrangements have developed without public marketing institutions. Most producers are relatively poor and depend heavily on income from livestock production, either consuming what they produce or selling surpluses to buy food staples (Hazell 2007). Production also occurs in remote areas with high transport and transaction costs. There are few formal information systems for market prices, and markets are poorly integrated.

Liberalization of the poultry market has precipitated the evolution of modest, small-scale commercial production. As in the fish industry, external pull factors—in this case, the spread of avian influenza, which threatened to wipe out the industry—led to quality management innovations. The governments immediately established the Poultry Development Board (PDB) to monitor poultry quality, as well as to advise the government on regulation and policy issues (Essegbey 2009). As a consequence, the poultry industry revived. The PDB's coordination and quality management functions are limited. The business organization of commercial poultry farmers, Ghana National Association of Poultry Farmers (GNAPF), which lobbies for government policies (Essegbey 2008), provides little coordination. In the formal value chain, veterinary providers, feed suppliers, and transporters provide support services. These secondary service providers, in collaboration with research institutes, have innovated in improving sanitary services such as vaccines, disease management techniques, and improved feeds for poultry.

However, to achieve critical mass in a large-scale industry, viable institutions for quality management and disease control, as well as links and coordination, are needed to successfully compete with cheaper poultry imports flooding Ghana as a result of market liberalization. For the livestock and poultry industries, the main concern is becoming more competitive against imports in the domestic market rather than producing for export markets. Low animal productivity and the high costs of disease control are further disincentives for livestock production (for example, cattle in Mozambique) (Hazell 2007). Given the insufficient economies of scale, small-scale, subsistence poultry production offers less profit potential and less incentive for private sector investment and coordination than in the fish industry.

The two industries illustrate the different dynamics, structures, and incentives associated with a mainly local subsistence product (poultry) and a major export commodity that is irreplaceable on the world market (Nile perch). In the Ugandan fish industry, agribusiness as well as production-level fish farmers take on the governmental role of facilitation, value chain enhancement, coordination, and quality management controls, whereas the livestock industry, such as Ghana's poultry industry, relies on government and NGOs, including agricultural research institutes, to provide extension services, insemination, veterinary services, quality management, and better animal breeds as well as animal feeds. Liberalization has brought about modest commercial production, but given the structure of the livestock industry and competition from cheaper imports, the country studies suggest a more prominent governmental role is necessary to bring about innovation.

Innovation in Fish and Livestock II: Dairy in Rwanda, Kenya, and Tanzania

The dairy industry in Rwanda, Kenya, and Tanzania has demonstrated significant private sector innovation, although it was not equally distributed across the industry of each countries. The cases suggest that market liberalization of the diary industry, when coupled with a growing domestic demand for the commodity and sufficient margins across the value chain, can create the conditions for potential growth. The dairy industry was liberalized in Kenya in 1991, in Tanzania in 1996, and most recently in Rwanda. In Kenya, the parastatal Kenya Cooperative Creameries, continues to operate, but has not radically affected market competition. With market liberalization, new private companies have taken over governmental roles, especially on the processing level and in input and support services, and established competitive dairy sectors. In Tanzania and Rwanda, the private sector dominates, although the Rwandan government gives significant support to the principal dairy cooperative, Umutara Dairy Marketing Cooperative Union (UDAMACO).

Dairy products, like horticulture and livestock, have a high income elasticity. Increased demand, in Kenya and the other countries studied, from increased urban population and income, has been a force behind increased innovation and production, which has led to increased returns. The high demand for fresh milk in all three countries has not been affected by competition from imports of powdered milk. In fact, imports into Rwanda have fallen over the last four to five years as domestic milk production has increased. However, the formal market for pasteurized milk in Rwanda is centered on the city of Kigali, a much smaller market than those in Kenya and Tanzania.

The value chain for dairy is relatively complex, since it accounts for the health, quality, and perishability of milk, its seasonality, and the logistics of daily assembly and bulking within a "cool" chain. These aspects apply to formal marketing channels. Processing in all countries constitutes only a small portion of fluid milk production. The Rwandan and Tanzanian local raw milk markets are more important, where farmers have effective access to collection points and cooling plants and where rural consumers do not have to pay the cost of shipping the milk to urban processing plants and then to rural consumption points. However, distance, as in Tanzania, can inhibit producers of raw milk from reaching markets, and cooling and collection facilities are not always close to the sites of production.

The informal and formal marketing structure for dairy products is a natural function of the high costs of distance in SSA, but it is also influenced by organizational responses to the distances. Expanding farmer access to formal marketing channels depends on innovative responses to distances and maintenance of the cool chain. Expansion is often limited to large integrated dairy units. Large-scale dairy companies in Tanzania have overcome bottlenecks in the value chain, such as the transport to the cooling facilities, by carrying out and coordinating all aspects of the value chain themselves (Mpagalile 2008). Supply chain management is more efficient where information shared within the integrated value chain eliminates costly demand shortages or oversupply. Rural consumption, however, will continue to rely on the informal, raw milk market, and the urban poor will be better served by peri-urban production.

Dairy expansion in Kenya and Rwanda differs from the Tanzanian example. In Kenya and Rwanda, growth in formal marketing of milk relies principally on smallholder production, and bulking in regions with sufficient production density. Higher production in turn justifies the investment in a cooling center, before delivering milk to a larger processing plant, usually located relatively close to the end market. Organizational innovations to reduce transaction costs and maintain quality control were particularly important in achieving greater efficiencies in the value chain. Farmers who were unable to deliver milk to distant processor collection centers and lacked sufficient economies of scale created cooperatives to collect at central locations, deliver, and sell milk on their behalf. The cooperatives, especially in Kenya, have vertically integrated the value chain and added value higher up the value chain through processing and creating new products such as yogurt (Odame, Musyoka, and Kere 2008).

Farmer cooperatives have also developed support service systems—particularly in veterinary services, artificial insemination, improved forages, and increased production of feed concentrates—to ensure smallholder participation in formal milk markets. Kenyan and Rwandan farmer cooperatives have provided financial services through savings and credit cooperatives (SACCOs). One milk processor has set up a revolving credit program among the firm, feed manufacturers, and farmers, so that farmers receive feed on credit and the dairy pays the feed supplier upon receipt of the milk from the farmers. In Tanzania, milk processing firms are experimenting with organizing transport from collection centers to processing plants. One Tanzanian firm has contracted with private haulers to do the collection. Another firm is expanding its own fleet of vehicles to ensure effective distribution, rather than collection (Mpagalile 2008).

The access to new markets is driving innovation. The spread of supermarkets beyond urban areas shortens distances for transporting perishable products, provides new outlets for products, and triggers innovations in product development, packaging, and batch numbering in cottage industries. In Kenya, the expansion of veterinary services and shops as a consequence of liberalization policies allows drug companies to enhance their distribution systems and provide farmers with improved access to drugs. The Kenyan dairy sector illustrates how innovative access to finance and credit can spur private sector expansion and more integrated and efficient value chains. Some examples are village banks that extend services to rural areas, contractual agreements with dairy processors that recover credit given to dairy farmers, and the easing of collateral requirement (Odame, Musyoka, and Kere 2008). Innovations that ease farmers' access to finance have resulted in increased private sector investment, and consequently in increased dairy production and more efficient value chains.

Milk processing plants primarily coordinate within the market chain, but cooperatives increasingly are creating links between farmers and input suppliers and engaging in value addition higher up the value chain. International NGOs that specialize in dairy development have aided cooperatives, but their role is more to facilitate the organization of farmers, to ensure access of farmers to appropriate productivity-enhancing techniques, and to expand the number of smallholders who can participate in the dairy value chain. NGOs provide a public good, as individual dairy firms face a free-rider problem in investing in downstream smallholder organizations. NGOs working closely with the industry in the development of smallholder dairies have replaced the public sector in providing advisory services and initial "cow" capital to initiate production.

The government's role in the initial stages of dairy subsector development is significant, for example, Rwanda's financial support for a large milk processing plant to foster growth in the dairy industry. However, with a healthy private sector following effective market liberalization, the public sector can withdraw to a more regulatory role such as the Kenyan government's creation of the Kenya Dairy Board (KDB) (Odame, Musyoka, and Kere 2008). The KDB has partnered with private laboratories (Ana-labs) to provide a diagnostics for milk quality, although the pricing of milk by grades has not yet developed. The Tanzanian Dairy Act of 2004 is an example of an ill-devised system and lack of clear governance that has led to overregulation and has hindered innovation and competitiveness (Mpagalile 2008).

Compared to staple foods and cash crops, the dairy subsector suggests a pattern of more evolutionary innovation at various points across the value chain, but without the requirement of coordinated innovation throughout the value chain. Incremental change is a response to high investment costs for smallholder participation in the market and the critical production density needed to justify private sector investment in collection points and cooling stations. The informal domestic market acts as an effective outlet for milk production in regions that are establishing a dairy industry. Smallholder integration into formal markets creates the cash flow incentives for further investment in enhanced production and productivity at the farm level and further scale increases at the bulking and processing level.

A major issue in the informal market, particularly in Tanzania and Kenya, is whether rural areas can be integrated into more formal market structures. Where the costs of bulking are too large to justify integration into the milk market, it might be possible to incorporate cottage industries for butter and cheese. Pilot integration attempts in northern Kenya have yet to reach a scale that would invite private sector investment in quality improvement, marketing, and packaging. Over time, the question of integrating all dairy producers into the formal marketing system depends on further investments in transport infrastructure and further refinement of grades and standards. Eventually price incentives rather than government regulations drive quality maintenance throughout the value chain.

The Importance of the Processing Scale in the Innovation Process

Farmers and commercial producers benefit from diversification into higher-value, knowledge-demanding, and innovative products in formal international and domestic markets. A greater demand for a skilled and educated workforce may reduce poverty as a consequence. Countries in SSA therefore have aimed, through liberalization reforms in the agricultural sector, to integrate smallholders into the formal market economy, to attract investment specifically in processing industries, and to add scale that increases value addition.

Agroprocessing assumes a key role to coordinating the supply, bulking, and marketing of agricultural commodities, and as such leads to organizational and technical innovations. An example from the dairy subsector is the processing businesses that, assisted by NGOs or the government, provide credit to farmers, organize stable supplies of raw products from farmers, and work out contracts with transporters to overcome the distance challenges.

The scale of operation determines innovation potential. Economists suggest that relative factor prices, particularly labor versus capital costs, and the technical underpinnings of economies of scale determine the choice of scale. However, in the context of agriculture in SSA, where transport costs are high and the transaction costs in assembly and bulking from smallholder producers are large, scale economies can be quickly counterbalanced by the costs of ensuring adequate stocks for processing, a common problem in seasonal and predominantly rainfed agricultural systems. Thus, scale economies, especially in horticulture, dairy, and livestock products, must be matched by reverse coordination through the value chain, reinforced through maintenance of product quality. Coordination usually involves some type of farmer organization in land-scarce economies and may involve contracts with large-scale production units in land-extensive economies, often reinforced by vertical integration. The market conditions, especially in the European Union, have influenced a shift, particularly in export crops and products (for example, vegetables and fish), to more integrated value chains represented by larger integrated exporters despite the trend toward smallholder contracting. Large-scale companies with strong links to end markets and producers through contractual agreements and ownership improve supply management through efficient information sharing within the integrated value chain that eliminates costly demand shortages or oversupply. Significant innovation can match appropriate processing scale with ways to maintain quality and ensure adequate raw material supplies at a reasonable cost.

Processing in staple food sectors. In the staple food sector, especially in informal markets, processing is dominated by small-scale operations, many integrated within the farm household, but increasingly within specialized processing units. Expanding markets, such as the gari market in Ghana, drive innovation process in the production, but still at a relatively small scale determined by cassava root perishability and bulk. To meet urban consumers' increasing demand for guaranteed quality, larger food processing firms operating within urban markets further refine the flour. A large-scale starch factory, such as the starch initiative facility in Ghana, has a particularly difficult time operating when it must compete for cassava roots with small-scale gari processors and has little flexibility in organizing assured supply chains.

To justify investments and create sufficient scale, some agroprocessors, such as cassava processors in Ghana, must acquire more generic technologies that go beyond processing a single product such as cassava and can process other foodstuffs, including staple foods and vegetables. As a consequence, these processing companies can participate in different value chains, create sufficient scale and revenues, and expand their role in agricultural markets.

Maize milling in Kenya offers an example of a dual processing structure, where small hammer mills serve rural communities and small towns and large mills provide higher quality flour to urban markets, thus reinforcing the informal and formal marketing systems. The formal market trade at the assembly and transport levels is attempting to enforce grades and standards for maize within the supply chain through the use of moisture meters that ensure storability and reduce fungal attack, but control over grades must usually extend back to the farm level, and sufficient price differentials are necessary to motivate farmer compliance. A warehouse receipt system with incentives for higher grades of maize, as well as farmer organization and quality-assurance training, allows maize smallholders to participate in the formal markets.

The market liberalization of maize in Kenya (and in other countries in eastern and southern Africa) has decreased the retail-marketing margin for maize flour; at the same time, maize flour consumers gain from competition and innovation in flour distribution. With the development of a warehouse receipt system[9] capacity, innovation in the maize marketing system will potentially match innovation in processing, with potential spillover into production technology and insurance of maize quality standards. Informal markets will continue to serve individual farmers with small surpluses and rural maize flour consumers, although the decentralization of large-scale maize milling out of the big urban areas potentially expands the market for quality, sifted flour.

Tanzanian sunflowers offer another example that reverses the usual direction of dual-processing technology with the recent introduction of the small-scale ram press that competes with existing large-scale factories. An NGO, Enterprise Works/Vita, introduced the ram press to Tanzania in 1985. The ram press decentralized processing, with a particular focus on local, rural vegetable oil consumption. When production increases reach a saturation point in the local markets, small-scale producers must compete with larger processors in urban markets, especially in terms of quality and market distribution. An innovative solution to market saturation and high transport costs is the decision to sell oil extracted from village-based ram presses to the larger mills, where the oil is further refined and marketed through the mills' distribution system. Given the high transport costs in Tanzania, producers find it more efficient to transport a less bulky, higher value commodity like unrefined sunflower oil rather than sunflower seeds, which compensates for the lower ram press extraction rate.

In Uganda, local efforts to further refine crude distilled waragi, a local alcoholic, banana-based beverage produced in small, rural distilleries, were unsuccessful. To satisfy urban demand, a large distillery bought crude waragi to further refine it for the urban market; however, it found that the costs of assembly and further refining waragi are high compared to importing alcohol based on sugarcane. Without government intervention to assist distilling companies in acquiring the necessary distillation technology, promoting the beverage nationally, and supporting the value chain in the initial phase, distilling firms could not profit from investment in the technology (Kibwika, Kyazze, and Nassuna-Musoke 2008). As a consequence, imported sugarcane alcohol has now replaced Ugandan waragi in urban markets.

Processing scale of export and cash crops. The Ghanaian government has focused on processing cocoa for export, with mixed results in competing with European marketing and distribution systems. Ghana is attempting to imitate the increasing success of Colombian coffee. Another interesting example is Mozambique's 1995 investment in large, mechanical cashew processing plants, protected by a high export tax on raw nuts (Cardoso de Barros, 2008). Mozambique's factories collapsed in 1999 after the government's revocation of the export tax under a World Bank loan condition. As a result, all raw nuts were exported to India for processing. However, since 2002, firms in Mozambique and also in Tanzania have increased investment in medium-scale processing plants relying more on hand labor. In 2005, the plants in Mozambique competitively processed about 9,000 tons out of a total production of more than 100,000 tons, using a similar technology as the plants in India. In the cashew processing example, relative factor prices determine the choice of scale and processing technique, as innovative solutions are developing.

Processing innovations allow product and market development for residuals and by-products that are being developed and sold to new markets. Here the larger scale allows efficient bulking and distribution of otherwise low-value residues, although in most cases, the by-products are a benefit and not the determining factor of choosing a certain processing technology. Processing companies in the fish industry in Uganda developed new products by processing by-products such as fish fat into cooking oil and selling them locally to poorer communities. Another example is processing vegetables that do not meet export requirements. Processing residuals opens up new domestic markets, creates income for processing industries, and supplies poor consumers with more affordable products.

In summary, agroprocessing is often a key source of both technical and organizational innovation within the value chain. Innovation balances economies of scale in processing and diseconomies in assembly, bulking, and quality control. Domestic markets are most often the principal driver in this process, often as a delayed response to market liberalization. The choice of an appropriate scale depends on the particular characteristics of the value chain and the economic context. The cases of cassava starch in Ghana and large-scale, mechanical cashew processing in Mozambique demonstrate the difficulties in preselecting the most appropriate processing scale and then adapting the supply and organizational systems to them. As innovation theory and examples of failed technologies suggest, SSA does not need the best technology, but rather the most appropriate technology that best fits with local conditions (Elliot 2008).

AGRICULTURAL INNOVATION SYSTEMS IN SUB-SAHARAN AFRICA: BEYOND THE VALUE CHAINS—SUPPORT STRUCTURES AND SERVICES AND THE INTERMEDIARY DOMAIN

Haggblade, Reardon, and Hyman (2007) suggest that growth in the nonfarm rural economy is due to growth in the service sector rather than growth in the processing or manufacturing sector. The service sector includes input supply, financial services, transport, marketing, and advisory services, in addition to health, education, and government services. The country studies do not generally support this assertion because transportation and financial services in SSA are lagging behind; processing is a major force of innovation as well as coordination within the value chain for most agricultural subsectors, yet there are some innovative service sector solutions such as new financial arrangements in rural Kenya. Innovations in finance in particular are pivotal to organizational innovations and links in SSA.

Agglomeration and Innovation in Support Services

Services based on farmer demand and purchasing power in SSA increase growth in the agricultural economy. Two processes are critical to generating growth. The first is supporting farm-level productivity growth from the availability of inputs, extension services, credit, and output markets—what economists call "interlinked markets." All of these services have high transaction costs in smallholder agriculture, particularly given limited transport infrastructure, and are only sporadically available to farmers. The second process involves the economies of agglomeration, a concept principally applied to urban manufacturing—and the more recent globalization of manufacturing and services (Collier 2007). However, it applies to the development of farm services in regional towns (Renkow 2007). The availability of banking and credit facilities reinforces the demand for and supply of farm inputs and advisory services, which then generate growth in production and demand for market services.

Kenya's Central Province and the Kilimanjaro region of Tanzania are examples of interacting and multiplying growth within the local rural economy. The model of input suppliers providing loans and credit to smallholder farmers recovering investments when farmers deliver products has become successful in the absence of access to finance from financial institutions. Economies agglomeration, however, affects the bigger urban areas such as Nairobi in Kenya, where farm services, including the provision of banking and credit facilities, have increased market services, and in some sectors, increased production (Odame, Musyoka, and Kere 2008)

Financial services. Access to finance contributes to growth through promoting entrepreneurship, innovation, and technology adoption. It covers innovation costs, supports incubation, and finances commercialization, as well as connecting smallholder farmers to inputs for production, technology, and knowledge absorption. According to a recent World Bank report (Honohan and Beck 2007), a coherent financial sector policy supports development goals for the SSA, including encouraging the adoption of modern technology and fully exploiting the benefits of organizational innovation and internationalization. At the same time, the private sector and banks must innovate in providing financial services to underserved farmers and agribusiness to alleviate the key constraints in agricultural financing in SSA.

Innovative financial services in SSA have lagged behind other service areas. High risks, the uncertainty of collateral, and high transaction costs for smallholder farmers or community-based processors have limited the extension of financial services into rural areas. Where banks do provide services, interest rates (as high as 15 percent in Uganda) and stringent repayment schedules—attempts to manage risks—have led to conditions that small companies and farmers can hardly meet, and therefore do little to raise capital and finance innovation. Because of loan conditionalities, even microfinance institutions, such as those in Uganda, have limited availability of financial services to agricultural entrepreneurs, much less to farmers. In Kenya, lenders developed an innovative way of providing collateral in the dairy subsector through the introduction of "social collateral," (Odame, Musyoka, and Kere 2008) where groups ensure that any loan obtained by a member is repaid accordingly, and through "chattel collateral," where collateral can be a viable business idea. Success depends on a proper loan evaluation and screening procedure for nontraditional collateral to minimize the risk banks face in financing innovation in SSA. An adequate support system, including the training of entrepreneurs to write business plans, is necessary for innovations to spread and become an integral part of the way commercial banks finance agricultural innovation.

An agroprocessor generally uses farmer credit as a mechanism to secure raw material supplies. For example, export horticulture in Uganda and dairy in Kenya and Rwanda used farmer credit where the timing as well as the reliability of supply are critical to the operation of the business. In Kenya, credit was linked to input suppliers and connected input, output, and credit markets. However, farmer credit arrangements still have to cover transaction costs as do micro-credit schemes. Where there is relatively tight integration between farmer groups and the processor-buyer, transaction costs are reduced and the processor is able to secure its raw material supply. In general, the country studies show that lack of access to financial services is a principal constraint to development, with little innovation in the provision of services.

Kenya is the exception in that financial service institutions have increased services to rural areas and to farmers through the expansion of well-established micro-credit banks, such as K-Rep, into larger rural towns. The growth in the dairy, export horticulture, and tea value chains and the significant increase in the number of SACCOs aided in the expansion of financial services to rural areas. The SACCOs kept transaction costs low and assured collateral by lending to cooperative groups, who then managed the disbursement and repayment with their members.

Cooperative lending has expanded in staple foods, especially where the warehouse receipt system is supported by financial innovations such as factoring. In Kenya, after delivering a product such as maize to an accredited warehouse, a farmer obtains a warehouse receipt that can be used as collateral for short-term borrowing at an Equity Bank to obtain working capital (figure 1.2). The farmer does not need to sell the product immediately to ease cash constraints. Because the market price of maize fluctuates seasonally, farmers can capture the margin from selling at a higher price at peak demand. In Kenya, unlike many other countries that fix prices between harvests, economic policy creates incentives for the warehouse receipt system and thereby introduces an additional financial instrument. The warehouse receipt system allows farmers to extend the sales period of modestly perishable products well beyond the harvesting season. The Kenyan country study and earlier studies (Lacroix and Varangis 1996) demonstrate how correctly structured warehouse receipts provide secure collateral for banks. A warehouse receipt system that comes out of a collaboration between farmers, growers, agribusiness associations, and agrodealers, ultimately reduces the role of government agencies in agricultural commercialization as the private sector is now responsible for purchasing, storing, and disposing of the physical stocks, as well as potentially providing receipts and credit for the producers (Lacroix and Varangis 1996).

Moreover, Kenya has restructured the Agriculture Finance Corporation (AFC), a government-owned financial institution that provides credit to the agricultural sector, but with a past track record of high losses. Not only did the AFC broaden its loan portfolio to include seasonal crop credit, but it also enhanced product delivery through process automation. It developed a financial delivery system geared toward wholesaling financial services, thereby abandoning its former retail model (figure 1.3).

Figure 1.2   How a System of Warehouse Receipts Works

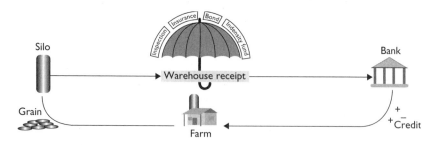

Source: Lacroix and Varangis 1996.

Figure 1.3 Financial Delivery Structure for the Agriculture Finance
Corporation

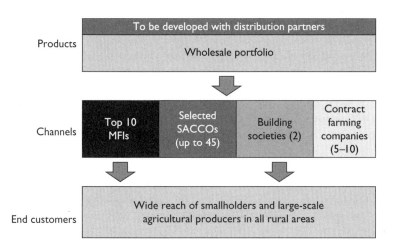

Source: Odame, Musyoka, and Kere 2008.

Possibly the most important innovation is the ability to receive and send money by mobile phone, an innovation instituted by K-Rep and Equity Bank in Kenya in cooperation with the mobile phone carriers. Identification of the sender and receiver is assured, and financial transactions can take place instantaneously across distances without requiring a bank account. This has enormously reduced the transaction costs involved in the financial end of market transactions.

The financial services sector is one of the few sectors where the public sector has failed to provide needed services, and the private sector, because of missing incentives, has only sporadically assumed this role. A common constraint across the country studies, except perhaps Kenya, is the lack of access to financial services and credit within most of the value chains. The private sector does not yet provide effective credit within SSA value chains, and this issue constrains innovation and investment in many markets. Rwanda and Ghana demonstrate the potential role of government in mobilizing private sector credit lines, but such investments need to be appropriately assessed for risk by banks and other financial institutions. Credit guarantees are an increasing incentive for financial mobilization because they spread the risk. Kenya provides an example of innovative financial services with prudent support by the government.

Input Supply and Distribution Networks. The poor transport infrastructure and the associated high costs of trucking have constrained building input distribution networks in SSA that serve smallholders. This situation is problematic in land-extensive rural economies such as Mozambique and Tanzania and in landlocked economies such as Rwanda and Uganda. Kenya, of the countries studied, had the deepest and most dynamic farm input markets, even for bulky low-margin inputs such as fertilizer and feed concentrates. Outside Kenya, stockist networks exist for hybrid seed and veterinary products, where margins are quite high and the products are not so bulky. Moreover, input suppliers tend to locate in areas of high population density, where there is greater demand for inputs because of high potential return on input use and lower transaction costs in serving high population density areas. In Tanzania, input distribution systems are evolving in the Kilimanjaro area.

Possibly the most dynamic growth, at least in eastern Africa, has been in the private seed subsector, especially in hybrid maize and hybrid vegetables in Kenya. The liberalization of the seed industry and the more transparent application of seed testing and certification regulations have spurred growth. However, Kenya was the only country with a functioning parastatal seed-producing firm that has a dominant role in the market and can exploit a competitive advantage. The seed sector is being liberalized within eastern Africa, and seed companies are looking to compete in a regional market. Nevertheless, while downstream seed networks have developed, the return on farmer investment is significantly related to access to fertilizer.

Developing fertilizer networks has proven more intractable outside Kenya. Input supply systems have developed within the value chains of high-value commodities such as dairy and export horticulture. Yet the potential to generate growth through increased productivity in staple food crops remains largely untapped. To a significant extent, increased productivity must build on the synergies inherent in farmer access to credit, improved seed, and fertilizer. Service systems must be independent of particular value chains, through services from small towns where agglomeration economies come into play. Experience elsewhere suggests that extending agricultural services into marginal and high-poverty areas will be unlikely without a basis for generating demand in these areas (Haggblade, Reardon, and Hyman 2007).

Equipment manufacturers. The only equipment manufacturers in the country studies were from Tanzania.[10] The innovation potential of these rural industries is often overlooked. They principally service small-scale processing, usually for local products. Two manufacturers developed equipment for cassava processing and the ram press for sunflower oil. Both were moving to stainless steel to prevent rust and maintain quality where the equipment came into contact with food. Local manufacturing capacity also provides for spare parts, maintenance, and further adaptive design. The two companies in the sample provided a range of equipment and were continually looking for new opportunities and market niches. A noteworthy innovation that exploited economies of scale was the production of more generic processing technologies that enabled manufacturers to sell to a larger number of processing companies from different subsectors and to respond to the demand by processing companies to serve different markets with a more generic technology. Manufacturers interacted with the engineering department at Dar es Salaam University in Tanzania and Makerere University in Uganda, where new designs and other equipment ideas could be tested.

Transporters. Transporting inputs to producers, raw materials to processors, and products to urban markets is one of the biggest challenges in SSA. Transport costs are generally high, exacerbated by the recent rise in fuel prices, and road infrastructure is often poor. Landlocked economies as well as those with a difficult terrain have an even harder time to overcome those challenges. Trucking and transport companies encounter many disincentives. To solve transport problems, large-scale agribusinesses, especially those targeting export markets, integrate transport services into their distribution or collection. In Tanzania, milk processors experimented with organizing transport from collection centers to the plants. One firm contracted with a private trucking company to do the collection. Through the spread of information and communication technologies (ICTs), especially cell phones, transporters have become more responsive and flexible to producers and input suppliers.

Innovations in the Intermediary Domain: Partnerships, Organizations, and Collective Action

The high transaction costs in agricultural value chains in SSA put a premium on organizational innovations. These innovations require cooperation in a context where the search for competitive advantage limits the information and collective action along the value chain. One dominant factor in cooperation and collective action across the country studies is the perceived returns from enforcement of grades and standards. The returns for collective enforcement are most apparent in export markets, such as perishable horticulture and livestock, where lack of compliance effectively limits national participation in that market. The case of Rwandan coffee is another example of collective action to meet higher quality standards, after participation in high-quality markets with significantly higher returns was constrained.

The value chains of export subsectors demonstrate considerable organizational dynamics on the processing and exporting level to provide sufficient coordination. Collective action, business organizations, and umbrella organizations have sprung up as a consequence. The Horticulture Promotion Organization of Uganda (HPOU) coordinates exporters and lobbies government for agribusiness.

With domestic markets evolving, coordination demands grow accordingly and further necessitate collective action, especially for quality management and marketing. The increasing market segmentation causes organizational changes, among them a fragmentation of umbrella organizations. In Uganda, the NOGAMU, the organization for producers of organic products, attempts to coordinate and streamline activities for evolving organic niche markets (Kibwika, Kyazze, and Nassuna-Musoke 2008).

With new demands by consumers and inadequate public-sector enforcement of regulations and standards, organizational arrangements have arisen to provide information, interaction with government, and increased industry self-regulation. Ugandan fish is an example of the increasing movement to self-regulation:

> To ensure competitiveness of Uganda fish exports, UFPEA, an umbrella association for fish processor and exporters (comprising 17 member companies) has constituted an independent technical committee to ensure adherence to minimum standards at the fish factory level. All members have signed up and contributed funds to facilitate the activities of the committee. The committee has unlimited access to all factories and imposes punitive measures on members who do not comply with agreed standards. For example, a first time of non-compliance attracts a one-week suspension; a second time of non-compliance attracts a one-month suspension and a third time attracts a three-months suspension. The punitive measures are affected through recommendation to the commissioner for Fisheries in the Ministry of Agriculture, Animal Industry and Fisheries (MAAIF). UFPEA also mobilizes resources and technical services to train quality managers of its member companies. (Kibwika, Kyazze, and Nassuna-Musoke 2008)

Similar types of collective action come from the input trade in Kenya, such as the Seed Trade Association of Kenya (STAK) and the Agrochemicals Association of Kenya (AAK). Although competition is quite intense in these industries, the motivating force behind the collective action is principally interaction with government in the area of regulation. The focus is on ensuring fair enforcement of quality regulations across the industry. The agrochemical industry is also organizing its members to develop a structured system for waste disposal and for safe use. In the case of seed, the Kenyan market is getting to the stage where farmers have choices and understand the quality requirements of seed. The market is competitive enough that seed quality is a principal determinant of competitive advantage. The seed industry is also discussing the possibility of self-regulation in seed certification and seed quality, reflecting maturity in a market where companies must compete on the basis of quality and where providing poor-quality seed will significantly reduce market share.

The other major area of collective action is among farm-level producers in formal market chains. Farmer organizations play a major role in marketing systems, but are also foci for technical extension and cost-effective channels for the public sector and NGOs to deliver services to rural farmers. The principal marketing benefit that farmer organizations offer to farmers is aggregating individual input purchases and produce sales so that farmers are able to engage in markets with much larger transactions (Dorward, Kydd, and Poulton 2008). Aggregated transactions offer the possibility of lower costs, more reliable relationships with larger traders, and sometimes better prices and access to financial services.

This need antecedent was particularly discernable in the smallholder dairy subsector, where participation in the formal marketing chain required access to a cooling facility to maintain quality and assembly required access to containers and transport. Maintaining quality, efficient assembly and bulking, and efficient distribution of inputs and services, including credit, motivated farmer organization. Organization also benefits processors because it guarantees continuity of supply at required quality standards. Processors gain ensured supplies of produce, and the farmers can compete for the firm that provides the best price and services. Tight vertical integration is needed to meet quality standards, for example, the direct link between producers and exporters in the export horticulture subsector. Who bears the costs of the downstream infrastructural costs, such as cooling facilities or coffee washing units, and how competitive the market environment is for raw material supplies often determine whether farmer groups contract with particular processors or compete for the best price. Cooperatives are increasingly investing in the downstream processing infrastructure, allowing them to bargain more effectively with the large-scale processors.

As the different country studies indicate, farmer organizations that promote market access are generally successful only where there are significant technical and market opportunities to engage in moderately high-return enterprises. In agriculture-based economies, these opportunities are more commonly found in export crops. Some farmer organizations with better communications or with particular agro-ecological advantages may be able to focus on livestock, fruit, or vegetable production for urban markets. A focus on intensive cereals productions will, however, rarely be profitable in agriculture-based economies unless this production is either a subsidiary activity to production and marketing of a more remunerative cash crop, is associated with an innovative and efficient irrigation system management, or is the focus of specific external support (Dorward, Kydd, and Poulton 2008).

The community establishment of BMUs at the production level of the Ugandan fish industry is an example of how export markets—when profit margins are potentially high—drive organizational innovation to enhance and leverage quality management. BMUs evolved as a community-driven effort to control fish quality after a poisoning incident led to the suspension of exports to Europe. This organizational innovation is described in Kibwika, Kyazze, and Nassuna-Musoke (2008):

> The fishing community mobilized and formed volunteer committees to supplement government efforts in enforcing regulations governing fishing activities. These committees have, since 2003, evolved into BMUs, which are now recognized by government and have taken over most of the regulatory activities on the lake and landing sites. Bylaws have been developed, and BMUs are, among other things, empowered to

- Ensure that illegal fishing methods and gears are not used;
- Ensure proper sanitation and enforce minimum standards by fishermen and traders at the landing sites;
- Coordinate the various stakeholders that operate on the lake and at landing sites;
- Collect revenue and issue movement permits and licenses to fish traders/transporters on behalf of government;
- Collect data and keep records related to fishing activities.

Collective action and organizational innovation is less frequent in the informal market channels for staple food crops. These markets are highly competitive but organizationally inefficient given the high margins needed to cover the large number of actors and transactions that characterize these markets. This dynamic also applies to small-scale processing of products such as gari in Ghana or banana beer brewing in Rwanda, where competition has overwhelmed the potential returns of cooperation. The costs of distance are also an inhibiting factor because there are fewer organizational innovations in Mozambique and Tanzania, where the high costs of transport and the long distances give a competitive advantage to larger production units. However, the introduction of warehouse receipt systems for smallholder grain producers, often facilitated by an outside NGO, offers the potential for improved efficiencies in staple food marketing and enhanced farmer incomes. In turn, such organizational innovations have the potential for a more direct impact on rural poverty, as poor farmers produce these crops.

Public-Private Interactions

The capacity of AIS, particularly an agribusiness, to innovate critically depends on interactions with the public sector (Hall 2006). Public-private partnerships (PPPs) have succeeded in research and development (R&D), technology transfer, and incremental problem solving—that is, the continuous process of minor adjustments and improvements that farmers and firms undertake to survive, improve profits, and compete domestically and internationally (Hall 2006). In a knowledge-based economy where the adaptation and transformation of knowledge into innovative processes is essential, public-private interactions stretch further than the traditional research-based PPP concept to include links in education, regulation, and extension services, among others. Often these interactions and partnerships must be considered as part of a broader web of actors because innovation often involves clusters or coalitions of organization (Hall 2006).

Interactions in standards and quality management. The country studies suggest several basic conclusions in the policy arena and interaction between the public and private sectors. Because policy makers have paid too little attention to PPPs and to the role of the private sector in government policies, there is little direct interaction between the private and public sectors and little perception by the private sector of government policies. The areas with the most interaction are regulation and quality standards. However, the private sector is increasingly moving toward instituting self-regulation, particularly in export value chains where maintenance of quality standards is essential to participation in those markets. A particular strong linkage exists generally in cash-crop industries such as cocoa in Ghana where both farmers and agribusinesses get assistance from COCOBOD on quality control and agronomic practices such as yield optimization of yields, disease control, and the maintenance of high-quality seeds (Essegbey 2009).

These interactions are primarily organized within formal marketing channels through umbrella associations of agroprocessors. Specifically relationships with ministries and government departments tend to take place through these umbrella associations. In Uganda, more so than in other countries, apart from specific regulations, these interactions are strongest in policy development, implementation, and resource mobilization for investment in infrastructure and services delivery (Kibwika, Kyazze, and Nassuna-Musoke 2008).

Interactions between NARIs and the private sector. Interactions between agribusinesses and the national agricultural research institutes (NARIs) tend to be limited. In Ghana, where most companies are not even aware of NARIs (Essegbey 2008), the basic function of NARIs as a source of knowledge, product development, and new technology is severely constrained. The weak links also lead to a significant disconnect between research priorities established by the research institutes and those demanded by the market. The lack of consultation with the private sector in setting the research agenda of public research institutions hinders the commercialization of innovations and inventions in technology, agronomic practices, disease prevention, and inputs that are crucial for the competitiveness, productivity, and innovative capacity of agribusinesses in SSA (World Bank 2007a, 2007b).

The area of research supporting small-scale processing, particularly local products such as gari and banana wine, is insufficiently financed by the private sector, and presents therefore a potential for the delivery of public goods. In Ghana and Tanzania, universities have developed equipment designs for improved processing efficiency that can be manufactured by local firms. Given the wide range of traditional food products in SSA, many of which are being adapted to urban markets, there is great potential for innovation. Scale, cost, and the potential for local manufacture are important to design such research.

The low rate of interaction between public research institutions and the private sector might be expected given the focus of NARIs on farm production technology and the reliance on the extension system in the delivery of these technologies. However, the extension system is often ill-equipped to transmit knowledge and technology to companies and farmers. With the lack of capacity for extension services, advice on agronomic practices and inputs for farmers as well as on technology dissemination and technical expertise for agribusiness is insufficiently passed on. In some instances, such as in Tanzania, farmers are not even aware of such services (Mpagalile 2008). As the Ugandan country study suggests, the lack of interaction between the public and private sectors is often due to the inability to effectively implement policies rather than to the lack of supportive policies.

Interactions between education institutions and the private sector. Agribusiness in SSA needs appropriately trained human capital to become competitive and innovative in the domestic and global economy. Instilling entrepreneurial values and managerial skills into a new generation of business owners together with educated specialists on agricultural technology, science, and production processes is an additional determinant to render agribusiness into an engine of growth and innovation in SSA. For this need antecedent to happen, educational institutions need to produce appropriately trained graduates and create sufficient links between the public and private sector, as a recent World Bank report (2007b) shows.

The employment of university graduates by firms within the value chain is a potential source of innovation, although only a few companies (in Tanzania, just 15 percent) (Mpagalile 2008) hire university graduates because of the scarcity of graduates and because of cost considerations. Only a few firms see graduates as an asset in innovating in the firm's production, marketing, and investing activities, but rather as lacking the appropriate skills to promote agricultural value chains. Agribusinesses in Tanzania and Ghana favor polytechnic and technical college graduates over business graduates from universities. The private sector favors graduates with practical skills and solid technical knowledge. Some governments, such as Ghana, have responded to private sector demands through educational reforms to boost the number of graduates in agriculture, the sciences, and technical subjects. However, the country studies suggest that success is hampered by two factors. First, educational systems and institutions often lack the institutional capacity and enough qualified teachers and professors—in Uganda, for example, only 36 percent of higher education agricultural researchers have a PhD (World Bank 2007b). Second, in some countries (for example, Ghana) private universities that offer mainly business and arts education undermine the broader educational policies and objectives of creating a skilled workforce for agriculture. A better dialogue between the public sector and private educational institutions is needed, including more active participation of private institutions and businesses in educational policy formulation.

Moreover, the universities and the private sector have not coordinated over setting skill development and competencies' targets for agricultural graduates, such as the precise skills and training to meet the challenges of the marketplace. This problem explains in part why agribusinesses are not satisfied with the current profile of university graduates. The country studies corroborate the conclusion of a recent World Bank report that "few institutions have so far made the major changes required to produce significantly different types of graduates" for agribusiness (World Bank 2007b). In Tanzania, the managing directors of major companies assisted in curriculum development and governance for the universities, but so far the efforts to produce more qualified students has not translated into measurable benefits for agribusinesses (Mpagilile 2008).

A further challenge is financing students for practical training and internships. Few institutionalized incentive and support systems exist to help place students in companies for internships. In Tanzania, the government has instituted programs that enable companies to hire and train students and foster links between educational institutions and the private sector (Mpagalile 2008). There are even fewer incentives to upgrade workers' skills, such as training workshops and seminars offered by either agricultural departments or public educational institutions. Companies and public institutions must invest more in continued learning and the adoption of new skills for employees.

Public investment in capacity building is essential to create the scientific personnel necessary to implement a country's strategy for agricultural development. The average allocation across the countries studied of just 2.4 percent of the government budget to the agricultural sector is alarming considering that agriculture is the chief source of income and jobs for the people of SSA (Eicher 2006). By comparison, India spent 10 to 20 percent of its government budget on agriculture in the 1970s, and Malaysia spent 20 percent (Eicher 2006). However, the country studies show that it is equally important to improve and strengthen the links between public institutions and the private sector to expand agricultural curricula to include agribusiness, entrepreneurship, rural finance, agricultural processing, postharvest technologies, and the marketing and distribution of agricultural products (Mpagalile 2008 for Tanzania). Without aligning agricultural education and training (AET) systems with national agricultural priorities and market requirements and low integration of AET institutions within national systems, AET cannot energize national AIS—a conclusion that other case studies of SSA corroborate (Davis and others 2007).

AGRICULTURAL INNOVATION SYSTEMS IN SUB-SAHARAN AFRICA: THE IMPACT OF PUBLIC POLICIES AND INSTITUTIONS ON AGRIBUSINESS INNOVATION

Policies

After the market liberalization of the 1990s, government has focused on broad sectoral policies and frameworks, such as the Plan for the Modernization of Agriculture in Uganda and the Agricultural Sector Development Strategy in Tanzania. These policies are usually linked to the Poverty Reduction Strategy Papers (PRSPs) in each country, with the principal aim of integrating smallholders into the market economy through a combination of service provision, especially a reformed extension system; support for agricultural research; facilitation of the private sector; and an appropriate regulatory environment. Policies support the farming community rather than the whole agricultural supply chain. Moreover, because of the PRSPs, public efforts tend to concentrate on the staple food sector. Rwanda is an exception because of its high population density and its distance from ports, and its policy has focused on high-value crops for export or the domestic market. In the other countries, policy has created a division of labor between areas of private sector investment and development, particularly high-value commodities, and areas lagging behind, such as staple foods, where the public sector has concentrated. In Kenya, more than in the other countries examined, government has continued to support parastatal operations in dairy, grain marketing, and seed production.

Where the sociopolitical climate has improved and macroeconomic fundamentals are relatively strong, the private sector has benefited from the recent liberalization policies. One element is the tax regime. Tax policies are not always aligned with broader growth strategies in the agricultural sector. As the country studies demonstrate, tax policies may be pivotal to the incubation phase of agribusinesses. In Ghana, domestic companies face significant barriers to entry as they are taxed before production and receive fewer investment incentives, including tax holidays, foreign exchange retention, and access to utilities, than international companies (Essegbey 2009). Recent export restrictions, taxes, and quotas during the food crisis have forced agribusinesses and smallholder farmers to sell their products below market prices; the lower profit margins are a clear disincentive to production.

When devising tax increases, governments must consider the actual profits made by companies and inflation, so that tax policies do not impede competitiveness and innovation as in Tanzania. Taxing the import of inputs, technology, and machinery can also act as a disincentive. Easy access to technology, inputs, and machinery is vital for a competitive industry, and high costs raise the bar for companies to become competitive. Import taxes on raw materials hurt staple food industries such as cassava and maize in Ghana and Tanzania, while at the same time, processing equipment, which is used in the horticulture and dairy industries, is not taxed.

Liberalization policy is not sufficient to lower input prices for fertilizers, gasoline, and seeds. Prices for those commodities have been continuously rising, which is a concern to staple food farmers whose major costs are incurred in inputs and whose production capacity depends on the high quality of those inputs. A prudent policy could revolve around providing assistance to farmers and agribusinesses in the initial phase to overcome those challenges. "Market-smart" approaches to jump-starting agricultural input markets include targeted vouchers to enable farmers to purchase inputs and matching grants to underwrite selected start-up costs for private distributors entering input markets (World Bank 2007a). In Kenya, further liberalization of the input markets and a diminished role of parastatal boards would likely decrease prices, even if additional measures are necessary to bring costs to an adequate level.

Success stories in other regions (Chandra and Kolavalli 2006), suggest that beneficial government policies are industry specific and include political commitment, specific policies, and initiatives in the subsectors; competition; and rewarding winners. Horticulture in Kenya, cocoa in Ghana, and fish in Uganda are all examples of the successful interplay of industry-specific institutions and policy programs—some supported by international public and private sector agents—to create the conditions to compete in international markets.

Public Investment

The states of SSA need to provide "public goods" to address market failures, especially in the seed and staple food markets, that have resulted in the withdrawal of the private sector. Market failures can arise from nonexcludable or nonrival goods and services, from externalities or spillovers from private investments, from difficulties in reaching sufficient economies of scale, and from informational problems (Dorward, Kydd, and Poulton 2008).

Governments must focus on investment in infrastructure, with some investments sector specific and others geared toward the whole economy. Economists identify poor transport facilities as a particular problem, especially poor-quality and low-density road networks. Investment in improved feeder roads is critical for improving farmers' access to markets and reducing trader and farmer marketing costs, especially in landlocked countries such as Rwanda or Uganda. As the country studies point out, transport costs in some countries may also be reduced by liberalizing transport services, lowering excessive import duties, and promoting more efficient management and operation. Tema port in Ghana, for example, has an improved infrastructure, including new cooling facilities for horticulture products paid for out of public investments, but handling and other operations are not yet streamlined, and cause delays and further transaction costs. Access to power and water is also difficult, and public investment in utilities is not adequate. A notable development in the ICT industry is the spread of cell phones following the liberalization of the telecommunications markets. Cell phones are vital to communication and information gathering, thereby significantly improving coordination and reducing transaction costs. Government investments are also necessary in specific production and marketing infrastructure such as village, district, and urban markets; warehouses; and cooling facilities for the staple food and horticulture subsectors, especially in the earlier stages of development.

If the processing industry is critical to innovation, coordination, and value addition, public investment and support in nascent industries where the private sector has recently gotten involved should be a government priority. To jump-start a processing industry and make it competitive, some initial PPPs and public investments might be needed, as the development of the Ugandan fish industry and Kenyan horticulture subsector suggests. The banana processing subsector in Uganda could have benefited from public sector support to acquire the necessary technology to realize profits; instead, distilleries stopped producing, and the product must now be imported from neighboring countries.

Public investments in R&D are also insufficient. Whereas investment in agricultural R&D tripled in China and India over the past 20 years, it increased by barely a fifth in SSA and has actually declined in half of the countries (World Bank 2007a). The countries in SSA are additionally disadvantaged because the specificity of their agro-ecological features leaves them less able than other regions to benefit from international technology transfers. The small size of many countries in SSA prevents them from capturing economies of scale in agricultural R&D at the national level. A disconnect between R&D institutes, agribusinesses, and farmers often misallocates resources to research that may not be conducive to a productive application by agribusiness. In only a few cases did agribusiness have strong links with public R&D institutes. Likewise, public education institutions and the private sector must coordinate in setting their agendas and curricula to better serve agribusiness needs. The general tenor of the country reports uniformly suggested that the numbers and qualities of graduates are not sufficient to satisfy the demands of the market.

Enabling Environment

The public sector plays an important role in establishing an enabling environment. Endemic in virtually all countries in SSA is the limited access of producers and agribusinesses to credit and finance. The lack of access hampers vital factors of production, including inputs for farmers or technology for the processing industry. The Kenyan financial sector is a notable exception, with significant expansion in the number of SACCOs in the dairy industry and microfinance banks into rural areas. The warehouse receipt system is another form of credit and finance for staple food markets. With the rise of more efficient integrated supply chains (especially in horticulture and high-value products) and contract farming, financial intermediation through interlinked agents such as cooperatives is becoming more common. But in general, access to finance is a major impediment to innovation in SSA.

The establishment of standards and regulations, as well as their oversight and enforcement, is critically important to the perishable horticulture and livestock subsectors geared toward export markets. What makes it easier for the public sector is that international regulations such as EuroGAP provide ready-made regulatory standards. Addressing the stringent sanitary and phytosanitary standards in global markets is increasingly challenging. The country studies corroborate the World Development Report's findings that "doing it well depends on the joint public and private efforts in policy (food safety legislation), research (risk assessment, good practices), infrastructure (export processing facilities), and oversight (disease surveillance)" (World Bank 2007a). Uganda and Kenya involved all stakeholders and value-chain actors even down to the farmer to pass along information on regulations, work out viable solutions, and facilitate coordination. Where agribusinesses and farmers are ignorant of regulations, policies, and standards, the public sector clearly has failed. Kenya's successful adoption of its own quality standard regulations and Uganda's adoption of UgandaGap standards are responses to both international market requirements and the new domestic and regional market requirements from supermarkets and consumers. The experience outside SSA indicates that private grades and standards should be adjusted and gradually implemented so that the cost of compliance does not lead to widespread exclusion (Berdegué, Biénabe, and Peppelenbos 2008).

The enforcement of regulations, such as the oversight of livestock diseases and quality management across the value chain, is equally daunting. Clearly in SSA, the public sector alone cannot handle regulatory oversight. Public sector institutions lack the skills and capacity to fulfill these tasks (Martinez Nogueira 2006). The Ugandan fish industry demonstrates how the prospect of higher profit margins in serving export markets can motivate organizing producers to provide quality management and surveillance in the absence of public institutions. But institutions are needed to coordinate the different actors across the value chain. In subsectors where the profit margins were high enough for the private sector to take over major functions across the value chain after liberalization, the state can withdraw to a regulatory function and concentrate its resources there. The Kenyan dairy industry is an example. After market reform, the Kenya Dairy Board (KDB) played a greater role in regulation and market promotion. To effectively execute these roles, it established a regulatory network of institutions at the national and regional levels where it partners with accredited laboratories and farmers to maintain milk quality. The network is also linked to the *Codex Alimentarius*, an international food safety body, which gives guidelines for food quality and standards (figure 1.4). With private sector assumption of major tasks and support from international stakeholders, Kenya could establish a relatively efficient system of regulation enforcement, surveillance, and quality management.

The public sector is increasingly involved in enhancing the performance of producer and other collective action organizations. Collective action by producer organizations can reduce transaction costs in markets, achieve some market power, and increase producer representation in national policy formulation. For smallholders, producer organizations are essential to achieve competitiveness and have expanded rapidly in number and membership to fill the void left by the state's withdrawal from marketing, input provision, and credit. Despite a number of successes, such as horticulture in Uganda and dairy in Kenya, producer organization effectiveness is frequently constrained by legal restrictions, low managerial capacity, elite capture, and the state's failure to recognized these organizations as full partners (World Bank 2007a). Support for farmer organizations is therefore critical and must focus especially on developing both technological and organizational capacity. However, providing assistance through subsidies remains a challenge. The country studies show

Figure 1.4   The Kenya Dairy Board Framework for Ensuring Quality
Standards and Promoting Dairy Products in Kenya

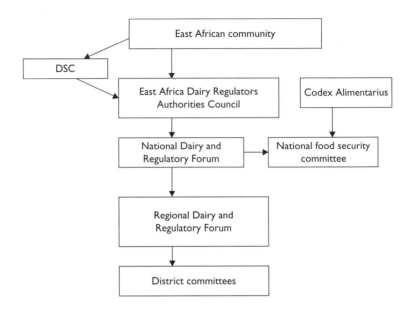

Source: Odame, Musyoka, and Kere 2008.

that collective action in staple food subsectors may warrant continued assistance to farmer organizations not only while they develop, but also while the economies and markets develop (Hazell 2007). The failed government programs for cassava starch in Ghana and large-scale, mechanical processing of cashew nuts in Mozambique are examples where the public sector preselected the processing scale and then relied on adapting the supply and organizational systems to the scale without considering the broader dynamics and structure of the respective markets.

Coordination and Facilitation

With the liberalization of markets, the entering of new private sector actors, and the proliferation of collective action, the state in SSA is pushed into a coordination and facilitation role. Strengthening the state in coordinating across sectors and partnering with the private sector and civil society in the provision of support services are critical for the success of the agricultural development agendas of spurring growth and production by supporting agribusiness, focusing on value addition and strengthening the whole innovation system.

So far, the state has coordinated higher-value chains and export cash crops in accordance with specific state policies and initiatives and an increased private sector role. Recognizing cocoa as a source of income and a major stronghold of the export economy, Ghana, for example, specifically supported the private sector and producers after deregulation and liberalization by providing major extension and other support services as well as by assuming a major coordination role. The state-established COCOBOD coordinated major aspects of the value chain. In production, the COCOBOD makes input supplies available to farmers. Furthermore, the various subdivisions of the COCOBOD such as the quality control division, the seed production unit, and the Cocoa Research Institute have established links to the farmers and cater to the extensive support needs of farmers (Essegbey 2009). As a consequence of COCOBOD's role, production levels have risen considerably. With the value chain becoming more competitive and efficient in these markets, the state focuses on providing coordination in marketing, and several marketing boards have been established to provide coordination and training on international regulations for export-oriented industries. However, apart from the COCOBOD, marketing boards in the other countries and sectors under examination have been less effective, partly because of insufficient management and design, partly because of inappropriate phasing such as with cashews in Mozambique.

Often, in these subsectors, export markets and regional markets with higher profit margins are sufficient drivers for the private sector, especially on the processing scale, to assume a major coordination role. The recent success of the Ugandan fish industry demonstrates that private sector and community-driven efforts can be effective if empowered and legalized by the state, as well as supported by international stakeholders. In this way new models emerge, especially given the limited capacity of the state to assume coordination, support, and implementation roles. Uganda also pioneered in contracting out agricultural advisory services, giving producer organizations a voice in awarding the contracts (World Bank 2007a). In staple food subsectors such as cassava and maize, and in the poultry subsector because of its informality and subsistence farming, coordination and support services are mostly sporadic. The private sector is slowly expanding its role, but market access for smallholder farmers is still a considerable challenge. The cassava starch initiative in Ghana indicates the difficulty in redirecting a whole value chain and creating economies of scale without being attentive to the dynamics and specifics of a staple food subsector characterized by different markets (informal, formal), different products (cassava, gari), and fragmentation across the value chain.

CONCLUSION

The markets for food staples are inherently different from the markets for many high-value products and need greater public attention. The private sector has successfully taken over many producer markets because of their higher profit margins, their greater integration into export and retail markets, and special governmental initiatives and tailor-made policy programs. The country studies point to the considerable challenge for the private sector in successfully taking over producer market chains for staple food during the early stages of agricultural development. As farmers struggle with low productivity and high subsistence needs, low input use, low incomes, poor infrastructure, and high risks, the amount of profit to be made in these markets remains unattractive for private sector investment. In high-value chains, in contrast, the state can assume a more facilitating and coordinating role while ensuring an adequate regulatory regime. Government has a key role in strengthening the innovation system and links between major actors and institutions. In general, the successes and failures in the country studies point to a number of different investment and policy priorities: greater investment in core research and transportation infrastructure, in institutional development, and in farmer organizations; more consistent and complete liberalization, especially in service delivery and seed markets; investment in fertilizer subsidies; improved access to credit, especially in rural finance; and intervention and support to overcome coordination failures and kick-start nascent markets (Dorward, Kydd, and Poulton 2007; World Bank 2007b; Rajalahti, Janssen, and Pehu 2007; Beyerlee and others 2008; Agwe and Kloeppinger-Todd 2008; and Umali-Deninger 2008).

NOTES

1. The commissioned country reports also included Mozambique and Rwanda in the original phase. To get a broader picture, one must reference these two reports in some instances. The six country reports in their original versions are accessible at http://ga.worldbank.org/MYRNMADDHO.
2. For a more detailed description of the methodology and the questionnaire for the interviews, see the appendix.
3. "Vertically integrated value chains" refer here to the formal value chains of the "new agriculture," which theoretically benefit poor farmers and are more equitable and possibly efficient, in contrast to formal value chains of the "old agriculture," which were colonial, exploitative, and possibly inefficient.
4. A World Bank report from 2006, *Enhancing Agricultural Innovation: How to Go Beyond the Strengthening of Research Systems*, also reviews the case of cassava in Ghana, but from the perspective of institutional arrangements between the public and private sectors and with a particular focus on public research institutions. The findings of the above-cited World Bank report complement the framework of our study but did not analyze many of the critical determinants within the value chains themselves.
5. The Partnership for Enhancing Agriculture in Rwanda through Linkages (PEARL) is assisting Rwanda in rebuilding from the civil war and genocide of 1994. PEARL works with rural communities across Rwanda to generate income through product development and market links. PEARL also works with grower cooperatives on the production and marketing of specialty coffee and cassava products and with Rwandan agricultural institutions to rebuild their educational and research capacities.

6. The Sustainable Uptake of Cassava as an Industrial Commodity Project (SUCICP) is a processing initiative for developing cassava-based industrial products such as flours, bakery products, and adhesives.

7. Gari is cassava with long, tuberous, edible roots and soft brittle stems.

8. A recent case study on Nairobi urban households (Musyoka and others 2006) estimates income and price elasticity for fruits and vegetables. Income elasticities are 1.21 and 1.03, respectively, and price elasticities are −1.63 and −1.66, respectively.

9. See the subsection on financial services for a broader discussion in this chapter on the warehouse receipt system.

10. While equipment manufacturers were not part of the sample in Ghana, they nevertheless exist. Some machinery manufacturers interact with knowledge centers such as the Food Research Institute and the Kwame Nkrumah University of Science and Technology.

REFERENCES

Agwe, Jonathan, and Renate Kloeppinger-Todd. 2008. "Pilot Innovations Could Reignite Anemic Rural Finance." *Development Outreach* 10 (3).

Berdegué, Julio, Estelle Biénabe, and Lucian Peppelenbos. 2008. "Innovative Practice in Connecting Small-Scale Producers with Dynamic Markets." Draft 2, Sustainable Markets Group, London.

Beyerlee, Derek, Alain de Janvry, Robert Townsend, and Paula Savanti. 2008. "A Window of Opportunities for Poor Farmers: Investing for Long-Term Food Supply." *Development Outreach* 10 (3).

Cardoso de Barros, Jorge. 2008. "Study on How National Public Policies Encourage or Impede Agribusiness Innovation: Cases of Cassava, Cashew, and Cattle in Mozambique." http://web.worldbank.org/WBSITE/EXTERNAL/WBI/WBIPROGRAMS/KFDLP/0,,contentMDK:21608036~isCURL:Y~menuPK:461215~pagePK:64156158~piPK:64152884~theSitePK:461198,00.html.

Chandra, Vandana, and Shashi Kolavalli. 2006. "Technology, Adaptation, and Exports—How Some Developing Countries Got It Right." In *Technology, Adaptation, and Exports: How Some Developing Countries Got It Right*, ed. Vandana Chandra. Washington, DC: World Bank, Washington DC.

Chandra, Vandana, ed. 2006. *Technology, Adaptation, and Exports: How Some Developing Countries Got It Right.* Washington, DC: World Bank.

Collier, Paul. 2007. *The Bottom Billion: Why the Poorest Countries Are Failing and What Can Be Done about It.* Oxford, U.K. Oxford University Press.

Davis, Kristin, David Spielman, and others. 2007. "Strengthening Agricultural Education and Training in Sub-Saharan Africa from an Innovation Systems Perspective: Case Studies of Ethiopia and Mozambique." Discussion Paper 736. International Food Policy Research Institute, Washington, DC.

Diao, Xinshen, Shenggen Fan, Derek Headey, Michael Johnson, Alejandro Nin Pratt, and Bingxin Yu. 2008. "Accelerating Africa's Food Production in Response to Rising Food Prices: Impacts and Requisite Actions." IFPRI Discussion Paper 825. International Food Policy Research Institute, Washington, DC.

Dorward, Andrew, J. Kydd and C. Poulton. 2008. "Traditional Domestic Markets and Marketing Systems for Agricultural Products." Background Paper for the World Development Report 2008. World Bank, Washington, DC.

Ducker, Michael, and Martin Webber. 2007. "Case Study: Uganda Nile Perch Quality Management and Certification." In *Using Value Chain Approaches in Agribusiness and Agriculture in Sub-Saharan Africa: A Methodological Guide.* Washington, DC: World Bank.

Dugger, Cecilia W. 2007. "Ending Famine, Simply by Ignoring the Experts." *New York Times,* December 2, 2007.

Eicher, Carl K. 2006. "The Evolution of Agricultural Education and Training: Global Insights of Relevance for Africa." Unpublished paper commissioned by the World Bank, Washington, DC.

Elliot, Howard. 2008. "Evolution of Systems Thinking towards Agricultural Innovation." International Food Policy Research Institute, Washington, DC.

Essegbey, George O. 2009. "Ghana: Cassava, Cocoa, and Poultry." In *Agribusiness and Innovation Systems in Africa,* ed. Kurt Larsen, Ronald Kim, and Florian Theus. Washington, DC: World Bank.

Fafchamps, Marcel. 2004. *Market Institutions in Sub-Saharan Africa: Theory and Evidence.* Boston: MIT Press.

Haggblade, Steven, Thomas Reardon, and Eric Hyman. 2007. "Technology as a Motor of Change in the Rural Nonfarm Economy." In *Transforming the Rural Nonfarm Economy: Opportunities and Threats in the Developing World,* ed. Steven Haggblade, Peter Hazell, and Thomas Reardon. Baltimore: Johns Hopkins University Press.

Hall, Andy. 2006. "Public Private Sector Partnerships in an Agricultural System of Innovation: Concepts and Challenges." Working Paper 2006-002. Maastricht, UNU-MERIT.

Hazell, Peter. 2007. "Case Study on Livestock." In *All-Africa Review of Experiences with Commercial Agriculture.* Background Paper for the Competitive Commercial Agriculture in Sub-Saharan Africa (CCAA) Study, World Bank, Washington, DC.

Honohan, Patrick, and Thorsten Beck. 2007. *Making Finance Work for Africa.* Washington, DC: World Bank.

Kaplinsky, Raphael, and Mike Morris. 2000. *A Handbook for Value Chain Research.* Ottawa: International Development Research Centre.

Kibwika, Paul, Florence Birungi Kyazze, and Maria Nassuna-Musoke. 2008. "How Public Policies Enhance or Impede Agribusiness Innovation: A Study of Fish, Banana, and Vegetables Value Chains in Uganda." In *Agribusiness and Innovation Systems in Africa,* ed. Kurt Larsen, Ronald Kim, and Florian Theus. Washington, DC: World Bank.

Kiggundu, Rose. 2006. "Technological Change in Uganda's Fishery Exports." In *Technology, Adaptation, and Exports: How Some Developing Countries Got It Right,* ed. Vandana Chandra. Washington, DC: World Bank.

Kydd, Jonathan, and Andrew Dorward. 2004. "Implications of Market and Coordination Failures for Rural Development in Developing Countries." *Innovation Strategy Today* 2 (1): 41–54.

Lacroix, Richard, and Panos Varangis. 1996. "Using Warehouse Receipts in Developing and Transition Economies." *Finance and Development* (September): 36–39.

Martinez Nogueira, Roberto. 2006. "New Roles of the Public Sector for an Agriculture for Development Agenda." Background Paper for the World Development Report 2008. World Bank, Washington, DC.

Mpagalile, Joseph. 2008. "Agribusiness Innovation in Six African Countries: The Tanzanian Experience." In *Agribusiness and Innovation Systems in Africa,* ed. Kurt Larsen, Ronald Kim, and Florian Theus. Washington, DC: World Bank.

Musyoka, M. Philliph, and others 2006. "An Analysis of Urban Household Food Demand in Nairobi, Kenya." *Eastern African Journal for Rural Development.*

Mytelka, Lynn K. 2000. "Local Systems of Innovation in a Globalized World Economy" *Industry and Innovation* 7 (1): 15–32.

Nyambo, Brigitte, and Ruth Nyagah. 2006. "Sustaining Kenyan Smallholders in Fresh Produce Markets." *Pesticides News* 71 (March): 10–11.

Odame, Hannington, M. Philliph Musyoka, and Joseph Kere. 2008. "How National Public Policies Encourage or Impede Agribusiness Innovation: Cases of Maize, Tomato, and Dairy in Kenya." In *Agribusiness and Innovation Systems in Africa,* ed. Kurt Larsen, Ronald Kim, and Florian Theus. Washington, DC: World Bank.

Rajalahti, Riikka, William Janssen, and Eija Pehu. 2007. "Agricultural Innovation Systems: From Diagnostics toward Operational Practices." Agriculture and Rural Development Discussion Paper 38, World Bank, Washington DC.

Renkow, Mitch. 2007. "Cities, Towns, and the Rural Nonfarm Economy." In *Transforming the Rural Nonfarm Economy: Opportunities and Threats in the Developing World,* ed. Steven Haggblade, Peter Hazell, and Thomas Reardon. Baltimore: Johns Hopkins University Press.

Rukazambuga, Daniel. 2008. "Agricultural Innovation and Technology in Africa: Rwanda Experience in Coffee, Banana, and Dairy Commodity Chains." http://web.worldbank.org/WBSITE/EXTERNAL/WBI/WBIPROGRAMS/KFDLP/0,,contentMDK:21608036~isCURL:Y~menuPK:461215~pagePK:64156158~piPK:64152884~theSitePK:461198,00.html.

Sivakumar, S. 2007. "Horticulture Supply Chains in India: A Private Sector Perspective." SASKI &SASSD BBL Seminar, World Bank, Washington DC, March 26.

Spielman, David J., and Regina Birner. 2008. "How Innovative Is Your Agriculture? Using Innovation Indicators and Benchmarks to Strengthen National Agricultural Innovation Systems." ARD Discussion Paper 41, World Bank, Washington, DC.

Temu, A., and Nyankomo W. Marwa. 2007. "Changes in the Governance of Global Value Chains of Fresh Fruits and Vegetables: Opportunities and Challenges for Producers in Sub-Saharan Africa." Research Paper 12, South Centre, Geneva.

Timmer, C. Peter. 1997. "Farmers and Markets: The Political Economy of New Paradigms." *American Journal of Agricultural Economics* 79: 621–27.

Tschirley, David, Miltone Ayieko, Mary Mathenge, and Michael Weber. 2004. "Where Do Consumers in Nairobi Purchase Their Food and Why Does This matter? The Need for Investment to Improve Kenya's 'Traditional' Food Marketing System." Policy Brief 3, Tegemeo Institute of Agricultural Policy and Development, Nairobi.

Tyler, Geoff. 2006. "Critical Success Factors in the African High Value Horticulture Export Industry." In *All-Africa Review of Experiences with Commercial Agriculture.* Background Paper for the Competitive Commercial Agriculture in Sub-Saharan Africa (CCAA) Study, World Bank, Washington, DC.

Umali-Deininger, Dina. 2008. "Linking Farmers to the Market." *Development Outreach* 10 (3).

Weatherspoon, Dave D., and Thomas Reardon. 2003. "The Rise of Supermarkets in Africa: Implications for Agrifood Systems and the Rural Poor." *Development Policy Review* 21 (3): 333–55.

Webber, Martin. 2007. "Case Study: Kenyan Green Beans and Other Fresh Vegetable Exports." In *Using Value Chain Approaches in Agribusiness and Agriculture in Sub-Saharan Africa: a Methodological Guide.* Washington, DC: World Bank.

World Bank. 2006a. *Enhancing Agricultural Innovation: How to Go Beyond the Strengthening of Research Systems.* Washington, DC: World Bank.

———. 2006b. "Horticulture and High Value Agriculture in ESSD-Africa." Presentation, AFTS4, World Bank, Washington, DC, March 10.

———. 2007a. *World Development Report 2008: Agriculture for Development.* Washington, DC: World Bank.

———. 2007b. *Cultivating Knowledge and Skills to Grow African Agriculture: A Synthesis of an Institutional, Regional, and International Review.* Washington, DC: World Bank.

———. 2007c. *Using Value Chain Approaches in Agribusiness and Agriculture in Sub-Saharan Africa: A Methodological Guide.* Washington, DC: World Bank.

Zachary, G. Pascal. 2008. "The Coming Revolution in Africa." *Wilson Quarterly* 32 (Winter): 50–66.

PART II

The Agribusiness Country Reports

CHAPTER TWO

Ghana: Cassava, Cocoa, and Poultry

George Essegbey

EXECUTIVE SUMMARY

Ghana's national vision is to become a middle-income country by 2015. Its development framework—the Growth and Poverty Reduction Strategy—emphasizes wealth creation and poverty reduction. The efforts to diversify the country's exports demand the exploitation of ample opportunities available in agribusiness particularly through innovations. A study of agribusiness that contributes to national development must examine policies and institutional arrangements, as either facilitators or inhibitors of innovation, and assess whether firms are innovative.

The Ghana country study evaluates the dynamics of innovation in the cassava, cocoa, and poultry subsectors by specifically looking at value chains and using the agricultural innovation system (AIS) framework. The commodities selected are important to Ghana's export strategies, food security efforts, and poverty reduction programs.

Cassava is one of Ghana's major staples, with production at more than 10 million metric tons in 2007. Cassava is consumed in almost all of the ten administrative regions of the country. The cassava value chain links farmers as primary producers to microprocessors such as gari producers, all the way up the value chain to traders, transporters, exporters, and consumers. The government's Presidential Special Initiative (PSI) on cassava starch aims to transform cassava into a major industrial crop, despite the challenges in production, processing, and marketing.

Cocoa is the leading foreign exchange earning crop for Ghana. Up to the 1980s, cocoa contributed about 45 percent of the country's foreign exchange earnings and constituted about 65 percent of total merchandise exports. The national goal is to produce a million tons of cocoa by increasing production from the current level of about 700,000 tons. The Ghana Cocoa Board (COCOBOD) is at the center of the institutional framework for managing cocoa production and marketing in Ghana. The content of processed and value-added cocoa in the total exports is still relatively low, constituting less than 20 percent of the export total. Ghana's objective is to process at least 50 percent of cocoa before export, producing cocoa butter, cake, roasted nibs, and chocolate. The current deregulation policy in the cocoa sector is enhancing private sector participation and creating agribusiness opportunities for innovation.

The poultry industry in Ghana contributes to the national strategies for food and nutrition and for entrepreneurship. Traditional village poultry farmers raise chickens for food and for income. The commercial poultry farmers operate a modern industry with links to veterinary services, input trading, poultry product retailers, and other stakeholders. The government set up the Poultry Development Board to stimulate the growth of the poultry industry, advise government on modernization, and institute regulation and monitoring.

According to the Ghana country study survey, most firms in the cassava, cocoa, and poultry value chains have tried new ideas and used new knowledge in the last three years. Innovations include new planting materials, products, production techniques, and machinery and equipment. The development of new products in the food processing industries involves experimentation and testing over a period. Technological hardware innovations included machines to grind cassava and presses to extract the liquid before processing into gari and other cassava products. The poultry industry has introduced the use of Moringa additives[1] in poultry feed to reduce mortality.

Innovations also occur at the processing level, in marketing, in organization, and in finance. Processing demonstrated innovations, which more often occurred in integrated, high-value chains such as cocoa, and less often in the staple food sector.

The agricultural research and development (R&D) system is a major source of innovation. For example, cocoa farmers plant seedlings developed at the cocoa research institute (CRI) of Ghana to be resistant against the virulent cocoa swollen shoot virus disease (CSSVD). Poultry farmers also maintained connections with the Animal Research Institute.

According to the responses from the field visits, the drivers of innovation include public policies, which stimulate business activities and open up new markets and entrepreneurial opportunities. The public sector plays a critical role in the enabling environment for innovation, including developing the country's R&D capacity, but also support systems such as road and transportation networks, public utilities, financial and banking services, and agricultural extension services. The diagrams of the commodity value chains highlight the relevant actors. However, public policies sometimes inhibit innovation. The liberalized market policies prevailing in Ghana have created an unfavorable climate for local producers, and most entrepreneurs (in fact, almost all the respondents in this study) complain of unfair competition in the domestic market. The influx of cheap goods, mainly from Asia, make local products uncompetitive in the market, and free-market policies have not created a level playing field for local industries and importers. Nevertheless, the export promotion policy, especially for nontraditional exports, is enhancing growth in some export businesses and has brought some innovations in products, machinery, processing techniques, and marketing.

In conclusion, the study of agribusiness in Ghana underscores the relevance of the concept of innovation as a dynamic system that is influenced by domestic and international policies and the enabling environment. The interactions and links among critical actors in policy institutions, knowledge centers, and agribusinesses affect the system's dynamics. The stakeholders must realize the interactive nature of the influences as well as how their own activities, interactions, and links with local and external agents determine economic outcomes.

BACKGROUND AND POLICY CONTEXT

The national development goals defined in Ghana's Growth and Poverty Reduction Strategy (GPRS II) (2006–2009) generally highlight wealth creation and poverty reduction. Agribusiness plays a crucial role in the attainment of these goals. Like most African countries, agriculture accounts for nearly 50 percent of the gross domestic product (GDP) and employs about 65 percent of the population, especially in rural areas (NDPC 2005). Given its importance, the GPRS II identifies agribusiness as one of the key areas of focus. The efforts to diversify Ghana's exports demand the exploitation of ample agribusiness opportunities, particularly through innovation. In this regard, this study of agribusiness policies and institutional arrangements, either as facilitators or inhibitors, assesses innovation and agribusiness contribution to national development.

The liberalization of Ghana's economy is generally traced to the Economic Recovery Program (ERP) introduced in 1983 with the support of the World Bank and the IMF. The perceived weaknesses of a state-controlled economy, even one that allowed some privatization, called for a revolutionary change in direction. The Structural Adjustment Program (SAP) of 1986, the Financial Sector Adjustment Program (FINSAP) of 1988, and other targeted policies facilitated ERP's execution. ERP's challenges in transforming a fundamentally state-controlled economy to one open to greater private sector participation were multifaceted. Socioeconomic policy initiatives included the divestiture of the state-owned enterprises (SOEs), which had become liabilities. From ERP's launch in the 1980s, through the 1990s, up to the present, economic laissez-faire policies have been sustained. The prevailing framework for economic activities places agribusiness at the heart of the economic development goals of wealth creation and poverty reduction.

The central goal of Ghana's economic policy as detailed in the GPRS II is to accelerate the growth of the economy for the country to attain middle-income status by the year 2015. Agriculture is expected to grow at an annual rate of 6 percent. The GPRS II stipulates that in keeping with the long-term vision of developing an agro-based industrial economy, interventions in agriculture sector will be complemented with appropriate interventions in trade and industry. The GPRS II spelled out the following highlights to promote trade and industry strategy:

- *Ensure proper integration of the nation's production sectors into the domestic market*—identify and promote opportunities for economically beneficial links along production and supply chains in new and existing productive sectors.
- *Increase agroprocessing*—promote and support the processing, preservation, and use of crops, animal, and fish products; develop and promote the use of standardized packaging materials; facilitate the establishment of small-scale agroprocessing industries for export.
- *Promote agricultural marketing*—develop farmer-based organizations (FBOs) capable of securing fair prices for products and encourage the private sector to set up produce-buying companies.
- *Increase industrial output and improve the competitiveness of domestic industrial products*—mobilize domestic and international resources for production of value-added products; enhance accessibility to productive infrastructure; assist exporters to comply with international standards required by selected export markets (NDPC 2005: 35).

Apart from the GPRS II, the Food and Agricultural Sector Development Policy (FASDEP) provides a holistic agricultural policy framework. FASDEP adopts the sectorwide approach to managing agricultural development as opposed to the discrete project approach pursued in the past. FASDEP provides a broad framework for agricultural development out of which detailed projects and programs address specific issues such as those in agroprocessing.

In recent years, the export of nontraditional export (NTE) commodities has increased significantly.[2] The annual total export value of NTEs grew from about $460 million in 2001 to $500 million in 2002 to almost $600 million in 2003. Since then, NTEs have steadily increased, reaching the high point of almost $900 million in 2006 (GEPC 2008). The increases result from new additions to the NTE list, as well as increases in volume of existing exports.

More importantly, NTEs lock Ghana and other developing countries into the export of primary commodities as these countries pursue similar policies of diversifying the economy through the exports of raw agricultural commodities. Value addition is a part of Ghana's development strategy but has not yet been realized. So far, governmental investment policy encourages more horticultural and other nonmanufacturing exports. The government attracts fewer investors to set up manufacturing businesses.

The goals outlined for the agricultural and industrial sectors provide a good reference point for analyzing the performance of the agribusiness sector and the potential for growth, especially with reference to innovation in the value chain. This study of agribusiness innovation in Ghana appraises the extent of competitiveness in the cassava, cocoa, and poultry subsectors.

AN OVERVIEW OF THE SUBSECTORS AND THEIR VALUE CHAINS

The subsectors differ in their importance to the larger economy as well as in the composition, structure, and efficiency of their value chains. The small-scale farmer is a critical production point in the cassava, cocoa, and poultry value chains. Generally, there are perceptible differences in the culture of small-scale farmers of these commodities. For example, although the traditional cassava farmer may produce cassava as a food crop, the cocoa farmer is primarily producing to sell for cash. The village poultry farmer quite often only keeps poultry in the backyard to supplement protein intake or to sell in times of need. The traditional farmer is important for the farm-level production of these commodities. However, because the Ghana country study focuses on the value chain, it deliberately focuses on farmers well above the traditional subsistence production level because these farmers are better linked into the processing component of the value chain.

The Cassava Subsector

Among the three commodities at the center of this country study, cassava is a major, if not leading, staple in Ghana, and it is consumed in almost all of the ten administrative regions of the country. Cassava's closest competitor is the yam, which is more often produced in the north. R&D for cassava actually goes back to the 1930s in the colonial era. Research included testing, yield increases, and development of new varieties, especially those resistant to the mosaic virus and those with good cooking qualities and yield increases (CSIR 1994; Tetteh and Taah 1989). Over the years, cassava production has increased significantly, reaching over 10 million metric tons in 2007 (MOFA 2008).

The Cassava Value Chain

The farmers producing cassava for micro- and small-scale processing are key components in the value chain, which links the farmers as primary producers to microprocessors such as gari producers up to traders, transporters, exporters, and consumers. Others in the value chain include dealers in agricultural inputs (certified seeds, fertilizers, pesticides, and herbicides) and agricultural extension officers of the Ministry of Food and Agriculture. Each of these actors support value chain activities and add value to the product. As figure 2.1 illustrates, farming inputs go to the farmers who produce for micro- or small-scale processors or for direct consumption. Produce also goes into the PSI on cassava starch. Transportation links almost all the actors in the value chain, and marketing is crucial locally and abroad.

The Cocoa Subsector

Cocoa is the leading foreign exchange earning crop for Ghana. Up to the 1980s, cocoa contributed about 45 percent of the country's foreign exchange earnings and constituted about 65 percent of total merchandise exports (Oduro 2000). Ghana's dominance of world cocoa production decreased over the years (accounting for 33.4 percent of total world cocoa production in the 1960s, but only 14 percent in the 2000s) for two main reasons. First, other countries such as Côte d'Ivoire, Indonesia, and Malaysia increased their cocoa production. Second, bush fires in the early 1980s, as well as drought, pests, and disease, reduced output and the significance of the cocoa industry. Nevertheless, cocoa occupies a strategic position in the Ghana's political economy, and no other cash crop is as important for Ghana's people (Appiah 2004).

Figure 2.1　The Cassava Value Chain

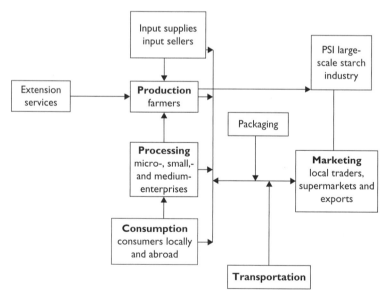

Source: Essegbey 2009.

The government is concerned with value addition and consumption of cocoa products. In the 2005–2006 cocoa year, Africa produced approximately 76 percent of the total world cocoa output and processed only 14 percent of the total output. Europe produces no cocoa, yet it processed 42 percent of the commodity. The comparative statistic for consumption is even worse; Africa consumes barely 3 percent of the world's cocoa. The challenge is how to increase the value addition of Africa's and Ghana's cocoa and also increase African consumption of cocoa products, especially because cocoa has nutritional benefits including high antioxidants and vitamins.

Ghana's cocoa production is targeted at a million tons annually, though currently production in 2002–07 has averaged about 700,000 tons annually. The objective of the cocoa industry is to process 50 percent of the cocoa before export, including cocoa butter, cake, roasted nibs, and chocolate. Cocoa processing firms include the Cocoa Processing Company (CPC) of the Ghana Cocoa Board, the West African Mills Company (WAMCO), Barry Callebaut, and Cargill. The CPC is not wholly state owned. The content of processed and value-added cocoa in Ghana's total exports is still relatively low, constituting less than 20 percent of the total. In 2002, Ghana earned $81.9 million for exported processed cocoa. The amount increased to $126.1 million in 2003 but dropped significantly to $21.1 million in 2004 (ISSER 2007: 93). The drop is attributable to the following factors: a drop in unit value per exported processed cocoa ($2,597.8 per ton in 2003 and $1,950 per ton in 2004) and a smaller volume of exported processed cocoa products because of institutional challenges in processing and exports. Earnings from exported processed cocoa products subsequently increased to about 78,000 tons in 2006, valued at $146 million (ISSER 2007: 93). See figure 2.2 below.

Ghana's cocoa industry made significant progress in boosting cocoa production in the 2000s. As figure 2.2 depicts, total cocoa exports increased in value

Figure 2.2   Total Cocoa Exports (US$ Millions): 2002–06

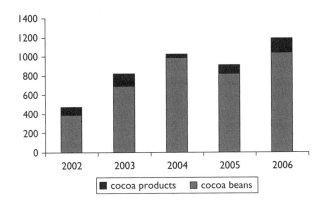

Source: Essegbey 2009.

from about $500 million in 2002 to more than $800 million the next year. It then increased to $1,000 million in 2004, dropped to about $850 million in 2005, and finally increased to about $1,200 million. The rise and fall in cocoa export earnings generally relate to the relatively unstable world market prices for all agricultural commodities. Nevertheless, these earnings are very significant for Ghana. However, to exceed this achievement and earn more, Ghana must innovate and transform a traditional cash-crop industry to a buoyant processing and value-addition entity.

The Cocoa Value Chain

Figure 2.3 illustrates the key components of the cocoa value chain, with inputs such as plants and pesticides going to the cocoa farmers who produce for the purchasing companies and COCOBOD to market. COCOBOD plays a dominant role across the cocoa value chain. In production, COCOBOD supplies inputs to farmers and the Produce Buying Company located in each of the cocoa districts to enable farmers to sell their produce at guaranteed prices. Licensed cocoa buyers and the processing, transportation, and trucking components of the value chain are also very important in the cocoa industry as shown in figure 2.3.

The Poultry Subsector

Ghana's poultry industry contributes to the national food nutrition strategies and to entrepreneurship and employment goals. A number of small and

Figure 2.3   The Cocoa Value Chain

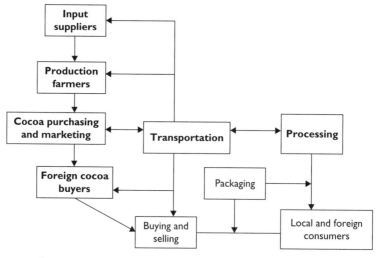

Source: Essegbey 2009.

AGRIBUSINESS AND INNOVATION SYSTEMS IN AFRICA

medium enterprises as well as traditional and modern entrepreneurs operate in the poultry subsector. Small-scale farmers with flocks of a few hundred can supply the domestic market with eggs and meat. Government economists estimate that chickens raised in rural villages account for about 60 to 80 percent of the poultry population (MOFA 2002; Gyening 2006). Aning (2006) estimates that the rural poultry population exceeds 25 million. The dominance of the rural village poultry population enhances food security and nutrition, provides livelihoods, and supports poverty reduction. The highest concentration of rural village poultry occurs in the poorest regions (Aning 2006).

The Poultry Value Chain

The poultry value chain brings together traditional and modern, commercial components of the commodity subsector. In the traditional component of the value chain, farmers rear various poultry breeds both as supplemental food sources and for income generation. Farmers sell directly to consumers or to poultry traders who sell to consumers on the open market. In the commercial component, entrepreneurs invest in poultry production, which is mainly based on exotic chicken breeds as a business venture. Products include eggs, live birds, and dressed chicken. The market consists of the traditional open markets, small retail shops, and big supermarkets. Commercial production is supported by veterinary service providers, producers of poultry feeds, transporters, and other support service providers. Figure 2.4 depicts the components in the value chain highlighting commercial and traditional production. The value chain illustrates the poultry feed, commercial poultry production, processing, and marketing components.

Figure 2.4 The Poultry Value Chain

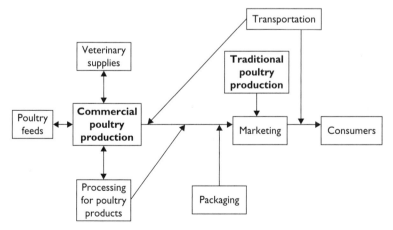

Source: Essegbey 2009.

INNOVATION IN THE SUBSECTORS: INNOVATIONS WITHIN THE VALUE CHAINS

According to the Ghana country study survey, most firms tried new ideas and used new knowledge in the last three years. Innovations included new planting materials, production techniques, and machinery and equipment. Due to lack of public financing, there have been only incremental innovations specific to the circumstances of enterprises and no "revolutionary" inventions. Incremental innovations show up in the new products developed for local or foreign markets and modifications in processing technologies. The development of new products in the food processing industries involves experimentation and testing over a period. For example at Selasie Farms, gari enriched with soybean and other protein-rich sources was developed and tested before the final product release.

Production-Level Innovations

Technological hardware innovations. Technological hardware innovations are the advances in machinery and industrial plants for making products. In the classical concept of innovation, these are the expected and obvious innovations. Innovations to machines and equipment in the processing component of the value chains include machines to grind cassava and presses to extract the liquid before processing into gari and other cassava products. Other mechanical innovations include machines for producing feed and for mixing or blending to make new products such as protein-enriched gari. Machines came from the local capital goods industry and were also ordered from abroad.

Farming practice innovations. Farming practice innovations are improved agronomic practices such as planting cocoa seedlings, applying fertilizer, spraying against capsids and other pests, pruning trees to enhance yields, inspecting and monitoring against infestations, and harvesting pods to maximize cocoa bean quality. COCOBOD extended a package of farming practices to cocoa farmers. Cassava farmers also used improved plants that were resistant to pests and diseases and delivered higher yields.

The agricultural R&D system was a notable source of innovation at this level. Cocoa farmers planted CSSVD-resistant seedlings developed at CRI. Cassava farmers producing for the PSI planted an improved variety, *Afisiafi*, which was developed at the Crops Research Institute.

In the poultry industry, there have been some innovations as well. For example, Asare Farms is experimenting with the use of Moringa additives in poultry feed to reduce mortality. Improved feed used quality protein maize variety from the Crops Research Institute, which has been widely extended to farmers. The Moringa additive is touted as having several health benefits, and Asare Farms Company used it on its 20,000-bird farm. Darko Farms Company controlled Gumboro disease on its farms using a concoction prepared from the bark of mango trees mixed with prekese, a tropical fruit. There were also innovations in farm management in how flocks were housed.

Processing Innovations

Process innovations signify the extent to which technology users have mastered the technological hardware. The West African Mills Company detailed process innovations implemented in the course of operating the plants (box 2.1). For example, the company developed a unique process for the crystallization of cocoa butter, and liquor (cocoa masse) was developed. WAMCO also enhanced the product in attractive color variations of redness or milkiness. Degumming used to be done with citric acid, which made some customers describe the taste of the cocoa butter as "flat" like cardboard. WAMCO substituted hot water and eliminated citric acid in the degumming process, which reduced costs, shortened the process cycle, and was more effective.

The processing component of the value chain shows a variety of entrepreneur-developed product innovations. There were processed local foods such as gari, cassava flour, maize flour, plantain flour, canned palm nut soup, meat products with local spices, soybean-enriched gari, Moringa-based health products, protein-enriched poultry feed, and herbal products for the Gumboro poultry disease, among others. The variety of product innovations in the three commodity subsectors illustrates the diversity of opportunities for product innovation in Ghana.

Marketing and Organizational Innovations

Marketing innovation. Several companies innovated their marketing strategies through radio and television advertisements, which also expanded in recent years; participation in trade fairs and exhibitions locally and abroad; and durable and attractive packaging and labeling. Some packaging techniques were innovated to suit particular markets, for example, changes to accommodate Japanese buyers of WAMCO products who requested clipped rather than folded packages to ensure maximum recovery of the cocoa butter at its destination.

Organizational innovation. Traditionally, farmer associations did not handle production and processing for cocoa production. However, to implement the PSI on cassava starch, farmer associations organized through the Corporate Village Enterprise (COVE) to mobilize farmers and enhance their roles in the PSI. The poultry industry formed a Poultry Development Board in 2005 to advise on enhancing industry performance. The Avian Influenza Working Group (AIWG), formed to fight against the avian influenza, included representation from stakeholders groups such as the Ministry of Food and Agriculture, the Ministry of Health, and the Noguchi Memorial Institute for Medical Research. Another organizational innovation is the evolution of a

Box 2.1 WAMCO as an Innovator

The West African Mills Company (WAMCO), established in 1947, processes cocoa beans at the three main factories producing the highest total value-added cocoa-export commodities—cocoa butter and natural cocoa liquor or cocoa masse. The total installed capacity is 75,000 tons, but WAMCO operates at 56,000 tons annually.

In the long history of the company's existence, there have been innovations relating to modifications in hardware, processing techniques, products, packaging, and general manufacturing practices. The drive for such innovations has generally been the need to remain competitive, satisfy customers, and meet the evolving international requirements for quality.

WAMCO maintains a quality assurance unit equipped with basic equipment such as autoclaves, weighing equipment, digital barometers, pH meters, and solvent extractors to enable the company monitor and evaluate product quality. The international standards are stringent. For example the microbial count for salmonella is zero, molds and yeasts should be less than 50, and the total plate count is limited to 5,000 colony-forming units. The moisture of the cocoa cake produced should range from 2 to 5 percent, and the free fatty acids is 1.75, though WAMCO imposes on itself the more stringent limit of 1.5 percent.

Technological hardware innovations have come from the successful installation and integration of machinery from different suppliers in Britain, Germany, and the Netherlands. Maintenance and repairs require that parts be changed, and without some of these innovations, the plant cannot work effectively. For example, the main barometric condenser must be produced with stainless steel to safeguard the quality of the products. The operation of the deodorizer was also an innovation. WAMCO is able to process all grades of cocoa—from the 2J super maincrop through the 2C super light crop to the SB remnant—unlike other processing companies, which only use high-grade cocoa.

The experiences in the operation, maintenance, and repair of the plants have produced a maintenance schedule and culture unique to WAMCO. The high point of internal innovation was the redesign and modification of the Soxhlet Apparatus to allow for recycling water. The innovator received an award.

In pursuit of good manufacturing practices, containers are fumigated prior to loading, then aired to clear fumigant. The container then is weighed with the truck, and the product is loaded with an appropriate WAMCO code for traceability. A multi-institutional gang supervises the process. At WAMCO headquarters, a joint production coordinating meeting every week reviews production, and employees are provided with manuals and training. Altogether, WAMCO provides an enabling environment and culture for innovation.

transportation and trucking company into a purchasing company. The Global Haulage Company Ltd. transported cocoa for the Produce Buying Company (PBC), a subsidiary of the COCOBOD. With the liberalization of cocoa purchasing, Global Haulage is now a licensed cocoa-buying company as well as a trucking company, and the new venture has significantly enlarged the scope of the company's operations.

SUPPORT STRUCTURES AND SERVICES

Innovation finance as a distinct business practice is almost nonexistent in Ghana. Across the value chain from production through processing to marketing, enterprises did not receive financial resources specifically for innovation. Expenditures incurred for innovations such as developing a new food product, adapting a particular machine to perform a specific task, or improving a given process in the enterprise used resources meant for the general operations of the enterprise. As a reaction, businesses made sure that money was plowed back in their business operations, and many saved out of their profit.

Financing Innovation

Financing arrangements and the products of financial institutions do not appear to be conducive to promoting innovation. National banks were not easy to deal with even in securing loans for business; the requirements for loans are too difficult to meet, although some enterprises succeeded. Marinoff Farm Ltd., based in Kumasi, indicated that it obtained loans for its poultry production from the Agricultural Development Bank (ADB), which was set up in 1973 to cater to the needs of agricultural practitioners, either to farmers or agroprocessors. ADB has been more responsive to the financing needs of the agricultural sector than other banks; however, Marinoff pointed out that the 15 percent interest rate on its bank loan was too high. Though 15 percent is one of the lowest rates in the country, loan repayment is difficult in a depressed market.

The difficulty in accessing loans is not only a problem with banking institutions. Other funding schemes have access conditions, which agricultural enterprises may not easily meet. Wad African Foods, a firm processing a range of food products including cassava, mentioned the unsuccessful attempt to obtain funding from the Enterprise Development Investment Fund (EDIF). The Food and Agriculture Organization (FAO) came to their aid with a grant that enabled the firm to acquire a dryer to dehydrate raw materials and reduce the moisture content.

There are other sources of finance for firms. For example, Kuafo Adamfo is a licensed buying company in the cocoa industry. It received assistance from COCOBOD to finance cocoa purchasing, but it had to supplement this assistance with a loan from Barclays Bank. Kuafo Adamfo did not obtain specific financial assistance for financing of innovations.

Education and Human Resources

The level of education for entrepreneurs in Ghana is high, with more than 60 percent of the sample having a postsecondary education in a country with a national adult literacy rate of 64 percent. The 2006 Education Reform aims at enhancing science education and improving the science enrollment to 60 percent, as compared to an arts enrollment rate of 40 percent. Currently the ratios are reversed. Attaining this ratio is a big challenge, because even though more private university colleges are being founded in Ghana, these offer courses mainly in business and the arts. The job market appears to favor business students, thus whipping up enthusiasm for science education and studies is a hard sell.

On the demand side, agribusinesses prefer hiring polytechnic graduates over university graduates for the practical technical work in their firms, despite the fact that university graduates seemed better suited for managerial functions and could be sources of innovation in administration. On the whole, however, agribusiness is rather dissatisfied with the quality of graduates from tertiary educational institutions.

The firms also gave internship and apprenticeship opportunities to post-secondary students, even paying a transportation stipend.

In some cases, agribusinesses were involved in policy formulation for training and research institutions. For example the managing director of Afariwa Farms is a member of the Council of Scientific Research Institutes (CSIR) which oversees all policy issues pertaining to CSIR research institutes. The managing directors of some companies were also involved in the curriculum preparation and governance for universities.

COORDINATION WITHIN THE INNOVATION SYSTEM: THE SYSTEMS APPROACH

The country study findings present a number of issues related to the systemic nature of agribusiness, which are summarized and illustrated in figure 2.5. The simplified value chain highlights the production, processing, and marketing components. The support activities interact and integrate with the value chain. Within each of the components, there are the identifiable activities, such as extension services, transportation, packaging, and storage.

Actors

A number of external actors affecting the firm's performance can be identified when examining Ghana's national innovation system. These actors include the government, other firms, business associations, the universities, research institutes, and local authorities. New knowledge generally comes from outside the firms, from relevant business enterprises abroad, and from local research institutes and universities.

Figure 2.5   Diagram of Interactions in the Value Chain and Environments

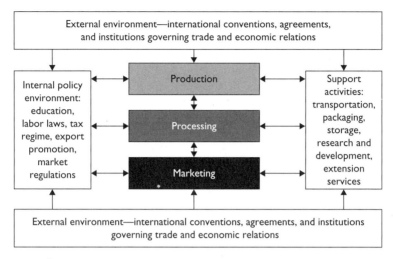

Source: Essegbey 2009.

Organization and Links across the Value Chains

The Ghana country study shows the interactions and links among the various enterprises throughout the value chain. Firms operating in a particular subsector are linked in their mutual interest. For example in the poultry industry, Ike Farms indicated that it did business with Afariwa and Darko Farms, large poultry hatcheries, for a supply of day-old chicks. Higher up the value chain, Lee Chemical Ventures, a firm processing gari and fufu flour for local and foreign markets, is linked to leading supermarkets, including Cayces Food, Savannah Imports and Exports, and Cecilia Afio Marts in the United States. Market links are critical to sustaining business activity.

The Ghana country study shows that knowledge transmission and application can be institutionalized as an organizational practice. In the poultry industry for example, there is the industry standard for raising poultry on the farm, and employees are trained in standard industry practices for feeding, maintaining strict hygienic practices, harvesting eggs, and monitoring poultry health. However, organizational practices vary; therefore eggs from one enterprise may be spotless and beautifully packaged, but eggs from another farm may not be so pristine. One farm may institute 24-hour surveillance to ensure bio-security, and another farm may be less stringent. The schedule for veterinarian visits may differ from farm to farm, even though basic practice acknowledges the need for regular veterinary visits.

Generally firms participate in local and foreign exhibitions and trade fairs to market their products and company, gain new knowledge, and share experiences. In Ghana, a number of trade fairs and exhibitions open to all businesses are held every year, among them agricultural shows, the Industry and Technology Fair (INDUTECH), the Ghana International Trade Fair, and grand sales. Firms that participate transact business and network, especially when attending trade fairs and exhibitions abroad.

Organization and links in the cassava value chain. The production of cassava for industrial processing comes under the PSI on cassava starch. The government's goal is to competitively position Ghana with other nations producing industrial starch for the global market. The government set up COVE, a limited liability company whose shareholders are farmers and strategic investors. To facilitate the sustainable production of cassava for the Ayensu Starch Company (ASCO) factory, COVE organized cassava farmers into an association and assisted them in cultivating large acreages. Farmers entered into contracts with the company, and the objective of the initiative was to orient the farmers toward cash crop production.

As was done with cocoa farmers, COVE supplied inputs, chemicals, and extension services for the production of the improved *Afiseafi* variety of cassava, and the contract stipulated a guaranteed price. But unlike cocoa, cassava is a staple food crop with alternative markets apart from the industrial raw material market, and depending on the market prices, farmers might not sell to the ASCO factory. That duality in the cassava market has led to problems both for the supply and demand sides. The factory, at the time of the interview (January 2008), was closed ostensibly for maintenance reasons. Yet problems beyond maintenance began in 2006, when the farmers diverted their harvests to the local food market because they could obtain higher prices than those in the ASCO contract. With the factory now closed, the farmers have lost an alternative market when the local food market is unable to absorb all their supply. More importantly, the farmers signed a contract with ASCO to sell cassava to the factory at almost twice the current market price. After the guaranteed prices stimulated production, farmers in surrounding areas complained that their cassava was going bad in the fields[3]—in some cases, up to 328 acres of cassava. Another problem was that the variety produced for the starch industry had higher starch content and was not favorable to traditional processing. Buyers for traditional processing therefore paid lower prices for industrial produce. In conclusion, the organizational innovation of contracting farmers to produce cassava as an industrial raw material was not very successful.

Nevertheless, traditional processing into gari, kokonte, and cassava dough offers a good alternative when industry and consumer demand ails. In recent times, R&D efforts have sought to enhance the efficiency in output and quality of traditional technologies. The Food Research Institute has set up an integrated cassava processing plant at Pokuase displaying processing technologies from the cassava grinding, through the water and starch removal, to roasting, bagging, and sealing. The plant demonstrates quality production of gari for the market with optimal standards for hygiene and industrial specifications, although the innovation has not been completely adopted. Even industrial cassava processors for export only have a few of these machines and produce according to their market requirements.

Food processing enterprises whose products include processed cassava have modernized traditional processing technologies to adopt better production processes, such as appropriately labeled packages for the export market. The enterprises operate generic technologies that enable them to process other foods such as plantain, maize, and legumes. The food processors, such as Selasie Farms, have strong links with institutions such as FRI-CSIR, which are engaged in business promotion and development.

Organization and links in the cocoa value chain. Cocoa farmers do not have to grapple with market duality because cocoa is solely a cash crop. Farmers primarily sell to purchasing companies whose business is to buy the cocoa beans from farmers for export. Until recently, the Produce Buying Company (PBC) of COCOBOD held a monopoly for cocoa purchasing. With deregulation of the cocoa industry, licensed buying companies have broken the monopoly. Cocoa farmers do not simply cultivate the crop and harvest. They ferment the cocoa bean to give it a distinct flavor. Cocoa farmers carry out this semi-processing and dry the cocoa for the buying companies. Farmers learn cocoa production processes in the cocoa farming environment. But cocoa production comes with extensive support services from various COCOBOD divisions, such as the quality control division, seed production unit, Cocoa Marketing Company, and the Cocoa Research Institute of Ghana. Quality control includes pests and diseases (capsids and blackpod disease) eradication efforts. A special unit addresses CSSVD. Even if the average cocoa farmer is usually small-scale and traditional, the cocoa industrial system and its institutions are quite large and shadow Ghana's political economy.

Organization and links in the poultry value chain. Poultry as a commodity differs from cocoa and cassava, and its differences are reflected in its value chain. The poultry market is basically local, and unlike cocoa, there is no poultry marketing board. Subsistence farmers dominate poultry production, providing live birds and eggs to the traditional consumer markets. The commercial farmers are of great importance to the poultry industry because they are organized as typical modern establishments—big farms with hundreds of exotic breeds, employing a number of workers, and using standardized feed, vaccines, and chemicals. The larger farms provide poultry products to modern market outlets. The commercial poultry farmers are organized into the Ghana National Association of Poultry Farmers (GNAPF) to lobby government policy makers and influence favorable public policies. Members of the association comprise small-scale commercial farmers (with flocks up to 5,000), medium-scale farmers (with flocks of 5,000 to 10,000), and large-scale farmers (with flocks of more than 10,000). In 2005, the government established the Poultry Development Board to advise on growth, modernization, regulation, and policy formulation in the poultry industry.

The poultry farmers that were the focus of the Ghana Country study mainly belonged to the Sector 2 or 3 FAO classifications, with flocks ranging from 2,000 to 20,000. Darko Farms and Afariwa Farms may be in Sector 1 if their subsidiary hatcheries and processing plants are counted. Until the avian influenza outbreaks, poultry farmers were holding their share despite the stiff price competition from cheaper products on the local market. However, between November 2003 and July 2007, there were a total of 319 confirmed human avian influenza cases worldwide, resulting in 192 deaths and a 60.2 percent mortality rate (Hong Hanh, Burgos, and Roland-Holst 2007). The panic over the avian influenza outbreak almost destroyed Ghana's poultry industry, as most consumers switched to other livestock products and fish. The timely reaction from the poultry industry and the government allayed fears and normalized the market for poultry products.

The market is important in promoting innovation. Industries face the challenge of finding consumer acceptance for new products. Local and foreign markets do not easily accept new products. Markets for traditional products produced in Ghana have generally become very competitive. The local poultry industries grapple with the liberalized open market, which allows an influx of imported poultry products.

Companies to business associations and farmer organizations. Farmers' associations ensure effective business practices for farmers. Associations such as the Ghana Farmers and Fishermen Council, Cocoa Farmers Association, Ghana National Association of Poultry Farmers, Ghana Feed Millers Association, and Association of Ghana Industries (AGI) unite firms or enterprises in pursuit of shared business interests. AGI is a well-known association with a strong lobbying capacity. The government has declared a "Golden Age of Business" to encourage private sector development. Some agribusinesses have criticized the government for not doing enough to encourage private sector development. Agribusinesses have lobbied for selective protectionist policies to shield the private sector from unfair foreign competition, but lobbying efforts for protectionist policies have not been successful, because the international trade regime—which has to be adhered to when targeting export markets—does not favor protectionism.

Companies to research institutes and universities. New knowledge generally comes from relevant business enterprises abroad and from local research institutes and universities. The few firms engaged in in-house R&D collaborate with a research institution or university science departments. For example, Marinoff Farm Ltd. collaborates with the Animal Science Department of the Kwame Nkrumah University of Science and Technology (KNUST). As Marinoff Farm seeks to develop improved feed for poultry, it engages the department to test new feed it formulates with soybean, fish, and other proteins. Afariwa Farms Company now collaborates with the Animal Research Institute for the production of breeding stocks for the poultry industry. (The company used to collaborate with KNUST.)

Afariwa Farms exemplifies the process of acquiring knowledge by interacting with companies abroad. Afariwa Farms is linked with the Hi-Line Breeding Company of India and serves as the market representative for Hi-Line in Ghana. Darko Farms Co. obtains its breeding stocks from a foreign company based in Zimbabwe. The Ghana country study also found links with outside knowledge centers, such as the collaboration between Asare Farms and the University of Florida on quality issues in poultry feeds. Locally the interaction and links come out of proximity, convenience, and shared interest. The international links come about through business dealings and personal contacts.

In the cocoa sector, the CRI of Ghana is the key center for new knowledge. For example, COCOBOD's Seed Production Unit obtains new genetic resources from CRIG, which also operates under COCOBOD. CRIG maintains demonstration farms to educate farmers and extension officers about new agronomic practices and cocoa tree cultivation.

Many enterprises are unaware of the existence of these institutions. Research institutes and the universities carry out very little consultation with businesses in setting out their research agenda. Knowledge centers infrequently contact businesses, and generally there are few incentives or funds for research.

Many firms do not place a high priority on R&D and knowledge creation. For example, WAMCO is a leading cocoa processing company in Ghana, but it has no research department outside of its quality control unit to ensure the quality of its products for the export market. WAMCO sometimes uses other, better-equipped laboratories for analysis. WAMCO's microbial load tests are done at the prestigious Effia-Nkwanta Hospital. The lack of R&D prioritization may be the reason for limited innovations.

Public-private interactions and partnerships. The government sponsors some expositions such as the Farmers Durbar held on the first Friday of every December, in collaboration with private sector companies, and thereby contributes to the acquisition of knowledge for agribusiness. Sponsorship of the various fairs and exhibitions could be significantly increased.

Public institutions such as the extension departments of the relevant ministries and organizations also transmit knowledge. For example, poultry farmers commended the veterinary services department of the Ministry of Food and Agriculture (MOFA) for its frequent visits and relevant technical advice. Farmers mentioned contacts with agricultural extension officers who advised them on agronomic practices and new inputs. In the specific case of cocoa, the farmers have strong links with either PBC of COCOBOD or with the licensed buying company operating in the vicinity. The quality control division of COCOBOD assisted the farmers in adopting good agricultural practices to optimize yields, control diseases and pests, and maintain good seed.

The quality assurance institutions also encourage good links with enterprises especially in relation to products destined for supermarkets and export markets. Processing companies linked with the Food and Drugs Board and the Ghana Standards Board. Ghana's Environmental Protection Agency (EPA) also contributes to good production practices by inspecting production premises to ensure compliance with the company's environmental action plan, which all companies are legally required to prepare and submit to the EPA.

PUBLIC POLICY INFLUENCE ON AGRIBUSINESS INNOVATIONS

In general, public policies in Ghana impede rather than encourage agribusiness innovation. The liberalization policies of the government, according to agribusinesses, have had a negative impact on agribusiness competitiveness and innovation. Liberalization appears to have flooded the market with an influx of cheap (and not necessarily better) foreign goods. Government science and technology policies generally do not support private sector efforts. The poultry industry especially believes that government policies have contributed to its uncompetitive performance on the local market and argue for limited market protection to enable local industries to compete.

The complaints concern specific policy instruments, which firms feel hamper their competitive practice, especially regarding foreign products and companies. One major criticism is that industries are taxed even before they start production. Industry lobbyists advocate for tax holidays to enable the infant industry to mature before taxation. Tax incentives would encourage investment in strategic processing industries. Ghana seems to grant better incentives to foreign investors in the form of tax holidays, foreign exchange retention, and access to land and utilities not available to local investors.

That these complaints are long standing points to the insensitivity of government and ineffective lobbying by business associations. Government needs to bring all the stakeholders together to brainstorm solutions to problems with market liberalization. However, stakeholders must understand that everyone will not be wholly satisfied with the outcome.

Problems with liberalized market policy regime amplify the critical role of public policies in the performance of agribusiness and other economic sectors. Even the innovations and performance of specific commodities are tied to government. A good example is the cocoa industry with its goal to produce 1 million metric tons by 2010. The Cocoa Abrabopa initiative to encourage the cocoa industry's goal is a package of agronomic practices and inputs approved by the CRI of Ghana to increase the cocoa yield by more than 300 percent. Among the recommended inputs are the Asaase Wura Special Cocoa fertilizer and pruning to allow sunshine and aeration and to discourage the spread of mold and insects. Cocoa farmer groups of between 10 to 15 farmers implement the Cocoa Abrabopa initiatives. Each group has a facilitator (the Cocoa Abrabopa Promoter) who provides technical information and advice. Model farms in cocoa growing districts demonstrate the effectiveness of the Cocoa Abrabopa initiative. In a country where cocoa farmers harvest up to three bags of cocoa per acre, the initiative is making it possible for farmers to harvest about fifteen bags of cocoa. Such phenomenal yield increases will multiply farmers' income and Ghana's foreign exchange earnings.

Public policies, however, must be systemic. For example, policies in the agricultural sector, even for single commodities such as cocoa, must dovetail with other policies such as R&D, information and communication, and local government. The harmonization of policies into a holistic approach has yet to be realized.

Infrastructure and Support Structure

In this context, infrastructure and support structure—which feed into agribusiness performance—are a main area the public sector has neglected, which has negatively affected agribusiness. A typical example is transportation, which affects all components of the value chain. Poor transportation infrastructure and facilities are major constraints on the supply side of agricultural outputs. The poor road networks are often impassable during the rainy season, and transport vehicles are often not roadworthy. It is estimated that transportation accounts for about 70 percent of total marketing costs (Aryeetey and Nyanteng 2006).

The challenges relating to roads and transportation also extend to ports and harbors. Clearly infrastructure networks either facilitate or constrain the movement of outputs from agribusiness production centers to local and foreign markets. The Tema and Takoradi ports have been modernized in recent years and are handling increasing volumes of cargo. The modernized Tema Port, which handles about 80 percent of the country's import and export cargo, has seen a steady increase of export cargo from 902,621 tons in 2000 to 1,949,950 tons in 2005. Import cargo also increased from 5,083,439 tons in 2000 to 7,748,169 tons in 2005 (Ports Overview 2005). Evidence suggests that the infrastructure for moving goods in and out of the country is improving. Handling services still need improvement to cut down on delays and congestion at the ports.

International Conventions and Policies

International conventions and policies also profoundly impact agribusiness. Effective and durable packaging protects the products from atmospheric elements and pests, maintains quality, and adds attraction for the prospective buyer. Industries produce packaging materials of polythene, plastics, cardboards, paper, and wood, but the importation of raw materials is a constraint. Ghana is a signatory of international conventions on labeling such as the CODEX convention, which falls under the auspices of the World Health Organization and FAO, and Ghana must comply with the labeling rules and regulations. The packaging industry has strong ties to the advertising industry. Ghana's packaging industry has yet to mature, though significant improvement has been made in recent years.

Ghana's opening to external markets has required greater adherence to international conventions on social accountability and human rights, especially concerning child labor in the cocoa industry. In narrow business economics, addressing these issues may lead to higher short-term costs of doing business; however, there are the social payoffs from more people-centered business practices. All members of the Cocoa Producers' Alliance have ratified a council resolution in Brazil in 2000 and International Labor Organization Convention 182, which deal with the worst forms of child labor and abuse. COCOBOD has established child labor desks at the head and all regional offices to monitor child labor in the cocoa subsector, advise management on the worst forms of child labor, and collaborate with other stakeholders to mitigate the practice (COCOBOD 2007). That these issues now appear in national policy and programs for Ghana's cocoa industry shows how important the issues have become for the international cocoa trade.

Implementation

On the implementation side, quality assurance in exported commodities, such as cocoa, is an important issue that underlines the increasing role of regulatory bodies such as the Food and Drugs Board (FDB) and the Ghana Standards Board (GSB) in agribusiness. These institutions are meant to facilitate and not to impede access to markets, and now hold training workshops on international quality standards and address specifics such as the EuroGAP.

The Ghana Export Promotion Council (GEPC) and related institutions have helped facilitate the development of the NTEs and their export. The GEPC organizes training seminars for exporters and expositions on export requirements. The main challenges of access to international markets come not only from the stringent requirements for good manufacturing practices and quality standards, but also from tariff barriers. Ghana and other cocoa producing countries have complained of the high tariffs on cocoa products such as chocolate that are exported to Europe.

Facilitators and Inhibitors of Innovation

The Ghana country study ultimately tackles the central question of what drives innovation and shows that the main facilitators of innovation include public policies, extension services, firm incentives, R&D capacity, and market opportunities. With laissez-faire market ideas prevailing in Ghana, government economic policies have generally been liberal. While such policies enhance competition and stimulate innovation, they sometimes inhibit innovation. Firms have demonstrated productivity where there are incentives for innovation. Available skills in the industry can respond to the need for certain incremental innovations that enhance competitiveness.

Table 2.1 summarizes the drivers or facilitators of innovation as well as the inhibitors that came out of the field visits.

Table 2.1 The Facilitators and Inhibitors of Innovation and Policy Options

Facilitators	Inhibitors	Policy options
■ Public policies ■ Extension services ■ Firm incentives ■ R&D capacity ■ Market opportunities ■ Market competition ■ Donor initiatives	■ Influx of foreign products ■ Limitation of innovative capacity ■ Lack of knowledge and information ■ Inadequate funds ■ No market demand ■ High taxes ■ Lack of innovative finance ■ Lack of infrastructure	■ Policy incentives for innovations in the firms ■ Enhanced R&D capacity to support firm innovations ■ Strengthened links between critical actors in NIS ■ Supportive funding mechanisms

Source: Essegbey 2009.

CONCLUSION AND SUMMARY OF RECOMMENDATIONS

The study of agribusiness in Ghana has underscored the relevance of innovation as a dynamic system, in which domestic and international policies and the enabling environment influence innovation and agribusiness. The stakeholders must understand the interactive nature of the influences as well as the extent to which their own activities, interactions, and links with local and external agents determine the outcomes of their activities.

Each commodity subsector highlights the dynamics of innovation in Ghana's socioeconomic context and the influences from domestic and international sources. For cocoa, the backbone of Ghana's traditional exports, limited deregulation in cocoa purchasing and the drive towards value addition has spurred private entrepreneurship. COCOBOD still serves as the central point in coordinating activities for cocoa production, purchasing, and marketing. Cassava is produced primarily as a food commodity. A major policy initiative, the PSI on cassava starch, launched to transform cassava into an industrial starch commodity, has not been effective, mainly because of a dysfunctional market system. The cassava starch factory is not operating competitively on the international market, the farmers are not producing enough to sustain the operations of the factory, and their surplus produce is not currently being purchased by the starch factory. However, the small entrepreneurs processing gari are innovating their products to sell in local supermarkets and for exports. Cassava production illustrates the facilitative role of policy in promoting non-traditional exports. Commercial poultry is important for job creation and achieving the national goal of better nutrition and food security. Government initiatives in setting up the institutional framework to inspect poultry imports, monitor the poultry industry, and create public awareness saved the industry from collapse against the avian influenza threat. However, the governments' free-market policies permitting the importation of cheap poultry products are making commercial poultry farmers uncompetitive in the domestic market.

Agribusinesses have shown the potential for innovation to have a huge impact on Ghana's livelihoods and income earnings. However there are constraints in finance and policy. Entrepreneurs have to finance innovation from their limited resources. Policy instruments relating to imports, exports, and taxes present no incentives to facilitate innovation. More importantly, government needs to understand and seriously work at the interconnections in public policies and pursue a holistic approach. The major challenge in the formulation and execution of policies is forging the vital connections to ensure synergy and to optimize the positive impacts.

In this regard, government should examine its economic policies. While the underlying philosophy of such policies should remain, government needs to enhance the incentives for local firms to be more innovative and competitive. Public policies can address inhibitors of innovation through funding schemes devoted primarily to innovation, such as new products, adaptation of machinery and equipment, and improvement in processes.

The national R&D capacity, physical infrastructure, and human capabilities must be strengthened to provide more beneficial support for local firms. More importantly, the linkage between knowledge centers and enterprises should be strengthened for effective knowledge flow. As the systemic concept of innovation has highlighted, functional links among the stakeholders are critical, and all factors facilitating innovation must be in place to ensure success.

NOTES

1. Additives are based on the leaves of the Moringa tree.
2. Nontraditional exports are all other export items except cocoa, electricity, minerals, and timber. They include agricultural products, products from the manufacturing sector, and handicrafts. See http://www.efcghana.com/NonTraditional.htm.
3. When cassava goes bad, the tubers become unsuitable for cooking as fufu. In other circumstances, the cassava actually rots.

REFERENCES

Amoah, J. E. K. 1995. *Development of Consumption, Commercial Production, and Marketing.* Accra: Jemre Enterprises Limited.

Aning, K. G. 2006. *The Structure and Importance of the Commercial and Village-Based Poultry in Ghana.* Accra: Food and Agriculture Organization.

Appiah, M. R. 2004. *Impact of Cocoa Research Innovations on Poverty Alleviation in Ghana.* Accra: Ghana Academy of Arts and Sciences.

Aryeetey, Ernest, and Victor Nyanteng. 2006. "Agricultural Market Access in Ghana." Discussion Paper 30, Institute of Statistical Social and Economic Research, University of Ghana, Legon.

COCOBOD (Ghana Cocoa Board). 2007. "Editorial—Efforts to Combat Child Labour in the Cocoa Sector." *COCOBOD News* 3 (3): 3.

CSIR (Council of Scientific and Industrial Research). 2006. *NARS Newsletter* 4 (1), December.

Essegbey, George. 2009. "Ghana: Cassava, Cocoa, and Poultry." In Agribusiness and Innovation Systems in Africa, ed. Kurt Larsen, Ronald Kim and Florian Theus. Washington, DC: World Bank.

Food and Agriculture Organization (FAO). 2004. "Poultry Production Sectors." http://www.fao.org/docs/eims/upload//224897/fact_sheet_productionsectors_en.pdf.

GEPC (Ghana Export Promotion Council). 2008. "Data on Non-Traditional Exports." GEPC, Accra.

Ghana Ports and Harbours Authority. 2007. *Ghana Ports Handbook 2007–2008.* Essex, U.K.: Land & Marine Publications Ltd.

Gyening, K. O. 2006. "The Future of the Poultry Industry in Ghana." Paper prepared for the Ghana Veterinary Medical Association, Accra.

Hong Hanh, P. T., S. Burgos, and D. Roland-Holst. 2007. "The Poultry Sector in Viet Nam: Prospects for Smallholder Producers in the Aftermath of the HPAI Crisis." Research Report of International Support Group. http://www.fao.org/ag/pplpi.html.

IFAD (International Fund for Agricultural Development). 2004. *Root and Tuber Improvement Programme Interim Evaluation.* Report 1533-GH. Rome: IFAD.

ISSER (Institute of Statistical Social and Economic Research). 2007. *The State of the Ghanaian Economy in 2006.* Legon: ISSER.

MOFA (Ministry of Food and Agriculture). 2002. *FASDEP.* Accra: MOFA.

Mytelka, L. K. 2000. "Local Systems of Innovation in a Globalized World Economy." *Industry and Innovation* 7 (1): 15–32.

NDPC (National Development Planning Commission). 2005. *Growth and Poverty Reduction Strategy (GPRS II) (2006–2009).* Accra: NDPC.

Nweke, Felix. 2004. *New Challenges in the Cassava Transformation in Nigeria and Ghana.* Washington, DC: International Food Policy Research Institute.

Oduro, Abena D. 2000. "Performance of the External Trade Sector Since 1970." In *Economic Reforms in Ghana: The Miracle and the Mirage,* ed. Ernest Aryeetey, Jane Harrigan, and Machiko Nissanke. Oxford, U.K.: James Currey.

Roots and Tuber Improvement Programme. http://www.ifad.org/evaluation/public_html/ (accessed 20/02/2008).

Tetteh, J.P. and J.K. Taah. 1989. "Cassava Cultivation Practices in the Cape Coast District of Ghana." Paper presented at the Second Triennial Conference, Cassava-based Crossing Systems Group, Cape Coast, October 20–26.

World Bank. 2007. *Enhancing Agricultural Innovation.* Washington, DC: World Bank.

CHAPTER THREE

Kenya: Maize, Tomato, and Dairy

Hannington Odame, Philliph Musyoka, and Joseph Kere

EXECUTIVE SUMMARY

The dynamics of innovation are assessed through case studies of Kenya's maize, tomato, and dairy subsectors and value chains using an agricultural innovation system (AIS) approach. In this context, one specific focus is whether policies encourage or impede agribusiness innovation. Since Kenya's market liberalization in the early 1990s, agribusinesses have engaged in various innovative undertakings in raising and processing the three commodities. Maize and tomato farming have seen new inputs and production measures where new seed varieties, fertilizer blends, soil fertility analysis technologies, biopesticides, and new production methods like plastic "green" house have contributed to increased production. In *processing,* the use of moisture meters, diversification into new products, and proliferation of posho mills in rural and urban areas have yielded. *Marketing* has witnessed intense outreach innovations like packaging into smaller sizes and branding campaigns that make products acceptable to a wide range of consumers.

Organizational innovations like farmer clustering, training for agrodealers and stockists, information and communication technology (ICT) usage, implementation of the warehouse receipt system, service diversification, and strategic planning have occurred in the maize, tomato, and dairy subsectors.

The dairy subsector has implemented innovations at production and input levels with the creation of milk collection centers, use of animal feed pellets, and input packaging. Processing and marketing value-addition innovations like new milk products, packaging products with new materials, batch numbering in the dairy cottage industry, and market promotions are examples of what knowledge and modernization can achieve. Organizational innovations include dairy cooperatives and contractual arrangements for inputs and service provision such as artificial insemination (AI) service provision hubs.

There have been *innovations in financing* specifically in the dairy sector and through contractual models of financial service delivery. New banking products favorable to small-scale producers, such as simplified finance operational procedures and cheap security and collateral for credit and loans, have increased productivity. The "village banks"—where K-Rep Bank has moved from traditional in-house banking operations to embrace outside local groups and fund women and youth entrepreneurship guaranteed by the government of Kenya at low interest rates or no collateral—are some of the modernizations that have revolutionized agriculture for increased production.

The main sources and drivers of innovation in Kenya include research and development (R&D) within firms, customer feedback, market intelligence, trade shows, and networks. New ideas regarding entrepreneurship, market demand for milk products, seeds, input and output prices, corporate social responsibility (CSR), value chain clustering that includes production, processing, bank contracts, markets, regulations, and business and collective associations all drive innovation. However, the output market remains the main driver of innovation in Kenya. Links from company to company; public to private partnerships; company to intermediaries; company to farmers, farmer organizations, and associations; and company to knowledge organizations also spread innovations. In the maize subsector, the company-to-company partnerships were higher given the large number of input suppliers and millers; in the tomato subsector, links to company intermediating agencies such as NGOs were highest owing to the self-regulating characteristics of the industry. In the dairy subsector, links among company to farmer, farmer organizations, and associations, partnerships, and banks are the highest because of the integrated value-chain systems. However, there were weak interactions and links among universities and agricultural research institutes and agribusiness firms. The weakness of these links arises out of the mistrust associated with different modes of operation in the public and private sectors and weak apprenticeship programs that undermine sectorwide innovation.

Policies can impede or encourage innovation in agribusiness. Trade policies such as import and export regulations and exchange rates are crucial for agribusiness to innovate. Taxation policies like the zero rating of agricultural inputs and quality standards are good, but bureaucracy is causing delays. Exchange rate fluctuations and the punitive local government levies are hurting agribusinesses. Financial liberalization has enabled access to loans and credit, but the cost of borrowing is still high. The need for government to harmonize agricultural and related environmental, land use, and research policies to increase productivity is imperative. There is also the need for market-oriented extension policies. Other related policies that significantly influence agriculture and require reform include ICT policy, which facilitates agribusiness through information on finance and markets through text messaging and transfers of money via mobile phones. Despite efforts to improve infrastructure, the roads, railways, and telecommunication networks are still relatively poor, resulting in market obstacles and poor returns.

The Kenya country study discusses several innovative approaches for the maize, tomato, and dairy value chains. The dairy subsector has had the highest number of innovative financial services. Mobile phones facilitate access to finance and markets, but these need more penetration in rural areas. The current policy drafts include the innovation concept but do not articulate it in a systemic way. Some government policies and legal and institutional frameworks support agribusiness innovation whereas others impede it. Policy indirectly influences innovation through the operational environment of value chain actors. Business associations play an important role in coordinating links between policy makers and agribusiness firms. For this reason, policy makers must examine the direct influence of agencies that link actors in value chains throughout the entire agriculture sector, including coordinating agencies in the government, private sector entities, and civil society organizations, as the AIS approach has suggested.

INTRODUCTION TO KENYA'S AGRICULTURAL SECTOR

Like in any other developing country, Kenya's economy is largely agricultural. The agriculture sector accounts for 26 percent of the gross domestic product (GDP) and 60 percent of export earnings. The sector also directly and indirectly employs more than 80 percent of the population. Smallholders dominate the sector, with 75 percent of the total agricultural output and 70 percent of the marketed agricultural output.

Kenya's overall agricultural development has been guided by policy frameworks that have evolved from the import substitution era to the post-liberalization era. In the preliberalization period when the economy was protected to enhance domestic industry growth, government involvement and control in agriculture allowed strong monopolies to emerge. The challenges of a protected economy forced the government to embrace the Structural Adjustment Programs (SAPs) in the early 1980s. Although the SAPs implementation started in the early 1980s, the government's commitment to agricultural liberalization came in 1986 when it published Sessional Paper No. 4 of 1986 on "Economic Management for Renewed Growth." This paper set out the framework for liberalizing the entire economy. Gradual government divestiture from the agricultural sector culminated in the opening of the economy in 1992, and Kenya was pronounced "open" by the World Bank in 1993. Following liberalization, the government published the Sessional Paper No. 1 of 1992 on "Development and Employment in Kenya," which sought to improve economic management, accelerate national development, reduce poverty, and increase food security.

The postliberalization policy documents that have had an impact on agricultural development include the Poverty Reduction Strategy Paper (PRSP) of 2000, which formed the basis of Economic Recovery Strategy for Wealth and Employment Creation (ERS-WEC). ERS-WEC emphasized the government's commitment to reviving and revamping agriculture, sentiments echoed in the more specific Strategy for Revitalizing Agriculture (SRA). In the SRA, the government's role in agriculture is confined to policy making. The SRA forms the overall agricultural development framework with sector-specific policies and strategies being developed within the overall framework.

OVERVIEW OF THE SUBSECTORS, THEIR VALUE CHAINS, AND INNOVATIONS

The Kenya country study examines agribusiness innovation in the maize, tomato, and dairy subsectors. Innovation refers to the application of techniques, processes, or organizational forms in the search for improved profits and incomes and results in enhanced firm or system productivity (World Bank 2006). The Kenya country study discusses innovation at the various levels of the value chains for the maize, tomato, and dairy subsectors.

The Maize Subsector

Maize is a major staple food crop in Kenya and is central to food security, since about 90 percent of Kenya's population depends on maize as a food source and as an income-generating commodity (Nyangito and Nyameino 2002). Maize is both a subsistence and commercial crop, grown on an estimated 1.4 million hectares, which is more than 30 percent of the arable land, by large-scale farmers and smallholders. More than two-thirds of the maize produced comes from small-scale growers (approximately 3.5 million) producing on farms that are less than two hectares in size. The remainder of the maize crop is produced by approximately 1,000 large-scale farmers who own large tracts of land mainly in the Trans-Nzoia and Uasin Gishu districts of the Rift Valley (ACDI/VOCA 2007).

The Maize Subsector Value Chain

Maize is produced in almost all parts of Kenya for home consumption whereas the surplus is marketed for cash. The average maize production for the last five years (2002–07) is 2.4 million tons for a population of 31 million people and constitutes 3 percent of GDP. According to the Ministry of Agriculture

(MOA), National Cereals and Produce Board (NCPB), and other sources, maize consumption in Kenya is currently estimated at more than 30 million bags per year. Most of the produce is retained for home consumption.

Maize production is usually characterized by high costs of inputs and low yields. On average, the production cost is K Sh 11,774 per hectare and the yield rate is 1,334 kg per hectare. Improvements in agricultural inputs, primarily seed, fertilizer, and chemicals, can have an enormous potential to leverage the efforts of farmers. Used appropriately, improved inputs can mean the difference between a good harvest and starvation. The most obvious result of improved inputs is a dramatic increase in production and a greater profit.

Milling is the main component in adding value to maize, the main staple food for most Kenyans. There are two types of mills serving the maize sector (see table 3.1). These are the hammer/posho mills and sifted maize mill. The maize milling industry is divided into three categories: large-scale sifted maize millers, small-scale granulated maize millers, and hammer/posho millers (whole-meal maize millers).

The country study shows that it is critical for Kenya to increase its maize production by increasing yields on existing maize areas. Improved policies will lead to improved technologies, improved varieties, increased fertilizer use, and the application of new management.

Table 3.1　Key Characteristics by Miller

Characteristics	Large-scale sifted maize miller	Small-scale granulated maize miller	Hammer/ posho miller
Capacity (tons/ month)	900–10,800	270–1,800	<100
Number of employees	>20	4–10	3–5
Main products	Sifted maize meal	Partially degermed maize meal	Whole meal
Extraction rate	74–84%	65–70%	99%
By-products	Germ, bran, and waste	Mixed germ	None
Source of maize	Framers, private, traders, NCPB, imports	Farmers, private traders	Service providers
Shelf life of products	2 years	1–2 years	2–5 months
Mills for	Urban consumers	Institutions and traders	Individuals and institutions
Type of mill technology	Roller	Huller	Hammer

Source: Nyameino and others 2003.

Kenya liberalized the maize market in December 1993 to phase out the monopoly of NCPB in the maize market and subsequently reduce milling costs. The NCPB previously controlled the marketing and transport of maize in Kenya and was legally empowered to purchase strategic grain reserves and famine relief stocks, which often distorted market prices for farmers. Farmers were able to sell their maize only at the below-market prices recommended by NCPB. The government's involvement undermined efficiency in the production and market development, induced uncertainty, and curtailed development of the maize value chain in production, processing, and marketing.

Under the liberalized market regime, there are many different ways in which maize reaches the consumer. The maize marketing channels vary depending on location. The main actors along the maize value chain include small-scale maize traders (15 percent), medium-scale agents/lorry traders (40 percent), NCPB (25 percent), other large-scale maize traders (40 percent), and maize millers (10 percent) (Nyameino and others 2003).

Table 3.2 depicts the actors in the maize subsector.

Innovations in the Maize Subsector

Improved inputs. The high costs of improved inputs and low yields characterize Kenya's maize production. The average cost of maize production is over K Sh 11,774/ per hectare, whereas the yield rates remain at 1,334 kg per hectare. The price of agricultural inputs, especially fertilizer, chemicals, and seed, have more than doubled since 2007—thus becoming a major expense for smallholder farmers. Yet, access and appropriate use of improved inputs will significantly increase farmers' yields. Improving input supply is more than introducing new seeds and fertilizer; it includes innovative ways to incorporate input supply into the value chain and make the chain itself more competitive. For instance, a value chain approach to improving input access could identify input suppliers with access to small-scale farmers and create a certification system that turns an input supply source into an agricultural information hub.

Seeds. Seeds are a critical agricultural input into agriculture that places an upper limit on productivity gains. Given the significance of seed production and the need to maintain a widely available and reliable supply of good quality seed, many Sub-Saharan African governments have historically tended to retain seed production within the public sector. In Kenya, the parastatal Kenya Seed Company (KSC) has until very recently controlled seed production. KSC had exclusive rights to the multiplication and production of varieties bred by the Kenya Agricultural Research Institute (KARI). KSC initiated its own breeding programs for hybrid maize. As a part of the liberalization of the early 1990s, the seed sector underwent significant policy changes and opened up to increased private sector entry. The

Table 3.2 Actors in the Maize Industry and Their Roles

Organization	Type of organization	Role
Farmers and farmer groups	Private	Maize production
Pest Control and Produce Board	Government	Quality assurance and registration
Kenya Plant Health Inspectorate Services (KEPHIS)	Government	Seed quality assurance
Kenya Agricultural Research Institute (KARI)	Research	Relevant research
Ministry of Agriculture	Government	Policy making
Agrochemicals Association of Kenya (AAK)	Business association	Lobbying policy issues
Agro dealers/stockists	Private	Input supply
Maize millers	Private	Add value to through milling
Supermarkets	Private	Retail outlets
ACDI-VOCA	NGO	Coordination of maize production and market links
KEBS (Kenya Bureau of Standards)	Government	Regulating quality standards
National Cereal and Produce Board	Government Parastatal-owned	Promotion of development of the industry, disseminating information on marketing
Kenya Millers Association (KMA)	Business association	Lobbying policy issues
Cereal Grain Growers (CGA)	Collective association	Lobbying policy issues
Eastern Africa Grain Council (EAGC)	Collective association	Promoting regional trade

Source: Authors' compilation, 2007.

Kenya Plant Health Inspectorate Service (KEPHIS), an autonomous regulatory body, began in 1996 to regulate the seed markets and enforce the Seed and Plant Varieties Act.

Over the years, a number of foreign companies have introduced hybrid maize seed varieties to Kenya. The new maize varieties are high yielding, disease resistant, weather resilient, and can be grown in different agro-ecological zones throughout East Africa. Kenya was one of the first countries in Sub-Saharan Africa to adopt hybrid maize.

Agricultural economists estimate that 45 to 54 percent of the annual total seed market of 30 million kg is commercial maize seed with only a limited amount of open-pollinated maize varieties. Hence, informal sources provide a sizable share of the market. Even after liberalization opened up the seed market, KSC continues to retain its dominating position and accounts for 86 percent of the maize seed market. Private seed companies, through their business association Seed Trade Association of Kenya (STAK) have lobbied for a more facilitative seed policy.

Fertilizer. Although many smallholder farmers use fertilizer, agricultural policy must increase fertilizer use and ensure that smallholder farmers understand how to use fertilizer in efficient and environmentally sound ways. Fertilizer use must be part of an integrated approach to soil fertility management that takes into account local soil and water resources and considers how organic matter, fertilizers, farmer cropping systems, and farmer knowledge can work in concert to restore soil fertility. Access to fertilizer is, however, equally difficult for Africa's small-scale farmers. Fertilizer cost has skyrocketed. For instance, the fertilizer DAP has soared from nearly $216 per ton on the global market in 2007 to about $680 per ton in 2009. It is this context that MEA has recently introduced the largest and most up-to-date blending facility and an ultra-modern soil and fertilizer testing lab in the East African region.

Chemicals. Chemical companies introduced biopesticides in response to food safety and environmental concerns and as part of their market strategy. For instance, Bayer East Africa's Green World flagship focuses on local stockists as the link between the company and farmers. There are 4,500 stockists in Kenya that are linked to about 60 agrodealers. In contrast to the strong link between Bayer and agrodealers, there seem to be an informational disconnect between stockists and farmers. Stockists sell products without understanding the needs of farmers. Stockists must provide better service to smallholder farmers. Bayer introduced an initiative to build stockist capacity by matching needs and best practices, including a regime for spraying that supports sustainable agriculture and the provision of green bins to stockists to collect waste. These green initiatives were motivated by concerns over adulterated products, inadequate environmental safety, and absence of links between product packaging and smallholder needs.

Linking small farmers to input suppliers is mutually beneficial because the small-scale producer gains access to improved inputs, and the input supplier enjoys greater business through a new role (see box 3.1). For example, input suppliers could further increase sales by holding farmer field days in which they demonstrate the appropriate use and storage of improved seeds and farm inputs. Buyers can also actively facilitate the availability of desirable inputs. In many cases, intermediaries in the value chain, such as processors or wholesale brokers, provide inputs on credit, with repayment due upon sale of the agricultural products. Value chain performance will seriously deteriorate if farmers use good seeds but underuse fertilizer, or if a fungus ruins the crop before it is harvested. Thus a full set of inputs with the associated services are necessary to ensure optimal results.

Production. Innovative activities in maize production in all regions of the country have one common denominator, that production is rain fed and

Box 3.1 The Coordinating Role of ACDI/VOCA

INPUT SUPPLY IN KENYA: ENSURING FARMERS ACCESS THE RIGHT INPUTS IN THE RIGHT AMOUNTS

Maize prices in Kenya are among the highest in Sub-Saharan Africa—the poorest quarter of the population spends 28 percent of its income on the crop. Inefficient production and marketing in the maize subsector contribute to economic stagnation and poverty. ACDI/VOCA's Kenya Maize Development Program (KMDP) is committed to ensuring that maize farmers use the seeds and the fertilizers that will increase production and offset these difficulties.

One method the project has employed is producing improved fertilizer varieties that balance the soil acidity and fit with the existing production practices. Through use demonstration plots, farmers can see the results firsthand. KMDP has also implemented a program to ensure not just that the right input varieties are available but that they are available in the right amounts.

In Kenya, fertilizer is usually sold in 50-kg bags. Even one bag is far too expensive for a smallholder farmer, not to mention far more than a small farm would require. KMDP began breaking the larger bags into smaller ones that were cheaper and appropriately sized for smallholder farmers. This effort, the first to target smallholders as a consumer market, has been expanded dramatically. With proof that smallholder farmers can pay for inputs in these smaller sizes, local shops have begun to adopt the practice, greatly increasing the number of farmers who can now access improved inputs at reasonable prices.

Source: ACDI/VOCA Web site.

characterized by high costs of seed and inputs and low yields. Although agricultural inputs, primarily seed, fertilizer, and agrochemicals have an enormous potential to leverage the efforts of farmers, access to inputs—especially inorganic fertilizer—is difficult for small-scale farmers in Kenya.

Kenyan farmers have increased the number of maize seed varieties they are growing. The high-potential maize growing areas have recorded the highest number of varieties while the diversification of low- and medium-potential areas remains unchanged. For instance, the number of varieties increased in high potential areas of western Kenya from 17 in 2004 to 26 in 2007. The liberalization of the seed sector is responsible for the increase in the number of varieties adopted for the high-potential areas. In particular, most seed companies such as Kenya Seed, Western Seed, and Lagrotech are concentrated in the western region of Kenya. These companies are also increasing product access to individual farmers through a network of agro-dealers and stockists who mediate between input suppliers and farmers' organizations. Government extension workers and NGOs facilitate the formation and functionality of farmers' organizations.

Fertilizer use in maize production has doubled in the last ten years. Areas of medium-potential yield areas have had the highest level of adoption. Despite the high rates of fertilizer adoption, the amount of fertilizer applied per acre of land has either remained constant or declined. In high-yield areas, for example, fertilizer application rate has generally remained high and at the recommended rate of 75 kg per acre. However, although medium-potential areas have recorded the highest adoption rate of fertilizer, the application rate has stabilized at slightly above 40 kg per acre. According to policy makers at the MOA, this application is 45 percent less than the recommended rate.

Farmers use a number of soil, water, and environmental conservation methods. Terracing, grass strips, and afforestation are the most common methods in low-potential yield areas. High-potential yield areas have a broader portfolio of conservation methods, but terracing, afforestation, and wind breakers are the most common.

Processing. Many firms used available machinery to solve particular postharvest processing problems and flour milling:

- Cimbria East Africa introduced and promoted the moisture meter as part of its Corporate Social Responsibility (CSR) program aimed to solve high-moisture content problems and reduce post-harvest losses in grains.
- Cimbria East Africa distributes postharvest grain storage and processing equipment.

Other innovations are as follows:

- Although the 20 largest maize millers in Kenya are required by the Kenya Bureau of Standards (KEBS) to process and sell unrefined maize meal (*ugali*), some firms are trying to diversify into breakfast cereal and porridge, which includes both maize and wheat.
- Corn Products Ltd is using starch hydrolysis to produce many value-added products, including new laundry and cosmetic products.
- Firms are organizing contract transport and road tankers to facilitate bulk transport and reduce costs.
- Because of the requirement to process unrefined maize meal (*ugali*), many large milling firms are focusing on efficiency in milling and product delivery. At the same time, small millers are enriching the nutrient value of maize flour. However, the main obstacle for milling firms is limited access to appropriate technology and markets to achieve economies of scale.

Marketing. Many firms have adopted new ways of doing business in response to existing market opportunities and threats to the operating environment of agribusiness firms. For instance, the Kenya Seed Company has clustered farmers in seed production to overcome the problem of land subdivision and reduce the isolation between fields. Also, many firms have established extensive distribution networks through working closely with agro-dealers and stockists. More effective networking has improved the education, business knowledge, and skills of dealers and stockists. Networking has also improved the professional and marketing edge of dealers, and stockists and customers are assured of a good quality product and timely service.

Other innovations include

- *Use of integrated pest management:* The chemical firms that sell biopesticides have changed from conventional uses of chemicals to integrated pest management (IPM). IPM changes how companies conduct product positioning and market orientation.
- *Use of ICTs as online links to markets for efficiency:* ICT is an important component of all the agribusiness firms interviewed. Staff use computers and the Internet to facilitate internal communication and e-commerce. For instance, some companies have set up the Enterprise Resource Planning software system to enhance connectivity to their branch offices and outlets. One milling company uses ICT in the formulation of food/feed rations and quality control.
- *Developing and implementing strategic plans that focus on business growth:* Many agribusiness firms have adopted new ways of doing business that reorganize market function. The parastatal NCPB previously waited for customers but now packages and brands its products and looks for customers such as millers and retailers. It also provides handling and storage services for third parties to use available grain storage facilities, including the recently launched warehouse receipt system.

Support services: Finance institutions. Financial institutions are proactive in developing and participating in new micro-credit facilities. Innovations include

- The government of Kenya runs a micro-credit facility for women and youth entrepreneurs, which subsidizes 80 percent of the interest payments and offers a reduced interest rate, in contrast to the commercial leading flat rate of 24 percent.
- The Nafaka loan by Family Bank aimed to assist smallholder farmers in offsetting cash-flow problems from delayed payment upon delivery of maize to NCPB. The loan is calculated at 80 percent of the total value maize delivered to NCPB. NCPB pays through the Bank, which makes deductions. This facility is currently suspended by Family Bank because of delays in receiving payments from NCPB. NCPB was not able to commit itself to the program through a contractual arrangement.
- Farmers, farmers' associations, and dealers collaborated to set up a credit scheme to facilitate transactions through the warehouse receipt systems (see box 3.2).

Box 3.2 Launching the Warehouse Receipt System

THE FORMER SYSTEM: SELLING AT A LOSS

For a long time, smallholder maize farmers have been miserable at harvest time. Despite the time, money, and energy spent tending their crops, they found themselves trapped in a cycle of debt because proceeds from the sale of their crops are never enough to cover the cost of farm inputs. Most local farmers sell their crops a price insufficient for their daily upkeep. Because they rely on the same weather patterns, they also sell all produce at about the same time as other farmers.

To the agricultural commodity market, however, this similar behavior by farmers only results in the fluctuation of prices—to the detriment of small-scale growers. For instance, farmers who dispose of their crops cheaply at harvest time can barely buy the same commodities back three months later when prices shoot up due to low supply in the market. For some time, the Ministry of Agriculture has been mounting campaigns in different parts of the country to persuade growers to stop selling green maize at the farms. But farmers who heed their advice are usually disappointed when the National Cereals and Produce Board (NCPB) either takes too long to respond or fails to absorb all their produce during harvest time.

THE INNOVATION: WORKING THROUGH THE WAREHOUSE RECEIPT SYSTEM

But now, there seems to be some light at the end of the tunnel with the installation of a warehouse receipt system. The Eastern Africa Grain Council (EAGC), in conjunction with Equity Bank, has set up a pilot warehouse receipt system in Kenya: In a warehouse receipt system program, farmers or traders can deposit maize at a certified warehouse between December and March when the market experiences a glut and receive a warehouse receipt. Depositors wishing to get money in the meantime can present their receipts at Equity Bank and obtain the cash as they wait to sell the maize in the stores when prices increase from between May and August. When the sale is finally done, the farmers are required to repay the loan and storage costs but retain some margin instead of selling during harvest period when prices are very low.

Source: Adapted from Omondi 2008.

The Tomato Subsector

Tomatoes are popular vegetables extensively grown in Kenya for the fresh produce market. Tomatoes are a nutritious source of vitamins A and C. Tomato cultivation is labor intensive and has the potential for creating rural employment. Minot and Roy (2007) note that tomato production requires 122 days of labor per hectare, as compared to maize, which requires only 29 days per hectare. Tomatoes can grow in different agro-ecological zones, either under irrigation or rain-fed conditions. Tomato cultivation is an important source of income for low-income households (Minot and Ngigi 2003). The value of Kenya's tomato crop in 2007 was K Sh 14 billion, with the Nyanza, Rift Valley, and Central Provinces contributing about 80 percent.

The Tomato Subsector Value Chain

Though the area dedicated to tomato production has been decreasing in the last three years, overall production has been increasing. Between 2004 and 2007, the area under tomato cultivation decreased from 20,743 hectares to 18,926 hectares, a 9 percent reduction. During the same period, the total volume produced increased by about 5 percent from 542,940 metric tons to 567,573 metric tons. The increase in production is attributed to farmers' extensive adoption of high-yielding varieties and other modern technologies. Previously the national average yield of tomatoes was estimated to be only 16.7 metric tons per hectare (Muendo, Tschirley, and Weber 2004) compared to recent yields of up to 60 metric tons per hectare.

Seed providers are important actors along the tomato value chain. Although some import seed only for local distribution and marketing, others are involved in R&D for new varieties. However, research often does not correspond to market needs. Kimani (2000) describes research trials on new varieties where tomato breeders only screened for a few attributes such as yield, whereas farmers' selection criteria for tomatoes included about sixteen attributes. These attributes include, in ranked order, seed purity, disease tolerance, pest tolerance, yield, marketability, labor costs, harvesting period, drought tolerance, storability, fruit shape, fruit size, taste, and color. Some of the most successful seed providers are now conducting market-based research.

Tomatoes are mainly produced under irrigation conditions by small-scale producers. An estimated 30 percent of households grow the crop for domestic consumption or for cash (Minot and Ngigi 2003). Farmers also grow tomatoes on contract. An emerging production system involved the use of plastic "green" houses for production. An estimated 70 percent of household tomato production is sold on the domestic market (Muendo, Tschirley, and Weber 2004), mainly marketed as fresh produce to processors and consumers. The main market channels include

- Producer to broker to wholesaler to retailer to consumer
- Producer to agro-processor
- Producer to middleman to agro-processor.

Wholesale markets are located in Kenya's major towns and cities, including Nairobi, Mombasa, Kisumu, Nakuru, Eldoret, and Kitale among others. Although tomatoes are produced in nearby regions, major sources of tomato production include the Kirinyaga district (Mwea area), the Meru central district (Mitunguu area and Isiolo region), Nyeri district, Nakuru district (Bahati and Kabazi region), and Taita Taveta district.

Retailers, particularly supermarkets, have divided the tomato market so that different products are sold in different markets. High-quality greenhouse tomatoes are sold in high-end markets at a premium, about K Sh 60 per kg compared to K Sh 40 per kg in other outlets. Nevertheless, to ensure value for consumers, the supermarkets regularly test their products for chemical residue levels. In the last eight years, the average wholesale price of a 64 kg crate of tomato averaged K Sh 1,300. However, the highest recorded average wholesale price was K Sh 2,800 in February 2007, at a time when processors and supermarkets started intensifying relationships with farmers to manage their raw material supplies.

Tomato processing in Kenya is carried out by large industries and small enterprises. Recently farmers have increased the value-addition of tomato by processing. Tomato processing industries fall under two main categories of the International Standard of Industrial Code, ISIC 3113: concerning the canning and preserving of fruits and vegetable; and ISIC 3114: concerning canning, preserving, and processing fish and vegetables. Currently there are fewer than 20 large-scale processors of tomatoes. More than 30 enterprises are engaged in tomato processing. Njoroge (2003) noted that because of the numerous informal operators, the level of competition in the tomato subsector is high. The large tomato processors identify the high cost of raw materials, seasonality of production, and competition from cheaper imports as the main constraints. The processed products are mainly marketed locally though the large producers, who also export a substantial amount in the COMESA region. Table 3.3 summarizes main actors in the tomato industry.

Innovations in the Tomato Subsector

All the actors in the tomato industry value chain who were interviewed confirmed having tried new ideas and or experimented with new forms of organization in the recent past. The innovations observed along the tomato value chain include:

Improved inputs. Quality inputs including seed, fertilizer, and chemicals constitute the largest cost element in tomato production. Consequently, the access to good quality and affordable seeds and chemicals has been a challenge for smallholder farmers. Responding to the challenge of access and the changing market demand for specific attributes, input supply firms have developed innovative products and mechanisms to ensure that inputs are widely available to consumers. The innovations include

Seeds. The development of new high-yielding and disease-tolerant tomato varieties adaptable to a wide range of environmental conditions. Firms use two main approaches to develop high-quality tomato seed:

- Enhanced collaboration with international companies to import high-yielding, disease-tolerant varieties. Firms have developed innovative packaging into affordable quantities for a wide market reach within Kenya. An

Table 3.3 Actors in the Tomato Industry and Their Roles

Organization	Type of organization	Role
Farmers and farmer groups (such as Kyevaluki Self Help Group)	Private	Tomato production and some processing
Pest Control and Produce Board	Government	Quality assurance and registration
Kenya Plant Health Inspectorate Services	Government	Quality assurance
KARI (Kenya Agricultural Research Institute)	Research	Relevant research
Ministry of Agriculture	Government	Policy making
Agrochemicals Association of Kenya	Business association	Lobbying policy issues
Agrodealers (such as seed and agrochemical suppliers)	Private	Input supply
Processors (such as Trufoods, Premier foods)	Private	Add value to tomato through processing
Supermarkets (such as Uchumi, Nakumatt)	Private	Retail outlets
Kenya Organic Agriculture Network	NGO	Coordination of organic tomato production and market links
KEBS (Kenya Bureau of Standards)	Government	Regulating quality standards
Horticultural Crop Development Authority (HCDA)	Government owned	Regulation of industry, promotion of development of the industry, disseminating information on marketing.

Source: Authors' compilation, 2008.

example of a product that has been marketed thus far is the Fortune Maker tomato variety.

■ Seed companies are increasingly engaging in seed research in collaboration with international and local researcher organizations. Through an arrangement with the public research organization CIMMYT, which enabled access to its germplasm, Simlaw Company set up lines for new tomato varieties. Simlaw's research involves developing seed with the desirable attributes, testing it various parts of the country, and bulking it to gain the required quantity. Their products are then marketed through field days, demonstrations, and mass media that reach a wide population.

As with maize, new legislation protecting the plant breeders' rights has spurred research in seeds.

Chemicals. Biopesticides are the other new products introduced into the market. The technology is mainly imported, tested, and registered for the local market. Innovations in branding and marketing have led to wide usage. Increased interest in organic farm methods has been the single most important trigger to this innovation.

Innovations in marketing and distribution have emerged to ensure that the new products reach a wide population. Firms such as the Osho Chemical Company are increasingly collaborating with other stakeholders by providing extension services to promote their products (box 3.3). Firms use product promotion campaigns in the mass media to increase outreach. Firms sponsor radio farming programs in native languages, place commercials on the television and the Internet, produce brochures and technical handbooks, and actively train stockists and farmers.

Processing and marketing of tomatoes and tomato products. The tomato industry is characterized by seasonality in production. During periods of glut, farmers experience high losses due to the perishable nature of the product. The government's policy of promoting common interest groups has triggered a move towards the processing of various agricultural commodities, including tomatoes, at the farm level.

Processing at the cottage industry/farm level. Such processing includes the following:

- Formulation and processing of tomatoes to produce new products, including tomato jam, tomato paste, and tomato sauce. In addition to mitigating against losses, agroprocessing aims at capturing higher value than the sale of raw tomatoes alone. Processing is generally small-scale, but the practice is carried out nationally. These products are mainly in the local markets. Some groups and small enterprises are in the process of seeking certification to sell to the bigger supermarket chains.
- Other innovations include product branding and labeling to capture the uniqueness of a group's product.

Industry-level processing. For the large tomato processing companies such as Trufoods, the constraints on the acquisition of adequate supplies of high-quality raw materials and increased competition from cheap imports are the main motivation for innovation. Innovative responses of the large processors include

- The development of new tomato-based products. Most firms have diversified tomato products by combining tomatoes with other agricultural products to develop new products, including include tomato crisps, tomato chili sauce, tomato garlic sauce, and whole tomato paste. Innovations have also aimed at enhancing product quality and safety.

Box 3.3 Kenya Initiates Plastic "Greenhouse" Tomato Farming

Greenhouse tomato farming is addresses the issue of seasonality and uniformity of tomatoes for improved marketing and increased smallholder incomes. The Kenya Horticulture Development Program (KHDP) and agricultural input suppliers Seminis Seeds and Osho Chemical Industries developed the program. A grower requires about 240 square meters of land and a greenhouse kit to get started. The cheapest kit, comprising a 500 liter water tank, irrigation drip lines, plastic sheet, seeds. and chemicals costs K Sh 150,000 ($2,239) for those participating in the project. A plot of land can grow 1,000 plants. The fourth demonstration site, for the Coast province, was launched last week at the Agricultural Training Center in Mtwapa, Mombasa.

The system enhances resource use and produces high-quality tomatoes, which have a longer shelf life of 21 days compared to 14 days for tomatoes grown in the open. In the system, one plant has a potential of producing up to 15 kg at first harvest, and increasing to 60 kg by the time it has completed its full cycle—recommended at one year. The plant vines are supported inside the greenhouse with sticks and strings and can grow up to 50 meters in height. If well looked after, the minimum plot of land under greenhouse production can yield up to 25,000 tons of tomatoes. Tomatoes are generally highly susceptible to disease and require heavy application of pesticides, but under greenhouse growing techniques, which come with basic training on hygiene, most common infections, as well as insects and weeds, are easily kept at bay.

Apart from huge savings on crop protection chemicals, which constitute a large part of production costs, less labor is employed in a greenhouse, whereas exposure to chemical toxins is minimized or eliminated altogether. The reduced reliance on chemicals is also good for the environment. In the partnership, Seminis East Africa provides the seed and Osho Chemicals provides free chemicals to farmers in the initial stages of planting as well as technical advice on application.

The introduction of greenhouse tomatoes in Kenya heralds a major shift from open pollinated farming to hybrid high-yielding methods, which if adopted in other sectors could lead to massive improvements in crop production, output, incomes, and ultimately self-sufficiency in food production. The increased adoption of improved planting materials in Kenya is a sign that farmers are keen to adopt new products and technology.

Source: http://www.nationmedia.com, publication date: October 5, 2007.

■ The development of niche products for high-end markets. There is a trend toward organic products, and processing firms are collaborating with NGOs involved in organic agriculture to develop an organic-certified tomato paste for the export market.

Marketing. Supermarkets are increasingly becoming an important outlet for fresh agricultural produce including tomatoes. Due to the intense competition in the retail business, firms have had to respond in innovative ways. These include

- Decentralized receiving of agricultural produce to enhance the decision-making process. For instance, in the Uchumi supermarket chain, each outlet receives its products and ensures that these meet high quality standards.
- Novel ways of displaying target products. Previously, most supermarket outlets sold tomatoes in prepackaged weights (kilograms); however, they have realized that prepackaging limits consumers. Consequently, consumers can choose the amount of products to purchase. Also, the supermarkets never used to display all of the produce, but have since realized that the more products on display, the more the consumer is likely to believe that the products are fresh and purchase more.

In both processing and marketing, constraints on supplies of raw materials have resulted in innovative supply chain management. Instead of relying on the market alone as the source of raw materials, firms are increasingly engaging the farmers as follows:

- The operation structure is reorganized to include agronomists who advise farmers and act as the link between the firm and the producer. These specialists often work closely with government extension service providers to advise and monitor farmers. Though the individual specialist is trained in general agriculture, he specializes in the production and marketing of the tomato. On the contrary, public extension providers normally handle agronomy issues related to the production and marketing of all other crops grown in the area.
- The producers and firms have also entered into contracts. Farmers normally enter into contractual arrangement with processors and retail outlets (supermarkets) for the supply of tomatoes.
- Processors and market retail outlets assist farmers' access to credit by providing them with guarantees. Firms assure lending institutions of their relationships with farmers, thereby enabling farmers to access credit.

Support services: Financial services. The Agriculture Finance Corporation (AFC), a government-owned, nonbank, development-focused financial institution, provides credit to the agricultural sector. Unlike other financial institutions, it is dedicated to agricultural development and receives its funding from the government, resulting in sustainability problems. Due to the challenges of outreach and sustainability, and to continue in existence, the firm has developed a new model for providing financial services, as well as new ideas and products, including

- Broadening their loan portfolio to include seasonal crop credit. AFC finances the development of nurseries; seed bed preparation; planting materials; greenhouses and equipment; water supply systems; electricity supply networks; harvesting; grading and packaging equipment; cold rooms and equipment; labor and other operational costs; and marketing for horticultural crops, including tomatoes.

- Automating business processes to effectively deliver and manage products and innovatively using automation as a platform for effective and timely executive decision making at its remote branches.
- Developing a financial delivery system geared toward wholesaling of financial services and moving away from the retail model. The new delivery system increases outreach and enhances sustainability of its operations. This model is depicted in figure 3.1.

AFC's innovations are borne out of the need to survive in an increasingly competitive and vibrant financial market. However, government policy does not fully support the changes because the government does not yet provide for the mobilization of resources from the economy in the form of savings.

The Dairy Subsector

Dairy cattle farming in Kenya is a dynamic enterprise with a mean milk production growth rate of 4.1 percent, accounting for about 3.5 percent of the GDP. Smallholder dairy production accounts for more than 70 percent of the total milk production and supports more than 600,000 smallholder dairy

---

Box 3.4   The Uchumi Supermarket and Farm Concern Partner to Ease Payments to Farmers

The Uchumi supermarket is one of the major retail outlets in Kenya with branch networks all over the country. The fresh produce section, which includes tomatoes, has an annual gross turnover of K Sh 30 million. Farmers supply the branches through the receiving area where the quality of the produce is checked and the transaction is recorded. According to company policy, payment is made after a fortnight. Due to farmers' immediate cash needs, Uchumi has entered into an agreement with Farm Concern International (FCI), a charitable development trust, involved in developing marketing models and strategic alliances to enhance economic growth among poor communities across Sub-Saharan Africa. This arrangement enables farmers who have supplied fresh produce to Uchumi supermarket to use the transaction record receipt to be paid immediately by FCI, instead of waiting for two weeks. When the transaction matures, the supermarket then transfers all due payments to FCI.

Source: Authors' compilation; http://familyconcern.net.

Figure 3.1   Financial Delivery Structure for Agricultural Finance
Corporation

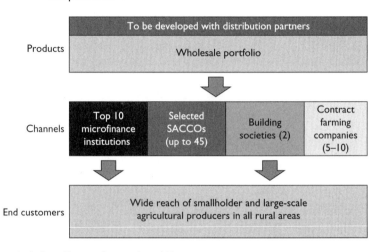

Source: Agriculture Finance Corporation of Kenya.

farmers. The total milk production in 2005 was about 3.2 billion liters, but there is potential for even higher production figures in subsequent years. Kenya is broadly self-sufficient in milk and milk products, with an annual consumption of about 1.92 billion liters. The country is self-reliant in milk and milk products except in years of drought (Export Processing Zones Authority 2005). The overall milk supply outstrips the demand, since consumption is estimated at 72 liters per capita per month against a production of 82 liters per capita per month (Karanja 2003).

The Dairy Subsector Value Chain

Due to poor distribution systems and infrastructure, Kenya's milk surplus is concentrated in regions where milk production is high, and it is not surprising to find regions with milk deficits. In high-production regions, much of the milk not absorbed into informal and formal channels goes to waste for lack of storage facilities.

The supply fluctuation in the late 1990s resulted from the collapse of the monopolistic Kenya Cooperative Creameries (KCC). However, recent evidence indicates that milk production is increasing owing to implementation of ERS-WEC, SRA, and industry reforms.

Milk consumption depends upon the level of household incomes, and therefore, Kenya's growing economy affects the overall effective demand for milk. About 55 percent of the total milk production is marketed through traders, cooperatives, hotels, and shops. An estimated 84 percent of the total milk production is sold in raw form, whereas 16 percent is processed. According to Karanja (2003), dairy producer prices have been declining while consumer prices have been increasing. This market distortion indicates that middlemen are exploiting the producers and consumers. Following liberalization, several new players have emerged, and there has been some degree of vertical integration, especially with cooperatives higher up the value chain.

Prior to liberalization in 1992, protectionist policies dating from independence guided the dairy industry. Before independence, the Dairy Industry Act was enacted in 1958, which established the Kenya Dairy Board (KDB) to regulate the dairy industry. The KCC had been formed in 1925 to focus on processing and marketing. With the act, KCC established its monopoly in the collection, processing, and marketing of milk. The KDB and KCC were heavily subsidized and, particularly following independence, were seen as central to encouraging a transformation of ownership, control, and production systems in the core farming areas of the Kenyan highlands. Following independence, the adjudication and subdivision of land saw the emergence of a strong small-scale dairy industry as against as large-scale industry. The growing economy, the inability of the dominant small-scale dairy industry to access markets, and the lack of alternative markets became matters of political and policy concern. Strong political support, together with a commitment to the smallholder sector, meant that for three decades a focus on a smallholder dairy industry was at the center of Kenya's agricultural policy. The government supported the expansion of the dairy sector through the provision of highly subsidized services to the subsector. The growth of the economy posed challenges, which necessitated the review of the roles of KDB and the encouragement of private sector participation in the industry. By the early 1980s, the implementation of SAPs, which sought to liberalize the markets, was initiated. The pace of implementation was gradual, and until 1992, the dairy sector had not been fully liberalized.

Following the Dairy Development Master Plan of 1991, the liberalization of the dairy industry in 1992, and the end of KCC's monopoly in dairy processing and marketing, new institutional arrangements in milk collection, processing, and marketing have emerged (Karanja 2003). Liberalization has brought about more involvement of the private sector and government divestiture from service provision. Since liberalization, new players have entered the dairy industry; in particular, the number of cooling plants, milk bars, and producers licensed to sell milk directly to consumers has increased significantly.

Table 3.4 shows the different institutional organizations and their roles following liberalization. The Kenya Dairy Board has undertaken regulatory and market promotion roles in the subsector. Several collective associations such as Eastern and Southern African Dairy Association (ESADA) now enhance regional coordination of the sector.

Policies. Veterinary services such as artificial insemination (AI) veterinary clinical services and tick control (dipping) were liberalized in 1991. The removal of the government-supported services led to the decline in the

Table 3.4 Players in the Dairy Industry and Their Roles

Organization	Type of organization	Role
KDB (Kenya Dairy Board)	Government	Regulation of quality standards, dairy market promotion
ESADA (Eastern and Southern Africa Dairy Association)	Collective association	Forum for discussing regional issues
KAM (Kenya Association of Manufacturers)	Collective association	Resolving disputes in processing
AKEFEMA (Association of Kenya Feeds Manufacturers)	Collective association	Regulatory
KARI (Kenya Agricultural Research Institute)	Research	Relevant research
Ministry of Livestock and Fisheries Development	Government	Policy making
Ministry of Cooperatives	Government	Promote cooperative movement
CAIS (Central Artificial Insemination Services)	Government	Provide AI services, maintain germplasm
DVS (Department of Veterinary Services)	Government	Regulate AI services
ILRI (International Livestock Research Institute)	Research	Relevant research
Private Banks	Private	Provide working/financial capital
KEBS (Kenya Bureau of Standards)	Government	Regulating quality standards
Private companies (such as World Sires, ABS-TCM)	Private	Provide veterinary and AI services
Farmer cooperatives (such as Undugu Dairies)	Farmers	Production, bulking of milk, and to some processing
Milk processors	Private	Milk processing and value addition

Source: Authors' compilation, 2007.

performance of the dairy industry, because the majority of the farmers could not afford to pay for the more expensive AI, dipping, and clinical services. Indeed, many farmers reverted to using bulls for breeding purposes, leading to a decline in milk production. The 1993 Dairy Development Policy dealt with challenges arising from liberation. The policy transitioned government away from the provision of some government-supported services, intensified dairy production systems, increased production in nontraditional areas and opened up milk processing to new investors. The divestiture of the government, though untimely, allowed private enterprise to competitively participate in service delivery. Since then, new players have entered the subsector at all levels of the value chain. The policy changes that have taken place strengthened the KDB to perform its regulatory functions effectively. There have been efforts to revive KCC following its collapse in the early 1990s.

The current dairy policy draft addresses the current challenges of the dairy industry and the crosscutting issues (environment, land, water, youth, gender, and HIV/AIDS) that were inadequately addressed in the 1993 Dairy Development Policy. In particular, the draft policy addresses the provision of support services and the supply of inputs including breeding, veterinary, clinical, and credit services. The new policy recognizes the role of goats, camels, and other milk-producing animals, especially in the arid and semi-arid lands (ASALs) and further examines how the product chain can best meet consumer needs at affordable prices while ensuring acceptable returns to the industry players. In line with the development framework envisaged in the Economic Recovery Strategy for Wealth and Employment Creation, Strategy for Revitalizing Agriculture, and the Draft Vision 2030, the new dairy policy reflects on the dynamism in the dairy industry and supports the interventions the government, together with stakeholders, will make in the entire dairy value chain. These interventions include dairy research; milk production; extension; marketing of milk and milk products; milk processing; milk consumption; human resource development and training; financial services; and institutional, legal, and regulatory interventions.

Innovations in the Dairy Subsector

Improved milk production and collection through collectives. Milk production, collection, bulking, and distribution have been an entry point into the dairy industry. The main incentives to innovation in this area are the economies of scale. With most farmers unable to deliver milk to distant processor collection centers, they find it appropriate to form cooperatives that collect, deliver, and sell milk on their behalf. The main objective of the formation of farmers' cooperatives and savings and credit cooperatives (SACCOs) is to provide services to local farmers. The dairy cooperatives come up with innovative ways to take advantage of economies of scale. Box 3.5 illustrates innovations adopted by cooperatives and processors.

Improved inputs: Animal feed. In the dairy sector, the feed industry is important as improved productivity cannot be achieved without proper feed. To compete effectively in the competitive markets, feed firms have engaged in innovative practices that ensure increased market share. Innovations include

- Providing pellet feed for the dairy animals
- Changing the active ingredients of the feed according to farmer preferences
- Changing packaging from big to smaller, more affordable packages
- Contracting agreements with dairy processors to advance feed to farmers on credit. Cost recovery occurs when the farmers deliver milk.

While most farmers are unable to deliver milk to distance processor collection centers, they find it appropriate to form cooperatives that collect, deliver, and sell milk on their behalf. Undugu dairies operate as a subsidiary of the Undugu SACCO Society. The main goal of the SACCO was to provide services to the local farmers. Currently the dairy SACCO serves an estimated 380 dairy farmers, collecting 700 liters of milk daily—an average of 2 liters per day per farmer. However, it is dependent on the lactation period of the herd. There are 10 employees and one six-ton collection and distribution truck. The dairy SACCO has developed innovative ways to enjoy the economies of scale, including:

- Value addition for milk: The dairy cooperatives have engaged in activities higher up the value chain, including processing and production of yogurt.
- Centralized collection centers: To operate effectively and minimize costs of operation, the cooperative has established 12 milk collection centers that are accessible, and farmers deliver their milk from their homes.
- Service delivery systems: The SACCO facilitates access to inputs (feeds, animal drugs, and fertilizers) and other services (AI and financial) to their member farmers. To effectively provide service to their farmers, the SACCO has engaged the services of veterinary officers, animal feed companies (Century Feeds Ltd,) and AI service providers and banks (AFC) to provide credit.

Source: Authors' compilation.

Improved inputs: Animal drugs. The dairy industry is a health-sensitive sector. The supply and access to affordable animal drugs is crucial to increase productivity. To ensure a steady supply to ever-growing markets, drug firms have become innovative:

- Enhancing their distribution systems: Initially firms sold drugs to government-controlled veterinary services. Currently the firms have improved distribution by networking with veterinary clinics, which have become their outlets. In addition, some firms have their own regional sales agents/ representatives who market their drugs, coordinate supplies and maintain stocks at regional levels.
- Changing active ingredients: The firms have changed the drugs in response to changing disease and pest resistance.
- Enhancing drug packaging: Smaller packaging increases affordability.

Policies. Although dairy production has been impeded by several factors including poor infrastructure, poor access to inputs, services, finance, and drugs, the current National Livestock Policy and the Dairy Industry Development policy recognizes that addressing these constraints will improve milk output. Consequently the policy targets improving breeding services, dairy feeds, veterinary services and animal health, extension and advisory services, and dairy R&D.

Processing and marketing of dairy products. Dairy product processing experienced a tremendous growth following liberalization. The entry of many players in the processing and cottage industries has stiffened competition. Processors and cottage firms have to innovate to maintain their market shares. Key innovations in processing segment have minimized processing costs, improved product quality, lengthened shelf life, improved distribution, ensured a steady supply of milk, and sustained consumer and producer loyalty (box 3.6).

Policy influence: Diversification in the dairy industry has resulted from policy changes, especially liberalization, which ended KCC's monopoly. Liberalization has brought new private processors into the dairy business. The resulting competitive environment has opened markets for different innovations. There has been an increase in new and different brands of dairy products that fit consumer preferences. Dairy policy evolution from the era of market control to the era of deregulation has embraced more positive and private accommodation in the dairy subsector. Increases in population, urbanization, and income are driving the demand higher, and increasing demand spurs innovations in the subsector owing to increasing returns.

However, despite positive policy change, public processors such as the newly reconstructed KCC are still under the government's procurement policy. Regulations slow down the purchase of equipment to respond to any changes in the competitive market environment. The dynamism of the market outpaces the lapse between purchase and delivery of equipment such that by the time equipment is delivered, the market demands a superior technology. The procurement process thus slows down timely technology adoption and adjustments to market technological requirements. Technologies become irrelevant to market dynamics. Other prohibitive policies include tax policy, import policies, and clearing and forwarding procedures, which increase the cost of importing equipment and delay its delivery. In addition, exchange rate fluctuations affect the import and export of equipment and finished products. Despite complaints that only New KCC is licensed to powder milk, private processors lack the equipment used in milk powdering and have been encouraged to purchase the powdering equipment.

Support services: Artificial insemination. Perhaps AI service provision is one of the most innovative service delivery methods, considering market dynamics, quality requirements, and the unlevel market field. The players in this segment have capitalized on market dysfunction and succeeded in modeling

Box 3.6 Innovation in Kenya's Dairy Processing (New KCC and Spin-Knit Dairies)

Dairy products processing experienced a tremendous growth following liberalization. The entry of many players into the processing and cottage industries has stiffened competition, requiring innovation by the processors and cottage firms to maintain market shares. Key innovations in processing have centered on minimization of processing costs, improvement of the quality of the products, lengthening shelf life, improvement of distribution and supply of milk, and sustainably maintaining consumer and producer loyalty. Key innovations include

- New product development: The market has witnessed the development and marketing of new dairy products, such as *Shakalaka*, a whey drink developed by New KCC. Initially whey was drained away after processing, but now it has been reprocessed into a drink. *Tamu Milk (Maziwa Tamu)* is a new dairy product introduced in markets within regions where *Khat* is consumed. The firm (New KCC) pioneering this product followed the discovery that *Khat* consumers require a sugary drink while chewing *Khat*. *Tamu Milk* could be a substitute for soft drinks, which have gained wide acceptance with consumers of *Khat*.
- New packaging: New packaging innovations range from reduced affordable sizes to new packaging materials and processes. The new packaging processes include the Ultra Heat Treated (UHT) packaging, which is lengthening the shelf life of milk. There have also been brand and appearance changes in UHT milk including *tetraphenol* for semi-long lasting milk and *tetraclassic* for the medium-range (two months) life, which have enabled dairy processors to reach long-distance markets without product spoilage.
- Enhancing milk collection and processed milk supplies: The dairy processing firms have improved on transportation by using refrigerated trucks and establishing milk cooling plants in high dairy production areas. The processors have established distribution agents in every market region to maximize demand.
- Financial services: Processors and financial institutions have set up contractual arrangements to provide financial services to the farmers. The processors assume the risk of cost recovery for the financial institutions and recoup advances upon milk delivery by the farmers. Similar contractual arrangements occur in AI, drug, and feed provision services by NGOs and other private service providers.

In the dairy cottage industry, key innovations include

- Packaging and packaging material: The inclusion of seals, which give the products a sense of uniqueness. In cheese packaging, there has been a shift from vacuum papers to pro-biotic papers. Yogurt is also being packaged in plastic cans rather than papers.

(*continued*)

Box 3.6   (Continued)

- Shapes and sizes: Shapes and sizes have been changed to fit certain occasions and preferences of the consumers. Shapes include slices, cubes, and portions to suit the market preferences of the consumers.
- Batch numbering: The batch numbers, achieved through jet machines, have helped tracing efforts in the event of bad products.

Source: Authors' compilation.

a service delivery mechanism. Key innovations have targeted AI service demand and effective and timely service delivery. Two innovations include

- *The AI "service hub model":* AI service hubs have been an innovation service delivery mechanism to dairy farmers. The service hubs are created around the milk collection centers (cooling plant) where farmers deliver milk. Within the service hubs, there are service providers who bulk services, such as AI, veterinary, and extension services, and farmers can get timely services without traveling far.
- *Changes in product site:* Initially CAIS stored semen; however, currently AI service providers (private and NGOs) can store semen on their own. Regional distributors and regional representatives who coordinate with the head office create demand, and semen is sent by express mail service (EMS) after the bank transaction statement is faxed to the office.

Support services: Financial services. The dairy subsector cannot succeed without access to financial services. The capacity to innovate and engage in economically viable operations depends on access to working capital. Many innovative ways of providing financial services exist to provide easily accessible services at the least cost, while minimizing the collateral requirement and shortening the financial operation procedures. Some innovations target new and special products and means of transacting. Key innovations include

- *Account opening procedures and requirements:* Banks have improved on their service delivery, making affordable products and services available to the clients. These include simplified account opening and maintenance procedures, which have minimum deposit requirements and free passport-size photographing.
- *New banking products, services, and systems:* Cash banking services, such as e-banking and mobile banking systems, have been provided through mobilizing vans equipped with computers connected to a mainframe computer. Now people in rural areas and areas away from the bank's branches can

open accounts. IT changes through better communication and computer-based technologies include ATMs, M-transact money-transfer systems, and the "soko tele" of K-Rep Bank, which is a money transferring system that enables the sending and receipt of money.

- The requirement of collateral for loans has been replaced by "social collateral" where local groups ensure that any loan obtained by a member is guaranteed and repaid accordingly. Other forms of collateral include "chattel collateral," where the client does not necessarily have to possess physical collateral, but can put up valuable and viable business ideas. The banks accept proposals, which are prequalified through economic viability criteria, and then the clients receive loans.

- The "village banks," such as K-Rep Bank, have moved from traditional in-house banking operations to embrace outside local group working principles. The local rural groups work and conduct transactions like banks. K-Rep sponsors several of these groups, which also enhance service access to the local community. Each of the groups has an advisor from the bank.

- Contractual agreements with dairy processors have facilitated financial access to credit for farmers. The processors recover the money on behalf of the service providers after milk delivery.

The overall agricultural policy in the SRA realizes that service provision in agriculture is important in increasing productivity. In the dairy subsector, through the National Livestock Policy and Dairy Industry Development Policy, AI services and financial services have been identified as points that require intervention to stimulate subsector growth. The policy suggests various interventions to encourage innovation in service provision.

LINKS AND COORDINATION WITHIN THE INNOVATION SYSTEM

The section discusses the interactions and links within the maize, tomato, and dairy subsectors. The discussion uses the following typology of links: company to company, public to private partnerships, company to intermediaries, company to farmer/farmer organization, and associations and company to knowledge organizations. This typology is based on links that go beyond the typical public-private partnerships (PPPs). The section also highlights the key collective or business associations, which coordinate links between policy makers and agribusiness firms.

Interactions and Links Between Key Actors: Company to Company

Maize. Chemical companies facilitate maize innovation by providing access to seed technology. The plantation companies were bulk purchasers of fertilizer and provided a ready market for chemical companies. Traders, supermarkets, millers, and retailers also provided a market for maize and maize products. Transport companies facilitated the transportation of maize and maize products to market outlets. Microfinance institutions facilitated access to loans, micro-credit, and management. Input supply companies also provide technology and service to agribusiness firms.

Tomatoes. The links facilitating tomato innovation include those that involve companies that jointly collaborated in technology dissemination, for example, chemical companies and dealers. The chemical companies supported dealers and stockists by providing training, credit, and logistical support.

Dairy. A company-to-company link in dairy enterprise is evident among processing companies, banking institutions, and feed companies. These interactions reduce transaction costs of paying dairy farmers, solve the problem of delayed payments, and provide inputs to the farmers. Two examples are New KCC and Equity Bank, whereby dairy farmers who deliver milk to New KCC Dairy processors are paid in a timely way by the Equity Bank, and the bank can extend loans to farmers based on their production trends and volume. The link between Sigma Feeds and Brookside Dairies provides timely and needed inputs to farmers on credit. All the loans advanced to the farmers are recovered by the processors for the banks once the milk is delivered.

Interactions and Links Between Key Actors: Company to Intermediary Services

Maize. The intermediating agencies that facilitate the agribusiness firms were banks, dealers, AFC, transport companies, and NGOs. AFC and Equity Bank provided credit support and financial management to smallholder farmers in maize production. Dealers and stockists distributed seed and helped in accessing smallholder farmers. NGOs facilitated agribusiness firms by securing financial services for their farmers and facilitating government procurement.

Tomatoes. The main interaction between agribusinesses and intermediaries involved the provision of financial services and credit to producers. AFC, in implementing its wholesaling model, used private companies, including contract farming companies, to channel funds to end users. This enabled the end users to finance their innovations provided they are within the lending requirements.

Dairy. In the dairy industry, the company-intermediary link is prominent in the drug companies that contract with several veterinarians and animal drug stockists in various regions to act as retail outlets. The drug companies network with the chemical retailers and regional representatives and distributors to maintain and enhance the supply of animal drugs to the farmers.

Interactions and Links Between Key Actors: Company to Farmer Organizations/Associations

Maize. Farmer cooperatives have organized groups of farmers and facilitated bulk transportation of inputs and products. Seed growers and agents have played a key role in growing and distributing seeds on a contract basis. The Millers Association of Kenya has recommended maize milling companies to the government.

Tomatoes. Company–to–farmer organization interactions have been the most facilitative in terms of tomato innovation as they provided knowledge. For instance, Simlaw Seed Company used its membership in the International Seed Federation (ISF), African Seed Association, and ACP Seed Association to gain information invaluable to their innovation processes. Also, Kamumo Food's interactions with CGD enabled it to network with important stakeholders and improve on its produce. Farmers who have been organized into groups are also better placed to receive training and other technological support, greatly facilitating the innovation process. Trufoods, for instance, has contracted with individual farmers and farmers groups, enabling it to provide technical support for innovation. Farmer groups that are members of the KOAN have a platform for sharing the new knowledge necessary for innovation.

Dairy. Processors and financial institutions have come up with models of providing working capital to farmers. Formal contracts, which are witnessed by the Kenya Dairy Board, are the mode of interaction. The financial institutions, particularly the banks, provide credit and financial services to farmers who supply their produce to a processor. The processor recovers the money on behalf of the financial institution once the milk is delivered for processing. For example, Equity Bank partners with New KCC to offer dairy farmers financial services. New KCC then recovers the money on behalf of Equity Bank when the farmers supply milk. Similar arrangements occur with other input providers where farmers partner with feed companies to access animal feed on credit. Sigma Feeds have an arrangement with Brookside Dairies to supply farmers with feed. Several companies providing AI service have established what they call the "service hubs" formed around milk cooling and collection plants in rural dairy producing regions. The American Breeding Society Total Cattle Management (ABS-TCM) uses this model to provide AI services to farmers. Within these "service hubs," dairy farmers can access all the services, especially AI and veterinary services, which they require. Again, the cost of providing these services is recovered once the farmer delivers his milk to the cooling plant.

Interactions and Links Between Key Actors: Public-Private Partnerships

Maize. The contribution of public-private partnerships to maize innovation occurs with technology transfer and dissemination. Public research bodies such as CIMMYT and KARI facilitate technology transfer to agribusinesses by donating their germplasm for improving maize seed to companies including Kenya Seed Company and Pannar. The Ministry of Agriculture extension service has organized agricultural shows, field days, and exhibitions.

Tomatoes. The interactions between agribusiness firms and public organizations focused on product testing and dissemination. For instance, Osho Chemical Company partnered with KARI in product testing while Simlaw Seed Company engaged entomologists and pathologists at the University of Nairobi in seed validation trials. The Ministry of Agriculture collaborated with Trufoods and Osho chemicals to organize farmer extension outreach. Also, the private and public sector organizations were actively involved in stakeholder forums for knowledge learning and sharing.

Dairy. PPPs occur less frequently in the dairy industry because of lack of incentives that enhance private participation in the subsector. However, the Kenya Dairy Board has partnered with private laboratories (Ana-labs) to ensure that milk quality standards in the dairy industry are maintained. The dairy board has also partnered with dairy training institutes and Egerton University to ensure there are training standards. There have also been some links between private animal feed companies with public research institutes in developing animal feed.

Coordinating Links within the Value Chains

This section focuses on value chain coordination, especially the range of organizations established to coordinate various activities, including marketing, access to technical and financial capacity or services, assistance in meeting and setting quality standards, and political lobbying.

Maize. Under the auspices of the Kenya Maize Development Program (KMDP), an NGO, ACDI-VOCA coordinates links between small farmers and input suppliers for mutual benefits. The chemical companies are members of the Agrochemicals Association of Kenya (AAK), which ensures a level playing field for its members. AAK is useful in providing information and guidance to its members, especially with respect to government regulations and makes dealing with public officials much easier. For instance, while there are standards for weights, quality, and environmental safety, the problem is their enforcement. Also, there is a need for a structured waste disposal system and coordination between agrochemical companies and public extension service.

The seed companies such as Kenya Seed Company and Pannar are members of the Seed Trade Association of Kenya (STAK), which is an association of private seed companies. These companies are also members of the Kenya Association of Manufacturers (KAM). These associations lobby for policy change and gain from their coordination and access to information. The maize processing firms are active members of the Kenya Millers Association (KMA). KMA has a membership of twenty millers. The association levels the playing field in the procurement of maize and packaging materials.

The banks and financial service institutions participate in the Kenya Banking Association (KBA) to channel collective problems as well as lobby for policy change. NCPB as a marketing agency is a member of the Eastern Africa Grain Council (EAGC), which lobbies for maize trade policies in the East African region.

Tomatoes. Apparently, the tomato value chain does not appear to have a single institution coordinating links. Rather, coordination appears to be spontaneous and localized. In the processing and retailing stages of the chain, firms involved are more interested in ensuring a stable supply of raw materials and products respectively. Consequently, they have reorganized their operations to include departments that vet, recruit, and provide advisory services to tomato producers. Their main aim is to create a working and sustainable relationship with the farmers to reduce problems in the supply chain. Similarly, input suppliers are more interested in coordinating activities that enhance their sales to the producers. Each of these groups works separately and is not linked in any way. The AFC's plans to form an Apex body to facilitate access to credit for input supply and product marketing comes closest to performing an overall coordinating role. AFC provides credit to enable input supply to farmers, links the farmers with the market, and recovers its loans from the beneficiaries through the marketing institution. However, AFC is aimed at the dairy industry and not tomato growers, and is subject to a policy change in its cooperating policy (Act of Parliament). An NGO provides a more localized coordinating role in linking farmers with the tomato market and entering into an agreement with the buyer to pay the farmers in advance while waiting to recover its money from the buyer.

Dairy. Strengthening the KDB during the liberalization era was one of the key institutional changes that have had a great impact in the dairy industry. The KDB was strengthened to undertake a role in regulating market promotion and increasing milk production and value addition. To effectively regulate standards and promote the market, the KDB has established a regulatory network of institutions at the national and regional levels. This institutional network promotes dairy products in the regional and domestic markets and maintains quality standards. The network is also linked to Codex Alimentarius, an international food safety body, which gives guidelines to food quality and standards. At the national and district levels, institutions partner with accredited laboratories and farmers to maintain milk quality. This new institutional framework is part of the KDB reforms undertaken under the new dairy industry development policy. This is in addition to aggressive training programs tailored to fit the specific requirements of different actors. Figure 3.2 illustrates the impact of organizational innovation that aims to promote marketing.

The Board through this framework has harmonized regional quality standards. For instance, East Africa dairy standards have been harmonized. The Board has been able to promote the market to fill the production gap by reducing the imports of dairy products while promoting more exports: by 2005, exports had almost caught up with imports that decreased significantly.

Figure 3.2   Framework for Ensuring Quality Standards and Market
Promotion of Dairy Products in Kenya: The Case of Public
Institutional Innovation and the Kenya Dairy Board

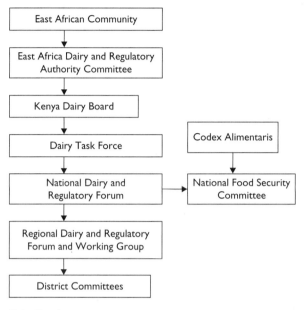

Source: Kenya Dairy Board.

PUBLIC POLICY INFLUENCE ON AGRIBUSINESS INNOVATIONS

This section presents the link between policies that are specific and relevant to a sector with innovations and innovation systems. The legal and institutional framework of a policy is assessed as to how it influences the operational environment of a subsector. Because Kenya is still undergoing economic reform, there are still policy drafts that have not yet been finalized. However, subsectors operate with best practices in line with the draft policies.

In this section, a general overview of the agricultural policy in the overall development framework will be given. This overview is followed by consideration of the maize, tomato, and dairy subsectors, in which the influence of policies in stimulating and enhancing innovation is assessed. The dairy subsector takes a relatively different format due to its unique characteristics, including a well- developed institutional organization and specific policy, unlike the other two subsectors (maize and tomato).

The agricultural sector in Kenya is governed by 131 pieces of legislation, many of which are obsolete, unenforceable, or inconsistent with current policy (MOA 2005) and the operational environment. The SRA spells out the current overall agricultural development framework, and *Vision 2030* adopts it. The current framework requires establishing sector-specific policies to address unique development issues that affect each sector. In addition, there are specific policies enforced in inputs such as fertilizer and seeds, which are important to agricultural production. For instance, the National Livestock Policy (NLP) governs the overall livestock sector. In addition to the NLP, the Dairy Industry Development Policy articulates issues specific to the dairy industry. The seed and fertilizer policies for maize and tomatoes address specific issues related to these inputs. These sector-specific policies are important in stimulating, encouraging, and enhancing innovation at the micro level.

Although not all sectors have sector-specific policies, analysis of the influence of policy on innovations is concerned with sector-specific policies, other relevant and related policies, and the overall macro policy. Incoherencies in policies may arise from inconsistencies in legal and institutional frameworks. Because of the legal and institutional incoherencies at the macro or micro level, it is difficult to determine whether a policy is facilitating or impeding innovations. Thus, it is useful to look at the influential role of particular policy elements.

Policy Influence on Innovation in the Maize and Tomato Subsectors

In the maize and tomato subsectors, lack of sector-specific policies confines the assessment to overall agricultural policy and other related policies, such as the tax seed and fertilizer policies.

The key policies with elements affecting maize and tomato agribusiness innovations included the following:

- Trade policy
- Finance and fiscal policies
- Agriculture policy
- Communication policy
- Legal guarantees.

In each of these areas, researchers cited either an element of the policy or a regulatory body as facilitating or impeding agribusiness innovation. By applying an augmented Dennis (2005) typology approach, the analogy of the key elements of the cited policies follows.

Trade Policy Regime

Facilitating: These policies have made the import and export of materials easy, thus enhancing and reducing the cost of production while expanding the market share for the finished product for agribusinesses and benefiting from the prices prevailing in the world market.

- *Quality assurance policy* has facilitated agribusinesses involved in importing agrochemicals and equipment by evaluating the quality of their products through Kenya Bureau of Standards to ensure good quality and food safety standards at reasonable cost.
- *Policies on value addition* enabled milling and processing firms such as Pembe and Corn Products Ltd. to add value to the raw materials through processing into various products. Among the most pertinent policies are the Strategy for Revitalizing Agriculture, which stresses the promotion of agroprocessing and rural industries; the investment policy and investment code, which facilitates the development of agroprocessing; and national food and nutrition policy, in which food fortification enhances value addition of basic products, for example, maize products.
- *Private-public partnership policies,* especially through business and collective associations, have reduced bureaucracy because some of the services were commercialized, and the long waiting process in the public sector could be eliminated by private partners.

Impeding: Trade policies through bureaucratic delays, high customs duties, and the requirement of relatively high international quality standards impede importation of seeds, equipment, and materials, and consequently, innovation. For instance, import policies have positive effects as agricultural inputs are zero rated, and there are tax exemptions on imported cooling equipment, but delays in the port can lead to delays in the adoption of technology.

- KEBS was commended for effectively enforcing standards such as the requirement to put company logos on manufactured products to reduce incidents of fake products. However, KEBS lacks sophisticated equipment for assessing and assuring food safety standards.
- While the zero rating of agricultural inputs facilitated the importation of chemicals and equipment, the taxation of experimental materials impeded their importation. This tax made experiments expensive, and many agribusiness firms were discouraged from carrying out various experiments that would improve their products and processes.
- Local authority levies' collection policy and modalities to enhance payment of levies and administration to curtail corruption were impediments.

Finance/Fiscal Policies

Facilitating: The liberalization of financial services in the country and the subsequent enactment of the Central Bank Act of 1996 have encouraged private players in the industry.

- The *Central Bank Act* led to the recognition of the microfinance institutions (MFIs) and the growth of several microfinance institutions. For instance, banks such as the Family Bank with agricultural-related products grew out of public sector reform policy, which have allowed financial institutions to provide loans to agribusiness firms, thereby creating a conducive business environment (see also the microfinance section under dairy subsection).

- *Policy on social services registration* enabled agribusiness firms to facilitate registration of self-help groups and give them a mandate to engage in income-generating activities that enhanced their performance (see, for example, the "Village Bank" model of K-Rep).

Impeding:

- Agribusiness firms were unable to access funding from most financial institutions because interest rates and the collateral requirements for loans were too high and cumbersome for small processing agribusiness firms.
- Taxation impeded technology upgrading by making technology acquisition burdensome.

Agricultural Policy

Facilitating: The *National Agricultural Policy* promotes technology and dissemination. Through this policy, agribusinesses and farmers were able to access information on new product development and to improve their production systems and the quality of production. For instance:

- The *Agricultural Extension* policy through the National Agricultural and Livestock Extension Program (NALEP) Focal Area approach facilitates performance by making it easier, cheaper, and faster for farmers and agribusinesses to access extension services and improve their production ability.

Impeding: The agricultural sector in Kenya, as discussed before, has by now an incoherent legislation system not aligned to the national economic strategy. Specifically:

- *The tension between policy and implementation* is illustrated by maize marketing (that is, liberalized markets facing implementation hurdles because of government intervention). Also, legal impediments are created by the Act of Parliament Cap 338 of 1995 governing operations of the NCPB. This act has not been revised. NCPB currently operates by using circulars and policy statements that are not legally binding. There is a need to revise Cap 338 in lieu of liberalization because NCPB is expected to raise its own revenue and serve as a third-party broker to stabilize the price of maize.
- *Land policy (or lack of it)* is another major impediment to technological investments and agricultural innovation. For instance, seed production by the Kenya Seed Company is currently constrained by land subdivision

especially among its contract farmers. This reduces the distances between fields, which is supposed to be 200 m. As a result, the company has been forced to cluster farmers to produce adequate stocks of certified maize seed.

ICT Policy

Facilitating: The *Information and Communication Technologies Policy* has made it easier for agribusinesses to access information on new product development through research and Internet facilities. For instance, ICT policies helped agribusinesses get information on finance and service provision through the Internet and telecommunication at affordable rates for agribusinesses. A majority of the agribusiness firms interviewed for this study used ICT for internal and external communications and to ensure sound financial transactions. ICT has facilitated access to finance and markets in the dairy subsector.

Legal Guarantees

Facilitating: The well-defined *Seed Policy Act* (Cap 326) governs the seed system. Also the Act is being revised to account for developments in the seed industry. For instance, the Act's support for the intellectual property rights for the protection of new varieties of plants has encouraged entry of private seed companies and subsequent development and deployment of new plant varieties. The process of seed testing by KEPHIS has become faster and more efficient.

- *Policy to distribute seed to stockists* appointed in conjunction with KEPHIS has made it easy for farmers to access high-quality certified seeds and for seed companies to distribute their products.
- *Quality assurance and food safety policies* have strengthened institutions and charged them with quality assurance responsibility. That is, KEPHIS and KEBS have respectively encouraged the production of quality products that are safe for human consumption and ascertained that market outlets like Uchumi supermarkets received good quality products.

Impeding: The major impediment of *policy on maize seed* is the monopoly of the KSC, KARI, and KEPHIS. Also, the seed input is strictly regulated, and seeds cannot be produced at the village level under duality declared seed, resulting in higher prices for farmers to obtain horticultural seeds.

Other cited policy impediments are:

- *Policy on inspection of production process* by local authorities deterred agribusiness performance, because most of them had not met all of the stringent and often outdated requirements by local authorities and had to hurriedly close business whenever the local authorities visited them to avoid penalties.

- *Environmental policy:* The environmental standards, especially those espoused by National Environmental Management Agency (NEMA), were high. The cost of meeting the standards required by NEMA for processing agribusinesses like Trufoods were high, thus increasing the production costs for their products.
- *Energy policy:* The high costs of electricity deterred the performance of processing agribusinesses and led to high production costs.
- *Disaster preparedness policies* were limiting because they did not adequately address the issue of supply during drought seasons, flood seasons, and off seasons, therefore leading to an unstable supply of products to markets.
- *Infrastructure policy and investment:* The main impediment for business is the high transaction costs because of poor road infrastructure and logistics. For example, poor infrastructure inhibits efficient milk collection, access to inputs, market information, and other important services, such as extension and AI.

Policy Influence on Innovations in the Dairy Subsector

The move to liberalize has brought positive changes to the dairy industry market. The number of private processors has increased, but informal milk selling has also increased and has brought the selling of low-quality dairy products into the markets. The resulting competitive environment has opened markets for different innovations. Different brands of dairy products and even new products that fit the consumer preferences have increased. The dairy policy has evolved from the era of market control to the era of deregulation and has embraced more positive and private accommodation in the sector. The dairy sector has been recognized by the ERS-WEC and SRA. The new National Livestock Policy (NLP) provides an overarching policy framework for the entire livestock sector, including the dairy industry. These policy frameworks have been adopted in the Draft Vision 2030, and the dairy subsector is recognized as important to poverty alleviation. The focus will be on encouraging more private participation and creation of incentives for public-private relationships.

The current draft dairy policy purports to make intervention over the entire dairy value chain. The draft dairy policy states, "Interventions will cover dairy research, milk production, extension, marketing of milk and milk products, milk processing, milk consumption, human resource development and training, financial services, institutional, legal, and regulatory issues." The main target of policy reform in the dairy industry and generally in agriculture has been the creation of an enabling environment within which actors can operate. For instance, liberalization opened up the markets and divested the market environment, which would otherwise encourage private participation. The competition resulting from the entry of more private actors was expected to enhance producer prices in agriculture while also enhancing consumer prices. Institutional reforms envisaged within the reforms package focused facilitation to market access rather than marketing the produce.

Innovation facilitating policies. Key innovation facilitating policies in the dairy industry include the Draft Dairy Industry Development Policy and the Draft National Livestock Policy. Although the NLP provides the overall livestock development framework, the draft dairy development policy prescribes specific important development policies to the dairy industry.

The dairy industry development policy encourages

- The entry of many players in the dairy industry market, which is in line with liberalization policy.
- Innovative ways of accessing animal feed: Although there are no government incentives to invest in the animal feed industry, the current dairy policy encourages and supports farmer innovation towards achieving access to animal feeds. The policy states that "Future efforts will be directed at ensuring availability of pasture and fodder seeds by encouraging large-scale range intensification and regeneration of existing pasture. Development of feed ration ingredients for every district is crucial to assist farmers to make their own feeds, as this would greatly reduce supplementation cost. The Government will also encourage cooperatives and farmer groups to put up small feed mills or purchase feed mixers for making homemade rations using locally available materials. Making bulk purchases for members would facilitate availability, price uniformity, and distribution."
- Harmonization of the various acts that govern the animal health and strengthening of the Department of Veterinary Services: The Draft National Livestock Policy and Draft Dairy Policy recognize animal health and veterinary services as key to the improvement of the overall livestock and dairy industry. Whereas previously the policy of the Cattle Cleansing Act recognized cattle dipping as the only way of tick control, the policy is being amended to accommodate other methods of tick control. Further, the amendments of the Veterinary Surgeons Act to allow para-veterinary workers with diplomas and certificate training to treat animals, and the Pharmacy and Poisons Act to allow veterinarians to dispense veterinary medicines, increase the access to veterinary services in the rural areas. This is enhanced further by the strengthening of the DVS to deal with epizootic diseases. Previously the government monopolized breeding services through the Central Artificial Insemination Services (CAIS). The target for the current dairy industry development policy is to revamp CAIS and commercialize its activities while maintaining the national strategic livestock genetic pool.

- Public-private investment in extension and advisory services: The government, while seeking to provide demand-driven extension services and involvement of the private sector, will encourage financing of private extension services by enforcement of a clear legal framework that will govern contractual agreements.
- The creation of the National Livestock Research Institute within which the Dairy Research Center will be incorporated. The policy encourages research in dairy product diversification as well as in packaging. In addition to technology development, the dairy industry development policy seeks to enhance technology development and transfer mechanisms for increased adoption. Research will be enhanced by royalties and contracts, including government grants, and by the commercialization of research products.
- Addressing the dairy business environment: The policy promotes ethical business practices that hinge on the development of contractual agreements and complementary legislation in the dairy industry. Markets are deemed important to innovation because they are the key pull factors. Innovation in dairy as in other subsectors responds to market returns positively. In terms of imports and exports, the policy targets ensure that cooperatives and processors develop sufficient capacities to produce and efficiently distribute dairy products to satisfy the domestic demand and also surplus for export markets. Market goals can be achieved through export market promotion, consistent and continuous production, and the inclusion of dairy issues in regional and international negotiations.
- Revival of milk marketing cooperatives: Cooperatives reduce marketing costs and consequently increase returns to farmers. The growth of cooperatives is attributed to the policy reforms. The policy encourages revival of cooperatives and emphasizes contractual engagements to facilitate marketing, inputs, and services access under economies of scale.
- Encouraging private participation in maintaining feeder roads regularly in milk producing areas, while encouraging private sector facilitation, speeding up the rural electrification program to encourage and enhance milk cooling, supporting and promoting more local milk processing, and allowing the dairy cooperatives and private sector operators to benefit from tax allowances on new investments. KCC facilitated the initial infrastructure of milk collection. Owing to the collapse of KCC, the milk collection mechanism has been poor. The policy aims to improve milk collection through the revival of farmer cooperatives and farmer groups that will facilitate rural milk collection. Several cooperatives and processors have set collection centers in rural areas. NGOs, such as Heifer International, and private companies have come into the dairy industry to facilitate milk chilling and service delivery. The rural milk, collection centers have been improved by installing chilling plants to preserve milk, especially where distances to the processors are long. The revival of cooperatives and farmer groups may increase incentives to promote ethical business practices and contractual agreements.

- Zero rating of taxes on inputs used in liquid milk processing with regard to a value-added tax. A tax exemption on equipment, especially those involved in powder milk processing, is important in the dairy industry to support processing. The policy recognizes that private sector operators will continue to benefit from tax allowances on new investments. Further inputs used in liquid milk processing are zero rated with regard to value-added tax.

Other positive measures that stimulate innovation within the dairy industry development policy include

- Promoting the development and adoption of acceptable cost-effective milk packaging that addresses health issues as well as discourages use of packaging materials that are environmentally unfriendly.
- Taking measures to ensure that dairy processors and manufacturers establish quality testing and assurance systems that conform to national and international standards.
- Implementing and enforcing the new management tenets embodied in the amended Cooperative Societies Act of 2004; encouraging partnerships between cooperatives and other private sector players, especially processors; promoting bulk purchases of farm inputs by cooperatives to minimize costs and improve competitiveness; and formulating ways of protecting producers and producer organizations from the effects of collapsed firms.
- Ensuring that adherence to quality standards for domestic and imported dairy products will be strengthened, while the level of participation in the development and setting of world dairy standards will be enhanced.
- Guaranteeing premium prices during dry seasons to processors.
- Promoting affordable long-life milk products and including dairy products in the stocks of national food strategic reserves.
- Implementing the ICT and the e-government policy to the fullest.
- Promoting strong links between universities and other research institutions. In addition, the government will set up a national dairy information center at KDB that will be equipped with a databank facility to collect, analyze, and disseminate information on the dairy industry.
- Implementating innovative ways of ensuring a sustainable environment, aligning the dairy industry with land policy, and implementing the water policy besides institutional changes that reform the KDB.
- *Financial service provision:* A current information and communication system and the liberalization of the financial sector has steered financial services access to the rural majority. The communications and information-sharing environment has been enhanced, and this has also prompted numerous and fast methods of making transactions. The Central Bank Act of 1996, which was geared toward encouraging private players in the industry, led to the recognition of the MFI and the formation of the Association

of MicroFinance Institutions. The growth of several microfinance institutions such as Faulu Kenya, Kenya Women Finance Trust, Jamii Bora Trust and even Equity and Family Finance Banks, which have come up with agricultural-related products, is attributed to Kenya's liberalization of financial services. The current Draft NLP and the Draft Dairy Policy all positively recognize financial service delivery as a key to increasing livestock productivity and to the growth of a vibrant economic livestock sector.

All these elements in the Draft Dairy Policy influence the operational environment of the actors over the value chain. Access and use of agricultural innovations can be improved in a favorable market environment. The positive influence enhances the actors' returns and enables them to invest more in innovations.

Innovation impeding policies. However, there are several policies that impede innovation in the dairy sector. Despite the availability of these innovations, there have been constraints in accessing and using these innovations. Constrained market returns inhibit innovation. Most firms reinvest their returns in enhancing and testing their innovations. In this case, policies that govern the trade and markets are the main points of contention, including county and municipal council's policies that impose a charge on animal feed sold in every county, the tax policies, and the infrastructure (communication and roads) policies. All of these policies increase the cost of production, which is transmitted to the markets as increased feed prices. Specifically:

- *Trade policies*:
  - *Import policies:* Although agricultural inputs are zero rated and there are tax exemptions on imported cooling equipment, delays in the port lead to delays in adoption of technology. Sometimes imported technology is overtaken by market requirements. Despite the companies incurring costs, the technology becomes obsolete.
  - *Exchange rates policy:* Unstable exchange rates greatly influence the prices of imported equipment especially whenever there is a delay. For instance, the New KCC, which is a public company, is still subjected to government procurement and tendering procedures. These procedures are the main causes of delays to adjustment in the dynamic market scenarios. Delays in importation of capital goods are sometimes grossly affected by exchange rate fluctuations.
- *Infrastructure and communication policy:* Milk is produced in regions with high potential. However, these regions are characterized by impassable roads especially during the rainy season. Poor infrastructure inhibits efficient milk collection, access to inputs, market information, and other important services such as extension and AI.
- *Financial access:* Although there has been a significant improvement in the communications and information sector, there is more to be done because

a vast rural area still needs financial access. The issue of collateral to access loans and credit services by the rural poor is still a barrier. The credit crisis is pegged to the land policy, which does not confer secure land ownerships that promote economic investment and sound environmental conservation and management. Trade policies (tax, monetary, fiscal, exchange, and interest rates) are disincentives to the provision of financial services because they increase the cost of doing business and thus the cost of loans and credits.

- *Land policy:* Land policy, which by failing to define sustainable land ownership, constrains capital and technological investments and consequently constrains innovations that would otherwise improve productivity.

CONCLUSION

This study entailed the assessment of innovation in the maize, tomato, and dairy subsectors by focusing on value chains using the AIS framework. In this context, a tentative conclusion can be made about whether national public policies impede or facilitate innovations. It is evident that policy in the institutional and legal contexts influences innovations in Kenya. The three subsectors are contextually different in terms of policy and geographical regions. The value chains, actors, and links are different. The influence of policy on the innovation thus varies over the value chains. Whereas the dairy subsector has a sector-specific policy that influences the environment of the sector, maize and tomatoes do not have such a policy, and thus their operational environments are influenced by other relevant policies within the agricultural sector.

The Kenya country study shows that there have been innovative ideas at the various levels of the value chains. Notable levels of innovation are at the inputs, value addition, marketing, and service provision levels. Policies that influence agriculture in Kenya and any other developing country are interlinked and have influence in at least one level of the value chain. Sector-specific policies, like that for the dairy enterprise in Kenya, are more comprehensive, specific, and have influence on the overall value chain. The entire set of policies focus on influencing innovation toward markets. However, conflicts arise and curtail innovation. Important policies in Kenya that relate to agriculture are trade finance/fiscal, agriculture, and communication policies, as well as legal guarantees. The sector-specific policies considered important in this country study were the overall agricultural development framework as defined in the SRA, the NLP, and the dairy policy. Although the SRA spells out the general directions of the sector development, the sector-specific policies that relate to specific inputs such as fertilizer and enterprises like dairy are more comprehensive and in touch with actual activities. The study identifies key drivers of innovation in all value chains: reduced cost of production through reduced input costs, available and affordable timely financial services, reduced barriers to markets access such as reduced taxes, improved infrastructure, and increased demand in the market as the population grows. Markets, especially in an open economy, serve as pull and push stimuli to innovation. The policy role will be to influence the push and pull factors of innovation.

Overall current policies in agriculture have had a positive impact on innovation, although they are not adequate to stimulate innovation. These policies have emphasized reducing costs of production through availing inputs, enhancing financial access, and reducing barriers to the market. Although policies have various effects on the value chains stimulating innovation, the current policy drafts include the innovation concept, but it is not well articulated in a systemic way. The need to stimulate innovations through adequate infrastructure that lowers cost of doing business in markets, reduced barriers to market access, and enhanced financial access in agriculture is imperative. All these aspects of the value chain increase production and enhance access to markets. Markets are the most important drivers, as they create incentives to innovate.

Within a government policy, some elements such as policy documents, legal and institutional frameworks support whereas others impede agribusiness innovation. These policy elements indirectly influence innovation through the operational environment of value chain actors and their attributes. Policy reforms and institutional arrangements are important in triggering innovations, in the way that liberalization fostered the entry of private players and opened the markets to external competition in the agricultural sector. The competition that resulted from these actions has positively triggered innovations. The collectives or business associations coordinate links between policy makers and agribusiness firms. We need to pay attention to the direct influence of agencies, which link actors in the value chains of the three case studies and the entire agricultural sector.

REFERENCES

ACDI/VOCA. 2007. *Kenya Maize Handbook.* Washington, DC: ACDI/VOCA.

CIMMYT (Centro International de Mejoramiento de Maíz y Trigo) Economics Program. 1993. *The Adoption of Agricultural Technology: A Guide for Survey Design.* Mexico City: CIMMYT. http://www.uflib.ufl.edu/ufdc/?b=UF00080103&v=0001.

Dennis, William. 2005. "Public Policy towards Small Business and Entrepreneurship: The American Approach." Paper presented at OECD workshop, "Understanding Entrepreneurship: Issues and Numbers." http://www.oecd.org/dataoecd/25/9/35579701.ppt.

Ekwe, Kenneth Chikwado, and Nwachukwu Ike. 2006. "Market Led Innovation in Agriculture: Sustaining Gari Marketing Enterprise for Rural Livelihood—Farmers' Indigenous Innovations in South Eastern Nigeria." Paper presented at the Innovation Africa Symposium, Kampala, November 20–23. http://www.innovationafrica.net/pdf/s7_ekwe_full.pdf.

Export Processing Zones Authority. 2005. "Dairy Industry in Kenya." Export Processing Zones Authority, Nairobi.

GoK (Government of Kenya). 2002. "The New Kenya Consumer Price Index: Users Guide." Central Bureau of Statistics, Ministry of Finance and Planning, Nairobi.

———. 2003. "Economic Recovery Strategy for Wealth and Employment Creation (2003–2007)." GoK, Nairobi.

———. 2007a. "The Draft National Livestock Policy." GoK, Nairobi.

———. 2007b. "The Draft Dairy Industry Development Policy." GoK, Nairobi.

———. 2007. "Vision 2030." GoK, Nairobi.

Karanja, Andrew M. 2003. "The Dairy Industry in Kenya: The Post-Liberalization Agenda." Tegemeo Institute of Agricultural Policy and Development, Egerton University, Kenya.

Kimani, Lilian W. 2000. "Women in Agricultural Research Policy and Management Today: The Case of Kenya Agriculture Research Institute (KARI)." Paper presented at Gender and Agriculture in Africa: Effective Strategies for Moving Forward, Nairobi, May 3–5.

Ministry of Agriculture. 2003. *Strategy for Revitalizing Agriculture 2004–2014.* Nairobi: Ministry of Agriculture, Government Printers.

———. 2006. "Strategic Plan 2006–2010." Nairobi: Ministry of Agriculture, Government Printers, Nairobi.

Minot, Nicholas, and Devesh Roy. 2007. "Impact of High-Value Agriculture and Modern Marketing Channels on Poverty: An Analytical Framework." International Food Policy Research Institute, Washington, DC.

Minot, Nicholas, and Ngigi, Margaret. 2003. "Are Horticultural Exports a Replicable Success Story? Evidence from Kenya and Côte de Ivoire." Paper presented at the InWent, IFPRI, NEPAD, and CTA Conference, "Successes in African Agriculture," Pretoria, December 1–3.

Miracle, Marvin P. 1966. *Maize in Tropical Africa.* Madison: University of Wisconsin Press.

Mukumbu, M. 1994. "Consumer and Milling Industry Responses to Maize Market Reform in Kenya." In *Proceedings of the Conference on Market Reforms, Agricultural Production and Food Security.* Egerton University, Policy Analysis Matrix, June, Nairobi.

Muli M. B., H. M. Saha, A. M. Mzingirwa, and K. K. Lewa. 2006. "Innovative Methods for Linking Farmers to Inputs Markets through Farmer Field School Networks for Increased Production and Food Security." Paper presented at the Innovation Africa Symposium, Kampala, November 21–23.

Mutuku, Kavoi M., and Tschirley, David. 2004. "Improving Kenya's Domestic Horticultural Production and Marketing System: Current Competitiveness, Forces of Change, and Challenges for the Future." Working Paper 08A/2004, Tegemeo Institute of Agricultural Policy and Development, Egerton University, Njoro, Kenya.

Njoroge, Peter M. 2003. "Enforcement of Competition Policy and Law in Kenya, Including Case Studies in the Areas of Mergers and Takeovers, Prevention of Possible Future Abuse of Dominance, and Collusion/Price Fixing." Monopolies and Price Commission, Ministry of Finance, Nairobi.

Nyangito, Hezron O. 1997. "A Review of Policies on the Maize Sub-sector in Kenya." Discussion Paper 008/97, Institute of Policy Analysis and Research, Nairobi.

Nyangito, Hezron O., and D. M. Nyameino. 2002. "Maize Production and Marketing in Kenya." Prepared for Oxfam Nairobi.

Nyoro, J. K., M. W. Kiiru, and T. S. Jayne. 1999. "Evolution of Kenya's Maize Marketing Systems in the Post-Liberalization Era." Working Paper 2A, Tegemeo Institute of Agricultural Policy and Development, Egerton University, Kenya.

Omondi, George. 2008. "Grain Farmers to Reap from New Receipt System." *Business Daily*, April 18.

Salasya, B. D., W. Mwangi, H. Verkuijl, M. A. Odendo, and J. O. Odenya. 1998. *An Assessment of the Adoption of Seed and Fertiliser Packages and the Role of Credit in Smallholder Maize Production in Kakamega and Vihiga Districts, Kenya.* Mexico City: Centro International de Mejoramiento de Maiz y Trigo and Kenya Agricultural Research Institute.

Schreiber, Catrin. 2002. "Sources of Innovation in Dairy Production in Kenya." Briefing Paper 58, International Service for National Agricultural Research, The Hague, the Netherlands.

Wagacha, Mbui. 2006. "Kenya's Trade Policies: Mainstreaming Strategies in National Development." Optimum Resources International, Nairobi.

World Bank. 2006. *Enhancing Agricultural Innovation: How to Go Beyond the Strengthening of Research Systems.* Washington, DC: World Bank.

Zoundi, Sibiri Jean, and Léonidas Hitimana. 2007. "The Challenges Facing West African Family Farms in Accessing Agricultural Innovations: Institutional and Political Implications Sahel and West Africa Club." Organisation for Economic Co-operation and Development, Paris.

CHAPTER FOUR

Tanzania: Sunflower, Cassava, and Dairy

Joseph Mpagalile, Romanus Ishengoma, and Peter Gillah

The concept of Agricultural Innovation Systems (AIS) recognizes a broader range of actors and sectors involved in innovation, including the private sector and its roles in the value chain. In recent years, the African continent has seen increasing technological innovation. However, there are many examples where technology investments in African countries have not been successful. Therefore, this study of agribusiness innovation in Sub-Saharan Africa (SSA) with a focus on the agriculture and food industry aims at a better understanding of the current situation and how it can be improved, especially through public policy. This country study of Tanzania looked at the policy framework/environment for innovation across the whole value chain for three commodities—sunflowers, cassava, and dairy—including production, management aspects, handling (processing, grading, and packaging) and marketing, with an AIS approach. The interviews involved agribusiness firms, representatives of nongovernmental organizations, business associations and applied research centers, and ministry representatives.

The Tanzania country study found that agriculture features well in Tanzania's policies and strategies. Tanzania already has a number of good agriculture-related policies in place. However, the main challenges and difficulties arise from policy implementation, and some policies lack implementation strategies and guidelines. Also, agribusiness awareness of these policies was low, especially with actors lower down the value chain, such as farmers who understand policy issues based on constraints and opportunities. Respondents pointed out that policies such as the Agriculture and Livestock, Cooperative, Small and Medium Enterprises, and Trade policies address issues that are important to agribusinesses. On the one hand, respondents applauded government effort to open markets for investment in various sectors. On the other hand, some policies were perceived to impede agricultural innovation, including trade, energy, land, and labor policies.

The majority of the firms tend to seek new ideas and knowledge as they innovate. Of the three value chains—sunflowers, cassava, and dairy—the dairy subsector is the most innovative. Examples include technical, product, and organizational innovations. In the quest to innovate, agribusinesses engage in networks. Various external actors influence agribusinesses in decision making, including consumers, the public sector, research and development (R&D) institutes, input suppliers, extension services, and business and farmers associations. In Tanzania, consumers, agribusinesses, and R&D institutes have driven innovation.

The Tanzania study concludes that most policies are positive but lack translation into actions and participatory evaluation at the local level. The Tanzania country study recommends that more effort is needed toward policy implementation and that the private sector should receive more priority in promoting agricultural innovation in Tanzania. Further, government must better support interactions between agribusinesses and drivers of innovations such as R&D institutions.

BACKGROUND INFORMATION

Agricultural Sector in Tanzania

Tanzania has great potential for agriculture development, yet it is among the poorest (ranked in the bottom 20) developing countries (UNDP 2004). Agriculture (including crop production, livestock, and natural resources) is one of the leading sectors of Tanzania's economy. Apart from providing food, agriculture is the main source of income for the rural population, which forms 80 percent of the total population and employs 70 percent of the active labor force. In 2005, agriculture contributed about 50 percent to Tanzania's gross domestic product (GDP). Crop production alone contributed 55 percent of the agricultural GDP followed by livestock, which accounted for 30 percent (MAFS 2005), and natural resources accounted for 15 percent. Smallholder farmers dominate agriculture, with farm sizes ranging from one to three hectares. A wide variety of crops can grow in Tanzania because of its wide climatic variation and agro-ecological conditions. Maize and rice are principal food as well as commercial crops, whereas cassava and bananas are important subsistence crops. Traditional export crops include coffee, cashew nuts, cotton, tea, and sisal. Other widely grown crops include beans, sorghum, millet, sweet potatoes, and a wide variety of fruits, vegetables, oilseeds, and flowers.

The Policy Context of Agriculture

Agriculture is the mainstay of Tanzania's economy, which is reflected in Tanzania's development vision, strategies, and policies. The Tanzania Development Vision (Vision 2025) envisages that the agricultural sector by 2025 is modernized, commercial, highly productive, and profitable; uses natural resources sustainably; and acts as an effective basis for intersectoral linkings. The National Strategy for Growth and Reduction of Poverty (NSGRP) recognizes the importance of agriculture in poverty reduction efforts. The NSGRP focuses on the aspirations of Vision 2025, and its strategy recognizes how the agricultural sector can contribute to poverty eradication. The NSGRP looks at nuisance taxes and levies imposed on farmers as well as backward and forward links to agricultural production.

The agricultural sector is the focus of the Agricultural Sector Development Strategy (ASDS) that set an agricultural vision for 2002–05. ASDS sought to create an enabling and conducive environment for improving the agricultural productivity and profitability.

In particular, the Agricultural and Livestock Policy (ALP) of 1977 aims to help accomplish the ASDS and NSGRP, specifically by ensuring basic food security, improving the standard of living in rural areas through increased income from agriculture and livestock production, increasing foreign exchange earnings, producing raw materials for local industries, developing new technologies, promoting sustainable use and management of natural resources, developing human resources within the agricultural sector, and providing support to the agricultural sector.[1] The policy covers important crops, including cash crops such as coffee, cotton, cashew nuts, tobacco, tea, sisal, and pyrethrum; staple food crops such as maize and rice; drought-resistant crops such as sorghum and millet; and other staples such as bananas, plantains, and Irish potatoes. Other crops given priority include fruits, vegetables, spices, oilseeds, and pulses. The ALP emphasizes the role of the private sector in achieving its policy objectives but limits government to public sector support functions. Such functions include policy formulation and supervision, research, training, extension and information services, sanitary regulations, quality control, environmental protection, and creation of an environment conducive to agricultural growth, specifically in the development of markets and marketing systems for inputs and outputs. The Cooperative Development Policy of 1997, which sets strategies for agricultural marketing cooperatives, rural financial services, and livestock and industrial cooperatives, supplements ALP's policies.

The National Science and Technology Policy of 1996 is another pivotal policy that relates directly to the agricultural sector. This policy aims at organizing and sustaining the technology capacity, as well as maximizing productivity through the introduction of improved methods of farming, such as enhanced seed varieties; better methods of food and crop processing, preservation, and storage; the development of agricultural mechanization and irrigation technologies; use of agricultural wastes (manure, biofuels); training of extension workers; as well as R&D in animal production and veterinary medicine.

A range of other policies impacts the agricultural sector. Among the most pertinent is the Land Policy of 1997, which gives some guidelines on securing the land tenure system to encourage the optimal use of land resources. Within the land policy, the government encourages multiple land-use techniques in areas of conflict. The policy states that agricultural land will be identified and set aside for agricultural use and protected against encroachment by grazers so as to avoid conflicts. The land policy covers issues related to rangeland management and livestock keeping. The National Higher Education Policy of 1999 gives agricultural-related disciplines high priority and calls for strengthening of laboratories as part of research and training effort. These laboratories conduct research that is oriented towards solving farmer problems.

Finally, the National Employment Policy of 1997 is intertwined with the agricultural sector. The policy stresses the use of appropriate technologies, development of employment in rural areas, involvement of women and youth in employment programs; and encouragement of self-employment activities. Moreover, because more than 70 percent of Tanzanians live in rural areas, effective use of labor force improves agriculture and livestock production. Other strategies include targeted investment in agriculture and issuance of land occupancy rights to nationals.

Several other important policies that influence agriculture include the Energy Policy (1992), Water Policy (2002), National Microfinance Policy (2000), National Trade Policy (2003), and the Small and Medium Enterprises Policy (2002). The overall goals of energy policy are exploiting the hydroelectric power sources, developing and using natural gas resources, developing and using coal resources, stepping up petroleum exploitation, arresting wood fuel depletion, developing and using forest and agricultural residues for power generation, and minimizing fluctuations in and stabilizing energy prices. Water policy aims to develop a comprehensive framework for promoting the optimal, sustainable, and equitable use of water resources for the benefit of all Tanzanians. The water policy addresses the allocation of water resources, prioritization of water uses, water conservation, water quality management, water and environmental pollution, and water resources management.

The overall objective of Tanzania's national microfinance policy is to establish a basis for an efficient and effective microfinancial system that serves low-income borrowers, and thereby contribute to economic growth and poverty reduction. The goal of Tanzania's trade policy is to raise efficiency and widen the links in domestic production and build a diversified competitive export sector to stimulate higher rates of growth and development. The policy on small and medium enterprises (SMEs) fosters job creation and income generation through creating new SMEs and improving the performance and competitiveness of the existing SMEs to increase their participation and contribution to the economy of Tanzania.

OVERVIEW OF THE SUBSECTORS, THEIR VALUE CHAINS, AND INNOVATIONS

The Sunflower Subsector

Sunflower is one of the most important oilseed crops in Tanzania. The crop is adaptable over a wide range of environments and is widely cultivated in Tanzania. Sunflowers are increasingly popular in the eastern, central, northern, and southern highlands of Tanzania. Current data show that local production of both factory and home extracted oils contributes to about 40 percent of the national cooking oil requirement with the remaining 60 percent being imported (ARI Ilonga 2008). Sunflower production in Tanzania from 2000–2005 increased almost 80 percent, from 80,000 tons to 134,000 tons.

Based on the importance of sunflowers, the Ministry of Agriculture, Food, and Cooperatives (MAFC) conducts sunflower research from the Agricultural Research Institute (ARI) Ilonga in Kilosa District. In 1999, the oilseeds research program at Ilonga imported 20 varieties for multilocation trials (ARI Ilonga 2008). Two of them, PI 364860 and PI 289624, recorded high yields and oil contents. However, the lack of seeds from high-yielding varieties is still a problem. Most farmers use their own seeds from previous seasons because of the high price and low availability of seeds from stockists. Inadequate funding for agricultural research and extension services exacerbates the seed shortages.

Postharvest management is an important aspect of sunflower production as well. Normally sunflowers are harvested manually. In the eastern zone, harvesting takes place in July through September, whereas in the central zone the harvest is between May and June. After threshing, sunflower seeds are pressed to extract sunflower oil, which is further purified into edible cooking oil. The cake is used as livestock feed. According to a recent study conducted at ARI Ilonga, the production cost for one acre is T Sh 380,000 and one acre can produce up to 16 bags of 70 kg to 80 kg each. If those bags are processed into oil, then the revenue from the sale of oil (T Sh 800,000) and cake (T Sh 59,520) totals T Sh 859,520. This calculation leaves a profit margin of T Sh 479,520 per acre.[2]

The sunflower subsector is faced with a number of constraints that include the following:

- Lack of improved and sufficient seeds, forcing farmers to use their own seeds
- Unreliable market and low prices for sunflower seeds
- Diseases such as downy mildew
- Insects and other pests before and after germination
- Inadequate improved tillage implements such as ox plow or tractors
- Unreliable rainfall
- Inadequate knowledge of improved sunflower production techniques due to poor extension services
- Stiff competition from edible oil imports.

Sunflowers as a cash crop can increase household incomes and security and raise the rural standard of living. Sunflower cultivation can ensure an adequate supply of cooking oil, and the increased installation of processing machines for oil pressing creates jobs that can reduce youth unemployment. With rigorous promotion, sunflower cultivation has the potential of contributing to poverty reduction. However, since one of the major constraints to sunflower production is the lack of improved seeds, the existing improved varieties should be popularized.

The Sunflower Value Chain

The value chain for sunflower subdivides into backward and forward links as figure 4.1 shows. Sunflower farmers link to other firms, such as agro-mechanic service providers. The farmer has a backward link with input suppliers for seeds, chemicals, and fertilizers. Farmers depend on farm machinery owners and operators on a contract basis for farm tillage operations. After harvest, the sunflower follows different routes to reach the processing shops. Farmers are forward linked to other firms that depend on farmers for services. Farmers may sell directly to the mills or through the middlemen who pass through the farms to buy seeds. Also at this stage, truckers transport the seeds to the mills. In some cases, the millers also own trucks, which collect seeds sometimes in conjunction with the middlemen with whom they might have a

Figure 4.1   Value Chain Links for Sunflower Oil Processing

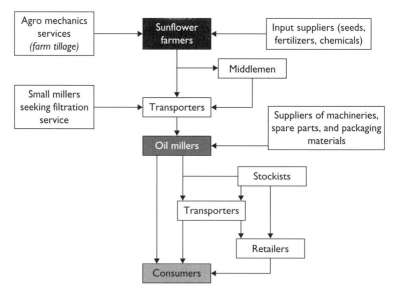

Source: Authors' compilation.

supply contract. The millers also link with suppliers of machinery, spare parts, and packaging materials.

Marketing activities start after oil has been processed, filtered, and packaged. This activity includes stockists or wholesalers, transporters, distributors, and retailers. Small-scale operators directly link to consumers who come directly to buy oil from the millers. Another relationship within the value chain is among small oil mills, which depend on one relatively well-equipped mill when it comes to filtering the oil. A few oil millers are equipped with filtration units, which allow them to offer services to other millers at a cost.

Innovations in the Sunflower Industry

The majority of sunflower farmers now use new ideas, knowledge, and inputs such as improved seeds, fertilizers, and new organizational procedures that they may not have used in the past. Farmers have organized small cooperative groups, which enable them to access inputs and services, to jointly market and improve their crops, and to have close supervision and improve quality. The cooperative enabled them to increase yield as they take charge of supervising, thus ensuring correct farming practices.

However, there is more testing of new ideas among the processors of sunflower oil than among farmers. Innovations included building stores, filter rooms, and better sanitation systems on their premises as well as facilities for the oil pressing that adds value. These innovations mean processors are able to increase the profit realized from the sale.

The Cassava Subsector

Cassava is a drought-resistant crop grown mainly in dry areas and contributes significantly to rural nutrition and livelihood. Cassava is more productive per unit of land and labor than even the highest-yielding cereals and sources of carbohydrates. Cassava plays an increasingly important food security role in areas where the risk of drought is high; it also provides a source of income to large numbers of the people who grow and market the crop in rural and urban communities (Mtambo 2007).

In Tanzania, cassava contributes on average 15 percent of the national food production and is second to maize, which is the leading staple food crop for many Tanzanians (Mtambo 2007). Cassava is mainly grown in the Mtwara, Coast, Mwanza, Kigoma, Tanga, Morogoro, Mara, Ruvuma, Shinyanga, and Lindi regions. Cassava is also increasingly becoming important in the fresh, boiled, roasted, and fried forms (Ndunguru and others 1994; Nweke 2003). Cassava production from 2000–05 slightly increased from 1,698,000 tons to 2,052,000 tons, mainly because of its increased use as a food crop as well as its use for production of starch and animal feed.

Cassava is used as a raw material in the manufacture of processed foods, animal feed, and industrial products. Even novel cassava products will continually be adopted as an ingredient in convenient fast foods for urban consumers or as an industrial material in some African countries (Mtambo 2007). The use of cassava as animal feed is expected to rise because the government of Tanzania is trying to encourage investment in livestock production and meat-processing industries, and the response from private investors has been positive (Mtambo 2007).

The Cassava Value Chain

As with sunflower, the value chain for cassava, shown in figure 4.2, is also similar in nature with the main nodes being the farmers, processors, and consumers, shown in figure 4.3. The backward link starting with farmers is towards the input suppliers. There is no established link to agromechanics because cassava is mainly grown on small farms, which are prepared using a hand hoe. Furthermore, cassava farmers are not sufficiently well organized to use service processors, as is widely done for other staples such as maize.

However, the need for improved planting materials, especially from agricultural research centers, is very high. The most common variety is Kiroba, which is high yielding and disease tolerant. Farmers link forward to middlemen involved in buying, retailers of raw cassava, transporters, agroprocessors, retailers of finished products, and consumers.

Figure 4.2 Value Chain Links within the Cassava Industry

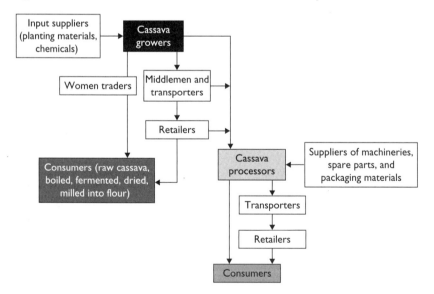

Source: Authors' compilation.

AGRIBUSINESS AND INNOVATION SYSTEMS IN AFRICA

Figure 4.3 Value Chain Links within the Milk Value Chain

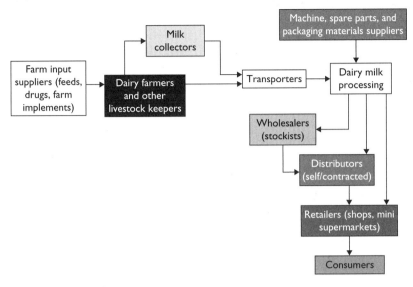

Source: Authors' compilation.

Innovations in the Cassava Industry

The cassava value chain involves farmers and processors. Only 29 percent of the farmers in the sample report having tested new ideas. Innovations included the use of high-yielding and disease-tolerant varieties (Kiroba), and in one case, farmers are participating in fertilizer trials together with researchers from ARI Mlingano in Tanga.

However, the level of testing new ideas and knowledge was considerably higher among cassava processors; at least 75 percent reported such testing. Processors used new dehullers (SB 50). Processors reported widespread organizational innovation to enable them to access new markets. In addition, they reported accessing new processing and packaging technologies. Whereas in the past processors were using manual processing technologies, they are now able to use small- to medium-scale processing equipment. Some processors innovated in blending cassava flour with maize and packaging it into smaller packages of one-, two- and five-kilogram bags. In particular, processors strengthened their marketing through the expansion of marketing departments, improved packaging and labeling, and participation in agricultural shows and trade fairs. These firms were able to develop new packaging and labeling based on consumer feedback (box 4.1).

Overview of the Dairy Subsector

Out of the total 88.6 million hectares of agricultural land in Tanzania, an estimated 60 million hectares are rangeland ideal for livestock grazing (Koggani

Box 4.1   Sample of Innovations at Power Foods Company

Power Foods Company is a small-scale privately owned firm that processes and markets cassava products. The firm is situated in the Kawe area in Kinondoni district, Dar es Salaam region. Its main departments are production, finance, sales, and stores.

The firm annually produces up to 26,500 kilograms of cassava products such as flour, which are distributed to different shops in town and also to individual consumers.

Power Foods has established a system of training farmers groups on better cassava handling and processing techniques from harvesting to processing to minimize cyanide and reduce aflatoxins.

The company accesses more customers through diversification of packaging by using smaller units as opposed to the old system of flour packages of 20 kg and 50 kg. Currently the firm sells its flour products in packages ranging from 1 to 50 kg to cater to different customer needs.

2005). However, only 40 percent of the rangelands are used for Tanzania's 17.7 million cattle; 12.5 million goats, 3.5 million sheep, 0.8 million pigs, 47 million poultry, and other species are also raised on Tanzania's pasture lands. More than 90 percent of the livestock population is indigenous breeds with low genetic potential. Also, the total contribution of the livestock subsector, including dairy, is 18 percent to the total GDP and 30 percent to the agricultural GDP. The subsector has the potential to contribute more. In recent years, private sector efforts are attempting to revamp the dairy industry establishing business association bodies.

The dairy subsector has a huge potential for poverty eradication in Tanzania. The major milk zones of Tanzania are the north (Kilimanjaro and Arusha regions); east (the Tanga, Coast, Dar es Salaam, and Morogoro regions); south (the Iringa and Mbeya regions); and Lake (the Shinyanga, Mwanza, Mara, and Kagera regions).

Milk production in Tanzania is divided into the traditional and modern production systems. The traditional dairy system is further divided into traditional livestock and modern dairy (Shem and Mdoe 2002). The traditional livestock system involves the highly mobile Masai and Barbaig people and the less-mobile cattle grazers known as agro-pastoralists (Shem 2004). Under the traditional livestock system, milk marketing is unorganized and often benefits intermediaries who buy milk cheaply. The modern sector raises exotic breeds from Europe and elsewhere. This system is characterized by commercial dairy farms, as well as medium- and small-scale smallholder dairy farms. The modern dairy subsector is concentrated in Arusha, Kilimanjaro, Kagera, Iringa, Mbeya, and Tanga, and in urban and semi-urban areas.

Sector-specific policies. In recent years, Tanzania has attempted to revamp the dairy sector. Efforts have included a Small-holder Dairy Development

Program (SDDP), which formed Tanzania Milk Producers Association (TAMPRODA). Other developments include the formation of Tanzania Dairy Board (TDB) and Tanzania Milk Processors Association (TAMPA). The dairy industry has organized itself at the national level around specific associations such as milk producers and milk processors, thus enabling it to address issues related to the industry. This arrangement is missing in the sunflower and cassava subsectors.

The Dairy Value Chain

The dairy industry in Tanzania involves small-, medium-, and a few large-scale actors. Several important stages within the value chain in the dairy industry include milk production, processing, and marketing of dairy products. Milk production is further linked to a supply of good cattle breeds and input supplies such as feed and drugs. If milk production is the center of the value chain, then one can establish backward and forward links. Figure 4.3 sets out the value chain for the dairy industry.

In dairy, farmers link backward on the dairy value chain to suppliers of farm inputs such as feed, drugs, and implements. Forward links involve mainly milk collectors, transporters, and dairy processors. Large firms may carry out all activities in the value chain by themselves and only subcontract to others depending on the processing capacities. Milk processors are linked to suppliers of spare parts and other consumables including packaging materials, transporters, distributors, and consumers. Distributors include retail shops or distributing centers where retailers obtain the products they sell. However, in some cases, the processors themselves have their own section to deal with marketing, including distribution to retailers.

Innovations in the Dairy Industry

The dairy farming industry is relatively more innovative than the other commodity subsectors in Tanzania. Dairy firms have been innovating at different levels and stages, though milk traders reported few innovations.

Two-thirds of the firms surveyed—milk collectors, processors, and marketing firms—carried out organizational innovations. Different types of organizational innovations sprang up within the dairy industry. For example, dairy farmers tried to access new markets. Other organizational innovations included starting small testing laboratories and strengthening their marketing section. Firms also participated more in agricultural shows and trade fairs to promote their products and establish contacts and networks.

Milk processors used honey as a yogurt sweetener and accessed new markets, such as supermarkets, by improving their product quality and packaging. Other innovations involved testing new forms of packaging, such as cups for yogurt. Firms collected information about consumer preference and upgraded their products accordingly (boxes 4.2 and 4.3).

Box 4.2 A Sample of Processing Innovations from TANDAIRIES Company

TANDAIRIES is a medium-scale milk-processing firm. The company's head office is in the Kinondoni district in Dar es Salaam region. The firm employs about 50 workers in five different departments: management, marketing, procurement, technical department, and storage. The company produces about 1,650,000 liters of processed milk products annually.

The company strives to become innovative. For example, due to difficulties in milk collection, the company has established six milk collection centers in Pongwe, Muheza, and Mkanyageni in Tanga region; Dakawa and Kimamba in Morogoro region, and Mdaula in the Coast region. TANDAIRIES subcontracts with private transporters to collect milk from the centers and deliver it to the factory as an innovative strategy to lower running cost and ensure timely delivery of milk through well-organized transportation logistics.

The firms researched in collaboration with researchers from local universities such as Sokoine University of Agriculture to develop, test, and launch a new honey-sweetened yogurt.

Box 4.3 A Sample of Processing and Marketing Innovations from ASAS Dairies Ltd

ASAS Dairies Ltd. is a medium-scale privately owned company that processes and markets milk products. The company is situated in Kibwabwa area on the outskirts of Iringa. The company employs 55 workers who operate under three departments: management and financing, marketing, and technical departments.

ASAS Dairies can produce nearly 144,000 liters of processed milk per year and is still expanding. The company adds value to fresh milk and yogurt products, which are packed in containers and sold.

The company has also developed some new products like cheese, butter, and skim milk. These new products help the company to expand its market base and are produced, packed, and distributed to consumers through middlemen who market them.

The company has established a transportation/distribution section and bought trucks for transportation of milk products as a strategy to expand its customer range through a wider distribution area. Such innovation has helped the firm in reaching more customers in cities such as Morogoro and Dar es Salaam. The company uses its experience and the network that it has established over the years within the transport industry, in which its other subsidiary companies are already involved.

FURTHER ASPECTS OF INNOVATION RELATED TO ALL SUBSECTORS

Innovations by Supply Actors to the Value Chains

Input suppliers. Most input suppliers are innovative. According to the survey, firms were organized to access new markets for their products. Also, they invested more in high-demand agro inputs, such as the industrial fertilizer Can, while reducing the amount of other inputs. The firms also diversified the input they sell to include small implements and inputs for poultry farmers. The firms repackaged inputs to appeal to the purchasing power of their customers and established their own seed farms.

Manufacturers of agroprocessing equipment. Manufacturers of agroprocessing equipment for cassava and sunflower (mainly chippers, graters, and slicers), innovated through the use of stainless steel foreparts that come in contact with food, whereas in the past they were using mild steel, which is not a food grade steel and is susceptible to rusting. The firms experimented with new forms of organizing activities or procedures since 2006, including accessing new clients through an expanding range of products and participating in trade fairs and agricultural shows.

Additionally, manufacturing firms worked closely with the universities to try new technologies developed by the universities. For example, some firms diversified into manufacturing agroprocessing machines for other commodities such as sorghum and nuts. Firms have tried to access new markets, including cassava processors in Mozambique and Malawi, such as Intermech Engineering Ltd.

Transporters. Because the Tanzanian economy is agricultural based, the transportation sector contributes significantly through haulage agricultural produce, as well as processed products. Transporters ferry inputs to the farmers as well as transport crops from the farms to market or to processors. Both farmers and input suppliers depend on transporters. However, the rapidly rising price of fuel and the failure of energy and trade policies to control the price of imported goods have created a huge disincentive to innovation.

Tax policy is viewed as a burden to transporters. For example, transporters are required to pay about T Sh 36,000 per year as a packing fee, T Sh 350,000 as a road license, as well as other municipal council fees that amount to T Sh 500 per each trip, whereas in villages they pay T Sh 1,000 as a vehicle levy per trip. Transporters also perceive increased operational costs as a major constraint. The increase in the price of spare parts and fuel is the most inhibiting factor, but the availability of customers and poor roads are also disincentives.

With regard to organizational innovations, transporters extended their links and networked with customers through the use of ICT, especially the mobile phones that they can use to call their contacts. Other organizational innovations include setting routines for timely maintenance of vehicles to avoid breakdowns. Box 4.4 provides additional examples.

To conclude, innovations could be noted at each stage of the value chain. Agroprocessing in general demonstrated greater innovative activity than could be discerned on the farm level. In particular, marketing displayed innovative dynamism. Most firms incorporated and applied new knowledge and innovation, especially in the dairy industry.

Box 4.4   Innovations among Input Suppliers and Agroproduct Manufacturers

- MANG'ANA AGRO VET (*input supplies*)
  This small-scale enterprise supplies agro inputs. The firm is located in Kibaha in the Coast region. The company supplies different inputs (chemicals, improved seeds, sprayers, garden tools).

  The firm established its own farms for producing vegetable seeds, rather than purchasing seeds from contract farmers. Seeds are now available in the right quantity and quality. After harvesting, seeds are processed (dried, sorted, tested, and packaged) and sold through shops owned by the firm.

- DEMACO ENGINEERING ENTERPRISE (*manufacturer of machinery*)
  This small-scale enterprise in Morogoro municipality manufactures oil processing machines. It has five employees working in an informal department. The firm annually produces seven complete processing machines.

  In addition to making small agroprocessing machines such as oil presses, the firm manufactures trailers, after it noticed that imported tractors had no trailers. The firm has since established trailer manufacturing as a new product line.

- INTERMECH ENGINEERING (*manufacturer of machinery*)
  This medium-scale firm, with headquarters in Morogoro, deals with the production of oil- and cassava-processing machines. The firm has seven permanent workers producing about 65 complete machines per year. The firm recently produced 60 cassava processing machines and 5 oil processing machines.

  After the firm grappled with rust in cassava-processing machines they were manufacturing, they had to address this problem. Working in collaboration with universities and other stakeholders, they developed an improved version whereby all parts that are in direct contact with food are made of stainless steel instead of mild steel.

SUPPORT STRUCTURES AND SERVICES

Financing Innovation

The study looked also at innovation in finance outputs and marketing. In general, the sources of investment finances were reported as follows:

- Credit from nonbanking financial institutions and individuals
- Personal funds raised from various sources
- Personal savings accumulated over time
- Accumulation from farming activities
- Loans from banks
- SACCOs
- Member contributions within groups.

Farmers, especially smallholders, finance relatively little through bank loans, but mainly through other accumulation and income.

Innovation cycle funding was used primarily for the following:

- Improving collection and transportation of raw materials
- Expanding the range of raw materials and improving the scale of operations
- Diversifying products and improving quality
- Acquiring new and innovative technologies such as packaging
- Enhancing marketing access.

For the vast majority (74 percent) of agribusiness firms, innovation finance does not provide sufficient funds for entrepreneurship. To accumulate funds for investment, firms strive to diversify their products to capture other markets. For example, instead of manufacturing a machine for pressing only one type of oilseeds, entrepreneurs are now manufacturing multipurpose machines for use with a wide variety of seeds. In the dairy industry, collection of milk to meet the required quantities is the main challenge.

In terms of finance innovation, some firms seek more institutional support to cope with a fast-changing market as well as form organizations, associations, or networks to ease a firm's access to loans. These networks may include just farmers or farmers and processors. Organizations lobbied to soften some loan conditions, such as the need of strict rules for collateral. Some firms suggested establishing a grant scheme that will specifically target SMEs in Tanzania, which shows that agribusiness firms are not aware of some of the recent government initiatives.

The reinvestment propensity of agribusinesses in general was high. The money put back into operations is used to purchase inputs such as fertilizers and seeds from input suppliers and services and products from research institutions, universities, and even overseas consultant companies.

Education and Human Resources

Currently, only 15 percent of the firms surveyed employed graduates in their firms. Firms saw university graduates as lacking the practical skills to perform adequately within the firms. Although education policy focuses on agricultural need, facilities for practical training are still inadequate for the number and needs of the students. The quality of university graduates differs from the quality of those from polytechnic and technical colleges. Graduates from universities generally lack practical skills although they seem to have competencies on theoretical aspects. Among the shortcomings of university graduates are lacking practical skills, having unrealistic salary expectations, and placing administrative duties over those related to their technical skills. University graduates may play a role as a source of innovation.

Government policies and programs. Tanzania provided incentives for financial support to students. Such support enables students to work without the firm paying a stipend. Firms can benefit without having to pay an allowance to the student.

To a lesser extent, government has been providing incentives to upgrade workers' skills, including an opportunity to attend seminars and workshops organized by the government or universities. The government also sponsors study tours within or outside the country and assists firms in participating in agricultural shows and seminars, where firms can learn of new innovations and also get access to new markets. In some cases, firms sponsor their employees to attend important courses.

The current education system can improve on education relevant to agribusiness needs in the following ways:

- Incorporating more practical skills through improvement of laboratory facilities and more support for apprenticeships or internships in industries for practical training
- Organizing farmer training as part of extension/outreach activities
- Enhancing technical and practical skills in the current teaching curricula
- Incorporating agribusiness entrepreneurship in the curriculum to make graduates more entrepreneurial and therefore more innovative.

Fairs and ICTs: Accessing Information and Knowledge

There are different levels of government sponsorship or facilitation in agricultural expositions. These facilitations and sponsorships reach about one-third of all agribusiness firms. Firms can exhibit their products in National Farmers' Day and the annual Saba Saba trade fairs. Additional avenues are the Small Industry Development Organization (SIDO) and Tanzania Chamber of Commerce, Industry and Agriculture (TCCIA) trade fairs, World Food Day, and other SIDO-organized fairs, which are under the Ministry of Industry, Trade, and Marketing.

The use of information and communication technology (ICT)—including mobile phones, computers, and fax machines—is widespread among larger firms. All milk-processing and agroprocessing firms regularly use computers.

In addition, the use of computers is common among cassava processors, though mainly for word processing and spreadsheets. The use of the Internet is limited, with about 27 percent reporting having access to Internet services where they search for new technologies and other technical information, especially on machines and spare parts. Milk processors, equipment manufacturers, sunflower processors, and some sunflower growers reported Internet usage. Some firms, such as Power Foods (cassava), ASAS (Dairy), and Intermech Engineering (agroprocessing machinery) have created their own Web sites.

Firms have been organizing themselves to identify and learn from relevant experiences through the following:

- Establishing communication with foreign companies and organizations
- Setting up or maintaining Internet facilities
- Creating a Web site to facilitate communication.

COORDINATION AMONG KEY ACTORS OF THE INNOVATION SYSTEM

Actors

The main external actors that affect a firm's performance and influence their decision making are public sector actors, such as utility companies, other agribusiness firms, input suppliers, consumers, and business associations. Other important external actors are research institutes, extension services, and the public in general, including farmers.

Companies—Intermediary Services

Input suppliers are included as main external actors that provide inputs for the firms. The input suppliers provide agricultural inputs such as seeds, fertilizer, raw materials, and packaging materials. Input suppliers tend to share new information and innovations with the firms that buy their products. Therefore the relationship is two-way. For example, seed suppliers inform farmers on availability of new high-yielding seeds, fertilizers, and even planting space. Farmers try these products in their fields and may later adopt them, depending on their performance. As for machine manufacturing, input suppliers share information about new raw materials and innovative fabrication techniques.

The majority of firms also have good working relationships with input suppliers to access knowledge and information. For example, about half of the firms have good communication systems with input suppliers whereas about one third have a moderate relationship with input suppliers. The remaining third report a bad relationship, mainly due to pricing issues.

Companies—Business Associations/Farmer Organizations

Business associations play a major role as external actors. Business associations share new knowledge and markets with agribusiness firms and are also involved in organizing business expositions. Some of the important business associations include Tanzania Food Processors Association (TAFOPA) and SIDO, which provide assistance with packaging and labeling materials. In the case of milk production and processing, TAMPRODA and TAMPA were mentioned as important associations. The manufacturers of agro-food processing equipment mentioned the Metal Cluster Initiative of the College of Engineering and Technology of the University of Dar es Salaam and Tanzania Chamber of Commerce, Industry, and Agriculture (TCCIA) as important associations.

Companies—Consumers

Consumers are also important external actors who buy and use products from agribusiness firms. Consumers provide feedback and share their experiences with firms about products such as sunflower oil, milk, yogurt, and cassava flour, which is useful information when companies try to innovate. Some consumers even share information regarding details of other competitors' products and marketing strategies and provide advice to firms.

According to the Tanzania study, the facilitation relationship among input suppliers, collective business associations, and consumers is good. Consumers sometimes complain about high prices that result from taxes and poor links, including infrastructure within the value chains. However, associations and consumers are seen as supportive to technical change and innovations.

Company—Research Institutes/Universities

There is less consultation among universities, technical institutions, and firms in setting their strategic priorities. Firms have low representations on the governing bodies of universities or research institutes. Certainly this affects the success of university-initiated activities that target agribusiness firms. University of Dar es Salaam (UDSM) and Sokoine University of Agriculture (SUA) in particular try to collect opinions from firms, including farmers' groups. However, private sector and university engagement needs improvement.

In recent years, SUA and UDSM have collaborated in research programs such as Tanzania Agricultural Research Project (TARP) II, Future Opportunities and Challenges in Agricultural Learning (FOCAL), and Program for Agricultural and Natural Resources Transformation for Improved Livelihoods (PANTIL), which involve farmers in the projects. Also, UDSM is involved in the incubator and cluster programs.

For most of the firms, the most useful outcome of these relationships is access to knowledge, markets, and the ability to create confidence among consumers of their products, which facilitates marketing.

To obtain new information and tackle technical problems, agricultural input suppliers have turned to SUA and fellow firms when they have technical problems. Cassava growers, however, tend to depend on their fellow farmers and agricultural research institutes. The dairy farmers tend to rely on research institutions such as SUA for solving technical problems. Collectors and processors of milk and sunflower oil rely on consultants from local universities, because they are easily accessed and do not cost much. Manufacturers of agroprocessing equipment consult UDSM in the case of technical engineering and manufacturing problems.

Two-thirds of the firms report that a good relationship exists among farmers, agribusinesses, and public agricultural research centers such as ARI Ilonga and Kibaha in the eastern zone, which enables them to access new knowledge and information. The following aspects of the relationship are perceived as the most useful:

- Accessing results of research activities via reports and Internet
- Creating awareness about appropriate processing technologies. For crops such as cassava, farmers benefit from technologies such as preparation of new cassava varieties, cassava chips, proper processing of cassava for human food, and fortification from SUA, ARI Kibaha, and UDSM
- Enabling firms to acquire better processing tools such as chippers, graters, and presses
- Enhancing entrepreneurship skills mainly through participation in training and exhibitions
- Improving sunflower production skills through improved agronomic skills at the farm level
- Advertising the link with research institutions and universities to create consumer confidence.

However, the relationship of small-scale cassava farmers with agricultural institutions is not as good as that of sunflower growers and dairy producers.

Public—Private Interactions and Partnerships

Generally public-private sector interactions are still low because there are no incentives for collaboration. This indicates that firms prefer to continue on their own and don't see much to gain from collaboration. Some of the firms collaborate with organizations such as SIDO to get access to technical knowledge, machines, and financial assistance. Other incentives for collaboration include market improvement, disease control, and access to loans and markets.

The main cause of poor links between the government and private investors is insufficient numbers of extension workers to meet a national demand. The lack of strong interministerial networking at lower levels and lack of strong PPP strategies has led to poor involvement of key players from both private and public sectors.

Government officials make contacts through their normal execution of duties. Respondents report contacts with local government on a monthly basis; however, they rarely meet with members of the national parliament or ministers. Government officials initiate most of these meetings; firms rather infrequently. The purposes of meetings include normal routine of inspections, taxation and licensing matters, assistance on technical matters/advice, inspection for safety and quality, offering agronomical advice, on-site training and sensitization, and financing and empowerment training.

The role of the public sector is to ensure availability of public services such as legal support, market promotion, and capacity building. Other important roles of the public sector include providing standards for quality control from the Tanzania Bureau of Standards (TBS) and the Tanzania Food and Drugs Administration (TFDA). Also, the public sector advocates and carries out activities that facilitate tax collection and compliance, that enable agribusinesses to carry out their activities uninterrupted. Other key governmental roles include issuing licenses and setting standards for quality control. These help firms to gain legal recognition and to run and operate profitably. Government also ensures the availability of public utilities, which facilitate firms' functioning.

Organization and Coordination across the Value Chains

Different levels of partnerships exist from one firm to another, and partnerships are absent among small-scale farmers. Firms with partnerships include cassava processors, agroprocessing machine manufacturers, and milk trading firms. The remaining firms revealed relatively weak partnerships.

Firms processing both milk and sunflower oil cooperated in partnerships for technical and investment matters. Conversely, dairy farmers and sunflower oil processors based their partnerships on technical matters. Input suppliers and sunflower processors have partnerships based on financial matters.

Government's Role in Coordination and Facilitation

Government generally assumes a facilitating role in these partnerships. The partnerships among cassava and sunflower growers are influenced by the government. The government influences input suppliers and dairy farming partnerships as well, whereas others coalesce around the need for raw materials or collective lobbying. The government encourages farmers to form and join small cooperatives so government and other groups can assist them through loans. Milk trader and sunflower processor partnerships are not influenced by government, but rather have links to other initiatives such as collective lobbying.

For government-facilitated partnerships, certain drivers are common. For example, the main motivation for sunflower grower partnerships include guarantees for loans, joint market access, and access to legal and business support. The partnership may be based on the need to cooperate and share experiences in technical matters or a shared investment of time and finances. Partnerships among input suppliers and cassava growers sought joint market access.

Moreover, firms facilitate these partnerships through the profits that they make especially given the lack of direct support from the government, as 67 percent of respondents reported. The government facilitation seems to be mainly in form of loan guarantees from financing institutions.

Some firms participate in networks and maintain communication with firms outside the country. Some overseas organizations mentioned included the following:

- European firms in Germany and the Netherlands, such as PACCO–Europe
- A Chinese parts supplier, CATIC (China Aero-Technology Import-Export Corporation) for spare parts used in agroprocessing machines
- Foreign firms based in Tanzania
- Farmers and entrepreneurs from neighboring countries, such as Kenya, Malawi, and Zambia, mainly to share information on marketing and agroprocessing innovations.

However, only a few firms, in particular input suppliers, manufacturers, sunflower and cassava growers, and cassava processors, currently participate actively in associations. Such associations include TCCIA, TAMPA, TAMPRODA, and MVIWATA (Mtandao wa Vikundi vya Wakulima Tanzania). The motivations for those who participate in such associations include the following:

- Accessing collective markets and exchange of market information
- Fulfilling a precondition for accessing loans
- Sharing business management skills and new technology information
- Getting an easy link to government for joint lobbying efforts.

THE IMPACT OF POLICIES

General Observations

Policies such as the Small and Medium Enterprises Policy (2002) and the National Science and Technology Policy (1996) attempt to establish a better environment and opportunities for higher income generation and employment that benefit poorer communities. However, although most of the policies favor agricultural innovation, the level of their implementation remains a concern. Many implementers do not act according to the stated objectives, and there is no compliance mechanism for measurement and evaluation. The lack of implementation is exacerbated by inadequate follow-up that is the result of inadequate government resources and funds. Public officials are seen as resistant, more interested in collecting taxes, and indifferent to policy implementation, though they sometimes are supportive of technological change in agriculture. In particular input suppliers, dairy farmers, agroprocessing machine manufacturers, and milk processors perceive a lack of support.

Lack of funds and human resources contributed to other problems such as inadequate networking and poor links. This hinders local entrepreneurs from being exposed to new ideas and innovations. There is a need to strengthen links among policy makers and other stakeholders at the grassroots level. The lack of national policy on innovations and intellectual property rights (IPR) impede agribusiness innovations in the country.

Unclear distribution of responsibilities among implementers results in confusion among the value chain actors. For example, dairy firms believe that the Dairy Act of 2004 overregulates the sector because about 17 bodies in Tanzania are mandated to regulate the milk sector, with each body regulating a certain part of the policy. As a result, dairy firms are responsible to the Tanzania Dairy Board, TFDA, and local government authorities through Regional Administration and Local Government (RALG), just to mention but a few. This creates difficulties for stakeholders.

Other policies, such as the National Science and Technology policy, are not widely known in most villages where farmers and other stakeholders are, which leads to more difficulties in implementation. This means more outreach is needed for stakeholders to understand the policy. Further, there is no strategic plan and implementation guidelines, which hinder the plan's effectiveness.

Impact of Specific Policies

The subsequent discussion highlights some of the major policies that encourage and impede agribusinesses and innovation in Tanzania.

Public policies benefiting agribusiness innovation. According to the Tanzania country study, several policy issues favor the private sector. At least one-third of the respondent firms saw incentives from the following:

- Access to seminars and trade fairs where new ideas, knowledge, and exposure are gained
- Fertilizer and seeds subsidies[3] to attract more investment and innovation
- Loan guarantees and insurance coverage, which mitigates risks for agribusinesses.

In terms of regulation, agribusinesses in Tanzania already use existing weights, quality, and environmental safety standards that are enforced. Some of the enforcing agents include TFDA, TBS, National Environment Management Council (NEMC), and Tanzania Scales and Weights Agency.

Agriculture and livestock policy is seen as highly commendable, but only if it is implemented effectively. Conversely, land policy is also supportive, especially when it comes to provision of title deeds whereas cooperative policy is supportive on issues of formation of cooperative societies. Efforts have been made to empower Tanzanian communities to fight poverty through the strategies stipulated in the Poverty Reduction Strategy Paper (PRSP),

National Strategy for Growth and Reduction of Poverty (NSGRP), and Property and Business Formalization Program (PBFP). Moreover, respondents applauded the government's effort to open markets for investment in agriculture and industries. This has promoted more investment that may bring more income and employment. In addition, the Dairy Act of 2004 is characterized as being an effort in the right direction in supporting the dairy industry, although more effort is needed to improve its operationalization. The act emphasizes promotion of the dairy industry and institutional support programs on livestock development. It also stipulates the role of dairy boards, despite not clearly delineating strategic implementation of the program.

With a view to improve the links between the public and the private sector, the government is recruiting new staff to fill the existing gaps, starting with the Ministry of Agriculture, Food, and Cooperatives, which has revived its agricultural colleges to enroll nearly 3,000 candidates per year. Furthermore, the Ministry of Regional Government and Local Governance (TAMISEMI) is currently employing graduates from universities such as SUA to train in colleges and to provide extension services at the district level. Also, existing incentives through funds such as National Fund for Advancement of Science and Technology (NFAST) are being strengthened. The government is also in the process of enacting a science and technology law that implements science and technology policy. Regarding support in research activities, government research institutions are mandated to conduct research not only for public services, but also to support private sector in achieving its objectives.

Public policies impeding agribusiness innovation. Trade policies seem to rather impede than encourage agribusiness operations and innovations. The reasons include high tax rates, which indirectly increase prices of inputs; lack of subsidies for veterinary inputs; a free market, which creates unfair competition from overseas products; high import taxes for raw materials that lead to higher and uncompetitive selling prices; and lack of policy awareness among firms.

Some dairy and agroprocessing manufacturers see trade policy as encouraging, in particular through tax waivers; government support through trade fairs,[4] which enables firms to display their products; and arrangements enabling local firms to access loans with affordable conditions for promoting local products such as milk.

Several other policies impede innovation. One issue is the legal constraints related to labor and land, which mainly affect milk collectors, processing and marketing firms, and sunflower farmers. The major impediment is a minimum wage being too high for processors, input suppliers, and milk traders. Yet land conflict is the main challenge for firms involved in farming activities. Other legal constraints for processors concern business regulations and licensing, land ownership, and environmental issues, including disposal of waste materials. Another constraint is the bureaucracy in registration of businesses, compliance with TBS regulations, high tax rates, and restriction on plastic container uses.

Proposals for reducing those constraints include the following:

- Reducing bureaucracy in land access and issuance of land title deeds for both farms and building plots
- Reducing unnecessary bureaucracy and prerequisites to promote investments
- Allowing negotiations between employers and employees on the minimum wage
- Enforcing the land laws
- Waiving some taxes, such as building and land taxes, as they are a burden to the firms
- Empowering farmers/processors organizations such as TAMPRODA so that they can speak on behalf of the farmers.

The tax system is another important factor affecting innovation. Higher income and import taxes discourage promotion of a firm's program and limit the firm's performance. The current high taxes offset profit margins. When income tax is not properly calculated, the agribusiness firms are deprived of income. Another constraint with the taxing system is automatic annual tax hikes without considering the actual profit margins obtained by agribusiness firms.

Furthermore, respondents report that prices for agricultural inputs are too high, thus discouraging firms from investing. High operating costs due to high energy bills also affect the economic performance of agribusiness firms.

Moreover, there is a weak link between National Agricultural Research System (NARS) and agribusiness firms because most NARS research emphasizes production rather than postharvest issues.

Policies, especially in the dairy subsector, have been changing unnecessarily. Such changes have led to inconvenience for the community and the nation from loss of revenue and employment opportunities. In addition, milk consumption is still low among Tanzanians despite a policy to encourage it, which means there is a need to look into the adequacy as well as the implementation of the policy.

Problems with land policy have mounted, when title deeds have been provided to private investors without full participation of the community. Furthermore, conflicts between farmers and grazers are another land issue.

CONCLUSION

Identifying the roles of the public sector and agribusiness for boosting innovation warrants a broader discussion on major drivers of innovation. The drivers of innovation include consumers, agribusiness firms, universities, and research institutes, and, to a lesser extent, firms from abroad. Research institutions consulting with agribusinesses in setting research priorities is vital for enhancement of innovations, but it does not happen enough. Agribusinesses lack representation on research institution councils and boards. However, research institutions do collect some data from agribusiness firms, which they then use in setting their research priorities.

Agricultural Innovation: Drivers and Constraints

The issue of firms testing new ideas and innovations before they are applied is also very important. The majority of firms carry out in-house research. However, the level and kind of research differ from one firm to another. Some in-house research includes research on new marketing strategies, effective means of minimizing cost, and research on new products. Other in-house research investigates the impact of better feeding practices on milk yield. In-house research has contributed towards improved income through reduction of production costs, increased yields, and increased quality.

Most firms do not contract with others to conduct research on their behalf. However, local arrangements where joint projects could be initiated with local existing institutions exist.

The low level of innovation is mainly contributed by such factors as the following:

- Inadequate funding for research
- Lack of time to conduct research
- Lack of knowledge to develop and conduct research queries
- Lack of institutional support in terms of research materials
- Lack of manpower and equipment or facilities required for conducting research.

The majority of firms did not receive any support as part of the incentive package for conducting private research. Only a few firms have received a limited amount of assistance to support research.

Outlook and Recommendations

This Tanzania country study assessed the dynamics of innovation in the sunflower, cassava, and dairy subsectors and their value chains in the AIS framework to gain new insights about whether public policies impede or encourage innovation. The study has shown that Tanzania has several good policies that recognize the importance of agricultural development, but the main problems are with implementation. The government's inadequate capacity to implement the current policies aggravates the situation. It is important to improve policy implementation and evaluation. There should be specific and defined policies and guidelines to avoid duplication of roles. Setting up a review process to make policies more effective is an important first step. Some of the policies are supposed to translate into action programs at the local government level, but limited capacities of local governments will make policy implementation difficult.

The majority of firms seek different levels of new ideas and knowledge, depending on the firm's size as it innovates. Of the three value chains, the dairy subsector is more innovative mainly because the dairy industry has the Dairy Board, TAMPRODA, and TAMPA to assist in subsector organization and support.

The study captured different ways in which firms innovate in production and marketing. Some aspects include the following:

- Opening of new sales offices in other towns where firms were not previously operating
- Innovating products, such as blending milk with honey
- Diversifying products, such as seeds and cuttings supplies
- Promoting sales of by-products like sunflower cake as animal feed
- Buying sunflowers direct from farmers
- Designing and fabricating new machines.

In the quest to innovate, agribusiness firms engage in networks and create links. However, such links are still weak and need to be strengthened through networking and collaborative research and dissemination of results into the communities. The government should enhance the involvement of agricultural stakeholders in policy formulation, implementation, and evaluation. The drivers of innovation—consumers (markets), agribusiness firms, and R&D institutions such as universities and research institutions—must be further supported through funding.

Constraints facing agribusiness innovators could be minimized by empowering agribusiness entrepreneurs to access resources for their investments. The government has initiated some interventions, such as the presidential fund, to support local entrepreneurs in the regions. The government should strive to reach more entrepreneurs, and a pilot study is under way to engage community banks in Mufindi, Mbinga, and Mwanga districts by linking them with farmers. The National Microfinance Bank (NMB) has entered into an agreement with the Ministry of Agriculture Food Security and Cooperatives to facilitate loan services to farmers. Several ongoing initiatives such as the Ministry of Communication Science and Technology's review of the science and technology policy to come up with an innovation policy and an implementation plan are necessary. Other initiatives include plans to form an innovation fund and to review NFAST. Issuing science and technology awards is another government initiative in the sciences. In addition, a strategy of the Ministry of Agriculture, Food Security, and Cooperative and the Ministry of Industry, Trade, and Marketing to waive taxes related to goods intended for agricultural investment is under way.

Another challenge is increasing funding for science and technology from the current levels, which is much lower than the target 1 percent of the government budget. Government bodies need to increase science and technology representation on governing bodies to encourage research. This can be done through forming a science and technology committee in the Parliament that may lead to speedier improvement of facilities and incentives for scientists.

NOTES

1. This policy is currently being reviewed.
2. US$1=T Sh 1200.
3. During 2004–05, the government had set aside about T Sh 14.5 billion for fertilizer programs. The Rukwa region alone was allocated about T Sh 19.5 billion for the same purpose in 2007. However, initiatives are limited by resource availability to cover operational costs like transportation. The government is also conducting a pilot study in the Kilombero and Mbarali districts to sell fertilizers to farmers under a special receipt (voucher) system whereby links between the NMB and farmers has been initiated to foster easy access to services. Such receipts (vouchers) would be recognized by NMB.
4. Such fairs are either free of charge or highly subsidized by the government or NGOs.

REFERENCES

ARI (Agricultural Research Institution) Ilonga. 2008. "Survey on the Status of Sunflower Production in Selected Regions of Tanzania." ARI Ilonga, Ilonga, Morogoro, Tanzania.

Koggani, D. M. K. 2005. "Study of Knowledge Gap Assessment in Linking Agriculture/Livestock/Natural Resources Production with Value Adding, Marketing, and Policy at Farmer's Level." Report prepared for the Regional Land Management Unit, World Agroforestry Centre, Nairobi.

MAFS (Ministry of Agriculture and Food Security). 2005. Budget Speech for 2005/2006. Presented at the National Assembly by the minister for agriculture and food security, July, Dodoma.

Mtambo, K. B. 2007. "Status and Potential of Cassava and Sorghum in Food Blending." Proceedings of the National Stakeholders' Workshop on Blending Technologies for Cassava/Sorghum with Other Cereal and Tuber, Kibaha, Tanzania, December 13–14.

Ndunguru, G. T., F. Modaha, F. Mashamba, P. Digges, and U. Keith. 1994. "Urban Demand/Needs Assessment Study of Non-Grains Starch Staple Food Crops in Dar es Salaam." NRI Report R 2195 (R), Natural Resources Institute, Chatham, U.K.

Nweke, Felix I. 2003. "New Challenges in the Cassava Transformation in Nigeria and Ghana." Paper presented at the InWent, International Food Policy Research Institute, New Partnership for Africa's Development, and Centre for Tropical Agriculture Conference "Successes in Africa Agriculture," Pretoria, December 1–3.

Kaplinsky, Raphael, and Mike Morris. 2000. A Handbook of Value Chain. Ottawa: International Development Research Centre. UK: Open University. http://www.ids.ac.uk/ids/global/man&hand,html.

Shem, Martin N. 2004. "The Dairy Industry Development in Tanzania: Lessons from the Past for a Better Tomorrow." Paper presented at the National Dairy Development Conference, Mwanza, Tanzania, June 3–5.

Shem, Martin N., and N. S. Y. Mdoe. 2002. "Dairy Production and Poverty Alleviation in Tanzania: A Historical Perspective." Paper presented during the Joint Meeting of the Society of Animal Production and Tanzania Veterinary Association, Arusha, Tanzania, December.

Steinfeld, Henning, Cees de Haan, and Harvey Blackburn. 1997. *Livestock-Environment Interactions*. Rome: Food and Agriculture Organization.

UNDP (United Nations Development Programme). 2004. "Monitoring Human Development." In *Human Development Report*. New York: UNDP. http://www.undp.org/hdr2003/indicator/indic_16_1_1.html.

United Republic of Tanzania. 1992a. *Food and Nutrition Policy for Tanzania*. Dar es Salaam, Tanzania: Ministry of Health.

———. 1992b. *The Energy Policy of Tanzania*. Dar es Salaam, Tanzania: Ministry of Water Energy and Minerals.

———. 1997a. *Cooperative Development Policy*. Dar es Salaam, Tanzania: Ministry of Agriculture and Cooperatives.

———. 1997b. *National Land Policy*. Dar es Salaam, Tanzania: Ministry of Lands, Housing and Urban Development.

———. 1997c. *Agriculture and Livestock Policy*. Dar es Salaam, Tanzania: Ministry of Agriculture and Cooperatives.

———. 1999a. *The National Science and Technology Policy*. Dar es Salaam, Tanzania: Ministry of Science, Technology, and Higher Education.

———. 1999b. *National Higher Education Policy*. Dar es Salaam, Tanzania: Ministry of Science, Technology, and Higher Education.

———. 2000a. *National Microfinance Policy*. Dar es Salaam, Tanzania: Ministry of Finance.

———. 2000b. "Poverty Reduction Strategy Paper." United Republic of Tanzania, Dar es Salaam, Tanzania.

———. 2000c. *National Employment Policy*. Dar es Salaam, Tanzania: Ministry of Labour and Youth Development.

———. 2001. *Agricultural Sector Development Strategy*. Dar es Salaam, Tanzania: Ministry of Agriculture and Food Security, Ministry of Cooperatives and Marketing, and Ministry of Water and Livestock Development.

———. 2002a. *Small and Medium Enterprises Development Policy*. Dar es Salaam, Tanzania: Ministry of Industries and Trade.

———. 2002b. *National Water Policy*. Dar es Salaam, Tanzania: Ministry of Water, Energy and Minerals.

———. 2003. *National Trade Policy for Competitive Economy and Export-Led Growth*. Dar es Salaam, Tanzania: Ministry of Industries and Trade.

———. 2005. *National Strategy for Growth and Reduction of Poverty*. Dar es Salaam, Tanzania: Vice President's Office.

World Bank. 2007. *Enhancing Agricultural Innovation: How to Go Beyond the Strengthening of Research Systems*. Washington, DC: World Bank.

CHAPTER FIVE

Uganda: Fish, Bananas, and Vegetables

Paul Kibwika, Florence Birung Kyazze, and Maria Nassuna Musoke

This study assesses innovations in three agricultural subsectors to understand how public policies enhance or impede agribusiness innovations in Africa. In Uganda, the country study focuses on the fish, banana, and vegetable subsectors and their value chains by taking an agricultural innovation system (AIS) approach. The study involved 6 producer firms, 10 traders and transporters, 5 processors and exporters, 5 nongovernmental organizations (NGOs) and service providers, and 2 policy makers.

The Ugandan government has put in place policies to support agribusiness growth, such as liberalization and privatization; structural reforms for infrastructure development; civil service reforms to improve public services; decentralization; land policies; and specific agricultural subsector policies. The policy-related constraints to agribusiness innovation are not necessarily due to lack of appropriate public policies, but rather inadequate implementation of well-intentioned policies.

The Uganda country study shows a clear correlation between the structure of the different value chains and the innovations within the value chain. A typical banana value chain is a short one that limits the range of innovations. The vegetable value chain and the fish value chain, however, are more complex. Innovations in the fish value chain relate to the participatory management of the fisheries resources through Beach Management Units (BMUs), quality assurance through the Uganda Fish Processors and Exporters' Association (UFPEA), primary processing for the local supermarket and hotel industry, and reduction of fish farmers' postharvest losses. In the banana value chains, innovations relate to organizing farmers for collective marketing, introducing new banana products and new markets, and shortening the banana beer brewing process by local producers. In the vegetable value chain, the innovations include introducing charcoal coolers to maintain freshness, new packaging for local markets, organizing producers to access services, and processing to reduce postharvest losses. Profit and entrepreneurial inspiration drive competitive innovation, as do competitive challenges for businesses, new market opportunities, and better access to information and exposure. The ability to organize interest groups is an innovation, but there are still weak interactions between those organizations and the knowledge and technology generators such as universities and research institutions.

Constraints to agribusiness innovation result from inadequate implementation and enforcement of policies for infrastructure development, credit to agribusiness firms, input subsidies, value addition to agricultural products, existing regulations and standards, and access and usage of lake resources. Stringent and ever-changing international market demands and high freight costs are also serious constraints to agribusiness innovation. Public policies enhancing agribusiness include nontaxation of agricultural exports, liberalization of trade and service delivery, and disposal of illegal fishing equipment to create a sustainable fishing industry.

Agroprocessing stimulates agribusiness innovation, but despite the emphasis in public policy, government facilitation value addition has been minimal. External markets and market conditions drive innovation in the value chains; however, quality standards, like those in EuroGAP, do overwhelm small-scale businesses and impede innovation. To enhance their innovativeness, agribusiness firms must also use electronic media such as the Internet to tap into global knowledge and to network locally and internationally.

BACKGROUND

In Sub-Saharan Africa (SSA), the role of innovation and technology development has increased significantly over the past decades. Many countries that relied on subsistence farming are investing in improved agricultural techniques, developing science and technology centers, and attempting to move up the value chain in terms of the quality and certification of products like coffee and tea. In Uganda, technology is having a great impact in aquaculture and organic farming.

This country study on Uganda assesses how public policies encourage or impede agribusiness in Africa, with a focus on the fish, banana, and vegetable value chains.

Bananas are a very important food and cash crop in Uganda and are widely grown in different parts of the country, but recent outbreak of the banana wilt disease has devastated production in some regions. Currently, the main banana-producing region is southwestern Uganda, where bananas and many other crops produced by smallholder farmers. Different varieties of bananas are grown for food and for beer brewing. There are two main categories of food bananas: the cooking variety and the dessert variety (apple banana). Other types of bananas—plantains—are roasted or baked. The cooking and dessert bananas are sold in almost all Ugandan markets, whereas the brewing variety is concentrated in specific locations.

The fish industry is one of the fastest-growing nontraditional export subsectors. Fish exports are the highest single nontraditional source of foreign exchange, amounting to more than US$140 million annually in Uganda. Several fish processing factories have proliferated since the 1990s, and currently UFPEA has 17 members. Most of the fish exports are destined for the European market, though regional trade for fish products is growing in the neighboring countries. Lakes are the main sources of fish, especially for export, but expanding fish farming is also targeting the growing local markets.

The Ugandan country study targets vegetables that are primarily for export. Smallholder farmers contracting with the exporting companies grow hot peppers, okra, and green pepper, with hot peppers becoming the most preferred in European markets.

Agriculture in a Policy Context

Uganda has experienced a dynamic policy environment since the mid-1980s. Like all other sectors, agriculture has been influenced by the broad economic and structural adjustment policies providing an economic environment conducive to private sector participation. The structural adjustment policies initiated in the early 1990s changed the context of agriculture and agribusiness in general. Several policies deserve particular attention. Macroeconomic stability, especially low inflation, has been desirable for agribusiness because it allows medium- and long-term planning and encourages savings and exports. Infrastructure reforms in electricity and road expansion are expected to further alleviate constraints for agribusiness.

Moreover, the liberalization of trade and the privatization of service delivery, including a no-subsidy policy for agricultural inputs, have led to the withdrawal of the government from marketing agricultural produce and supplying agricultural inputs. In a move toward decentralization, the government passed along responsibility to local governments for service delivery, including agricultural extension services. The national government has considerably revamped government by streamlining ministries and staff, as well as specifically by creating semi-autonomous organizations such as the National Agricultural Research Organization (NARO), the National Agricultural Advisory Services (NAADS), and the Dairy Development Authority (DDA).

Later, policy makers superimposed a poverty eradication focus onto the policy and development agenda. The poverty-focused development frameworks, namely the Poverty Eradication Action Plan (PEAP) and subsidiary plans such as the Plan for Modernization of Agriculture (PMA) have put another spin to policy dynamics. PMA (developed in 2000) is the major pillar in the poverty eradication strategy, as more than 80 percent of the population depends on agriculture, with the largest portion consisting of poor smallholder farmers.

The PMA is the comprehensive and multisectoral framework for agricultural development that targets poverty eradication through the commercialization of agriculture. This PMA's vision encourages a business orientation for agriculture, hence enhancing agribusiness. The PMA has seven priority areas for public action:

- Promoting agricultural research and technology development
- Improving access to and the quality of agricultural advisory services
- Promoting agricultural skills and knowledge through formal and informal education
- Improving access to and the availability of rural finance
- Promoting agroprocessing and improving access to markets
- Promoting the sustainable use and management of natural resources
- Improving supportive physical infrastructure such as roads, electricity, water, and communication.

The priority areas articulated in the documents, if implemented, present all the preconditions for a fast-growing agribusiness sector. The challenge is in the implementation and coordination of the interventions, which are scattered in various ministries and departments. Given the interdependent nature of the PMA's priorities, the greater challenge is adequate funding for a holistic implementation of the PMA. Without such implementation, the anticipated benefits and impacts aren't likely to be achieved.

In line with the PMA, a number of specific agricultural policies have been put in place, including the following:

- A new National Agricultural Research policy put in place in 2003 as part of realigning agricultural research into the PMA. The key principles of the policy include responding to market opportunities; empowering stakeholders; decentralizing agricultural research services; promoting participation of the private sector, civil society, and farmers; and assuring the quality of agricultural research services.
- The NAADS, a pillar of the PMA, creates a decentralized, farmer-owned, private sector delivery.
- Through Farm Power and Agricultural Mechanization, which also comes under the PMA, the government would promote the adoption and use of intermediate technology and animal traction under smallholder agriculture, and leave motorized farm power to remain a private sector activity based on individual farmer needs.

- *The dairy subsector*: The government has liberalized the dairy subsector. The DDA champions the dairy subsector with the guidance of a Dairy Master Plan.
- *The beef subsector*: Government policies for the beef subsector are contained in the Beef Master Plan, which provides the framework for increased production of meat for both domestic and export markets mainly through increased private sector investments. Of critical importance is the government's role in providing the necessary legal and regulatory frameworks, as well as standards for meat quality and hygiene.

Supplementary reforms on food security and land are currently being reviewed by the Ugandan parliament and will be discussed in the final section of the study.

INNOVATION ACROSS THE VALUE CHAINS

The Fish Subsector and Value Chain

The actors in the fish value chain are many and interconnected into a complex web. For purposes of analysis, a simplified value chain ordinarily involves the following categories: fishermen and input suppliers, management and regulatory agencies, fish traders and transporters, factory processors for export to premium markets, and processors for the local and regional markets. Figure 5.1 illustrates a simplified linear structural connection of the actors.

The fishermen and input supplier category includes fishmongers, boat owners and makers, and suppliers of fishing nets and other gears. These actors operate largely at the primary production level. The management and regulatory agencies include the BMU and the fisheries department. Some traders and transporters play two roles; those who supply factories for export to premium

Figure 5.1   The Fish Value Chain

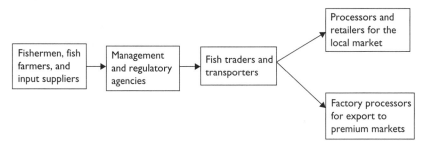

Source: Authors' compilation.

markets (Europe) and those who supply and process for the local and regional markets. Some traders are also processors and export as well.

Like any other food chain, the final product is influenced by the first level of handling. In this regard, international market policies and conditions demand changes in the management and handling of fish in the entire value chain, with an emphasis on the quality and safety of the product. Some of the quality measures are consumer initiated, stringent, and dynamic, requiring regular sensitization, monitoring, and control.

Innovations across the Fish Value Chain

Most of the so-called innovations in the fish value chain are driven by the need to comply with the policies and demands of the European markets. Some demands relate to technology adaptation and transferability to a modernizing local market in urban areas. The notable innovations follow.

Production and marketing: Reducing postharvest losses at the farm while ensuring customer satisfaction. Fish is a very perishable commodity and poses a risk of high postharvest losses, especially to the fish farmers who do not have facilities for preservation. Because of the limited scale, fish farmers target supplying the neighboring communities and rely on farm-gate marketing. A fish farmer came up with the idea of keeping harvested fish alive in a small, shallow pond at his home. The buyers choose the fish they want when they are still alive. With this innovation, the farmer can harvest his pond one time and sell his fish without any losses to consumers who are happy to purchase live "fresh" fish. The pond overcomes the challenge of preservation and brings a new way of marketing live fish to customers.

Alternative use of fish farming residues. The same farmer is not only earning money from the fish but also from the nutrient-rich waste water from his pond. After harvest, the farmer drains the ponds and sells the nutrient-rich drained water to organic farmers who use it as a fertilizer. This is an example of new market opportunities leading to creativity and usage of knowledge for new purpose.

Processing. The growth of supermarkets and hotels has created local niche markets with specific customer preferences requiring primary processing. The supermarkets and hotels prefer fish fillets with different specifications. For example, Asian restaurants prefer fish fillets with the skin whereas other hotels and supermarkets prefer fish fillets without skin. Fish fillet processing used to occur in the fish processing factories, but now fillets are made at the landing sites, ready for supermarkets and restaurants. Value addition at the source of production is an example of adapting a technology to different situations.

The bulk factory processing of Nile perch leaves behind bones and fat as by-product, which are processed and sold locally. The bones are smoked and sold mainly to the Democratic Republic of Congo, but the fat is processed into cooking oil and sold to the local community. The community use of the factory by-products illustrates the potential for integrating fish processing into multiple products.

Organizational innovation: comanagement of the fisheries resources. At the production level, the BMU was originally a community-driven effort to enhance monitoring and surveillance of fishing activities. The community effort was in response to fish-poisoning incidents, which suspended fish exports to foreign markets and severely reduced local fish consumption, threatening the sole source of livelihood to the fishing community and the fish subsector. Because the Ugandan government system was ill-equipped to monitor and control illegal fishing practices, the fishing community mobilized and formed volunteer committees to supplement government efforts in enforcing regulations governing fishing activities. Since 2003, these committees have since evolved into the BMUs, which are government recognized and have taken over most of the regulatory activities on the lake and landing sites. Government-endorsed bylaws empower the BMUs to prohibit the use of illegal fishing methods and gears, enforce proper sanitation and minimum standards on fishermen and traders at the landing sites, coordinate the various stakeholders that operate on the lakes and at landing sites, collect revenue and issue permits and licenses to fish traders, and collect data and keep records related to fishing activities.

Stakeholder-based collective action associations have emerged to advance their specific interests and aspirations and coordinate activities. Indeed, BMUs consist of a 14-member volunteer committee representing fishmongers, fish processors, fish crews, boat owners, boat makers, engine and net suppliers, and the district fisheries department. A total of 355 BMUs are found on Lake Victoria alone. BMUs generate revenue from licensing traders, issuing movement permits, fines, and user fees, and each fishing boat contributes one fish to the BMU at landing. BMUs retain 10 percent of the total revenue to facilitate their activities. Though recognized by the government, BMUs are not agents or employees of government. At a higher level, UFPEA has put into place a mechanism to curb processing of immature fish among its members as part of a comprehensive quality assurance system.

Quality assurance among fish processors and exporters. To ensure competitiveness of Uganda fish exports, UFPEA, an umbrella association for fish processors and exporters (comprising 17 member companies) has set up an independent technical committee to ensure adherence to minimum standards at fish factories. All members have signed up and contributed funds to facilitate the activities of the committee. The committee has unlimited access to all factories and imposes punitive measures on members who do not comply with agreed standards. For example, a first instance of noncompliance earns a one-week suspension; a second instance earns one month, and a third time earns three months. The punitive measures are carried out through a recommendation to the commissioner for fisheries in the Ministry of Agriculture, Animal Industry, and Fisheries (MAAIF). UFPEA also mobilizes resources and technical services to train quality managers for its member companies.

The Banana Subsector and Value Chain

Bananas are widely grown in Uganda both as a food and a cash crop. However, the banana wilt disease has severely affected banana production in some parts of Uganda. The main banana-producing areas in western and southwestern Uganda are now under threat. The disease is spread partly by the movement of infected bananas, and control efforts require movement restrictions and a quarantine of the infected plants. Bananas are mainly produced by smallholder farmers who grow different varieties, for brewing, eating (apple bananas), and cooking (matooke). Whereas most bananas are eaten in their cooked form, as matooke, other products are produced from bananas, including crafts made from banana stems and leaves. The other common banana products are alcoholic beverages, juice, and banana chips. Figure 5.2 is a simplified illustration of the banana value chain examined in this study.

Most of the bananas go directly from the field to market. Value addition in bananas comes from processing banana chips or brewing a crude spirit known as waragi. Banana exports to overseas markets are limited by the bulkiness of the product; exports would be enhanced if there was processing technology to reduce banana bulk.[1]

Innovations across the Banana Value Chain

A typical banana value chain is a short one that limits the range of innovations. The innovations in the banana value chain relate to making chips from bananas, shortening the brewing process, and organizing farmers to increase their bargaining power with traders.

Figure 5.2   The Banana Value Chain

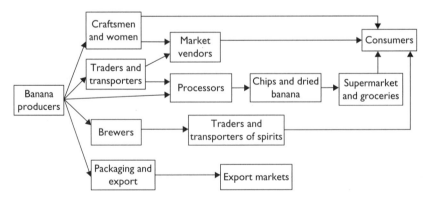

Source: Authors' compilation.

Production and marketing: new products and markets. Chips processed from bananas are a relatively new product that is increasingly popular among urban dwellers. Most supermarkets and groceries in Kampala stock banana chips, an innovation to cater to new urban lifestyles and eating behaviors. Urban dwellers find it easier to pack banana chips as a snack than ripe apple bananas. The processing and packaging add value and increase the shelf life of bananas. Dried banana chips are also exported.

Related to the banana chip export market are new markets for crafts made from bananas. Making crafts from banana stems and leaves is not new, but the quality of such products has tremendously increased and has attracted regional and international export markets. Most of these crafts are made by rural and urban women who supply finished products to wholesalers and exporters. The artisans organize a weekly auction market.

Processing: Shortening the waragi brewing process. The traditional method of brewing waragi from bananas involved ripening the bananas, squeezing the juice, adding yeast and fermenting, and distilling the waragi spirit. The extraction and fermentation steps are now combined. Ripe bananas are crushed and mixed with water and fermented before the distillation. The new process is shorter, yields more alcohol, and uses less labor and fewer additives. The new process doubles the alcohol yield as compared to the traditional method. The crude waragi is not processed any further and is consumed in the form it is produced. Direct consumption of waragi is a departure from the past, when crude waragi was further purified and bottled as Uganda Waragi. Uganda Waragi is no longer processed from crude waragi, but comes from imported sugarcane alcohol, because it is so expensive to purify crude waragi.

Organizational innovation: Farmer organization to reduce overexploitation by traders. For a long time, farmers have been vulnerable to exploitation by traders, who often took advantage of their poverty and lack of market information to purchase produce at very low prices. To minimize exploitation and gain collective bargaining power for their produce, farmers have locally organized to set minimum prices, making it difficult for traders to exploit individual farmers. This new type of arrangement has strengthened the role of brokers. The brokers link traders with banana sources for a guaranteed price for the banana produce. It is through such organizations that farmers begin to interact with the market and exchange knowledge that can lead to new innovations.

The Vegetable Subsector and Value Chain

The vegetables of interest in this study are the high-value varieties targeted for the export market. Hot peppers are the most common vegetable grown on a small scale by companies and outgrower farmers. Outgrower farmers produce for specific export companies on a contractual basis. The firms also provide a variety of services to the outgrowers, including credit—which is recovered when the growers sell the produce—and advisory services to ensure quality production and handling. Stringent EuroGAP (now known as Global Gap) conditions have considerably reduced the number of farmers who can fulfill the requirements to produce for export. The regulations assume that farmers are elite, resource endowed, and professionally managed. The export companies have to employ more professionals to provide quality services and advice, thus increasing expenditures. Because of the strict regulations, the value chain for vegetables is very short, with many outgrowers dropping out and some exporters becoming producers and transporters. Export companies directly handle farmers' produce for export, or farmers supply produce directly to the supermarket for the local market.

Innovations across the Vegetable Value Chain

In the context of global trade policies, innovations are driven by the need for compliance with the market conditions. The innovations identified in the vegetable industry relate to improvising for cold-room handling and new packaging for the local market.

Production: Implementing charcoal coolers to improvise for cold-room storage. Of the major challenges in the vegetable export business is the maintenance of a cold chain for storage to ensure freshness. The vegetables are produced by farmers in remote areas with no electricity, and providing cold-chain facilities is a big challenge. One vegetable producer invested in the construction of a charcoal cooler, which uses charcoal and water as the cooling system. This system gets vegetables into the cold chain as early as possible and enables on-farm sorting and packaging, after which the produce is transported directly to the airport. This innovation benefits the exporter, as well as provides employment to rural communities. The charcoal cooling technology requires substantial investment, but it considerably cuts down an exporter's expenses if adequate volumes are raised. The reduction in the number of farmers who can produce for export has curtailed effective use of the cooling facility because the exporter cannot regularly raise adequate volumes for export.

Processing: Processing to reduce postharvest loses. There is a high level of postharvest losses in hot peppers because the produce that does not meet export market standards is thrown away. One firm processes the rejects into chili sauce and extracts oil from the seeds, but is currently finding supply difficulties because many farmers who cannot meet EuroGAP requirements have dropped out because it is no longer profitable to sell produce at prices lower than they would get for export products. The processing of rejects otherwise adds value, expands the range of hot pepper products, and widens the market.

Marketing: New packaging for the local market. The new and ever-changing regulations make exporting vegetables for European markets more difficult. Many exporters are exploring the local market, focusing on attracting new elite consumers in and near urban centers. One firm innovatively packages an assortment of vegetables in a single basket for the convenience of supermarket shoppers. The customer preference for this type of packaging is overwhelming, and the firm cannot meet the demand from the supermarket. The challenge then becomes ensuring a consistent supply of high-quality produce. Discussions between the processing firm and one of the supermarkets resulted in an experiment in which the supermarket subleased space to the firm to sell vegetables. The firm then employed a salesperson for its vegetable stall to guarantee quality and to obtain direct feedback from the customers. The arrangement has worked very well for both the supermarket and the vegetable firm. The supermarket gains through customer satisfaction and rents, while the vegetable firm has a guaranteed outlet for its products and direct contact with consumers. This arrangement has extended to several other supermarkets, with a very high potential for the local market.

Organizational innovation: Producer organization into cooperatives. The stringent market conditions make it difficult for individual smallholder farmers to survive independently. The need for collective action is apparent, and farmers join cooperatives to conduct joint production and marketing activities. Some of the producer organizations are registered as legal entities that share facilities and the cost of services. Within a cooperative arrangement, internal mechanisms for adherence to established standards are put into place and enforced. This method makes it possible to certify the cooperative as an entity rather than certifying individual farmers. Through their cooperatives, farmers can collectively bargain for better prices, equipment, or services. Box 5.1 describes an example of a cooperative arrangement.

LINKS AMONG KEY ACTORS OF THE INNOVATION SYSTEM

For a value chain to function, coordination is essential among actors in the chain, implying that actors at various levels are organized. Many innovations are organizational and basically come from the need to interact with other organizations. It is at the interfaces of these interactions that information and knowledge translate into economically and socially beneficial innovations.

Links within the Value Chains

The fish value chain. All value chains exhibit some form of organization, although some are more elaborate than others. In the fish enterprise, there are several informal associations of actors at the production level. Associations perform several functions including collective articulation of needs and interests, social support, and joint savings, which are sometimes used as a revolving credit fund. No organization for traders and transporters exists. A more formal organization of processors and exporters, the UFPEA, exists. The mission of UFPEA is to strengthen participation of its members to promote

Box 5.1   Benefits of Farmer Cooperatives

At their own initiative, a group of six hot pepper growers in the Binzi village, located in the Mpigi district, formed a cooperative and registered it as a legal entity. As a cooperative, the farmers negotiated a contract to supply hot peppers to an exporter. To meet their contract with the exporter, the farmers synchronize their planting and other farm operations to raise the volumes and bulk produce required by their client. Farmers explained the benefits of the cooperative, including:

- Sharing information and experiences in various practices and learning more about pests and diseases and how to manage them within the guidelines of EuroGAP. As a group, the farmers also secure training sponsored by their client.
- Jointly procuring inputs like pesticides, sharing facilities and equipment like chemical stores and sprayers, and hiring someone to spray all their plots in one day. The person who sprays comes with his own protective gear, and farmers only pay a fee for his services. Combining spraying services ensures a single spraying regime and allows farmers to pick their peppers on the same day.
- When their client is not able to take their produce, farmers are informed in advance and can find another buyer for their produce. This situation is possible because the buyer is assured of quality and a reasonable volume of the produce. Similarly, farmers are able to engage a technical person to offer them advisory services if they needed it.
- Having mechanisms to monitor and enforce adherence to standards. If a member deviates from those standards, sanctions are applied.

Uganda fish products, foster a partnership with government on policies and programs for fisheries, promote sustainable use of fisheries resources, and assure quality in fish processing.

In some cases, the fish traders provide boats and fishing equipment to fishermen; thus fishermen get operational facilities at no cost and, in return, are committed to sell all their catch to that particular trader. The trader benefits by raising an adequate volume to supply the processors. Similarly, some processors provide insulated trucks and ice to their suppliers as incentive for traders to maintain their supply to the company. This credit system facilitates operations within the value chain. These transactions are based on informal agreements and rely on mutual trust.

The fish processors/exporters interact via UFPEA with regard to policy, quality assurance, and upstream training. Interorganizational interactions for innovation are limited by cutthroat competition. Organization is blocked at the operational level, though UFPEA provides a platform for joint learning related to general aspects of the fish industry. How each firm applies the knowledge and skills is zealously guarded.

Organization and links in the vegetable value chain. In the vegetable value chain, smallholder outgrower farmers are organized in cooperatives clustered around the exporter. At this level, the cooperatives enable farmers to bulk their produce, jointly procure inputs and services, and facilitate training and learning. The exporter extends credit to the outgrowers to purchase inputs, and the exporter recovers the loan when the farmer sells the produce. The exporters also extend training and technical support to their outgrowers.

In most cases, the exporter is also a producer but does not fit in the smallholder outgrower cooperatives. For some time, producers have been organized into a national association called Horticultural Exporters' Association (HORTEXA). HORTEXA is a broader coalition than just vegetables; it embraces all other horticultural producers including fruit and flower growers. This umbrella organization sometimes causes confusion over the specific interests of producers and exporters of various horticultural products.

A new organizational arrangement is in place to streamline roles and responsibilities between producers and exporters. HORTEXA now addresses horticultural production-related aspects. The Association of Fresh Produce Exporting Companies (AFPEC) addresses export-related aspects, and all export companies have aggregated into the Federation of Associations of Ugandan Exporters (FAUEX). An umbrella organization, the Horticulture Promotion Organization of Uganda (HPOU), coordinates these other organizations. Another organization, National Organic Movement of Uganda (NOGAMU), organizes producers of organic products. HPOU is the voice of the fruit and vegetable industry and coordinates activities and responsibilities of its subsidiary organizations. Each exporter, however, has a direct link with the market, and the associations only coordinate issues of common interest.

Organization in the banana value chain. The banana value chain is not as elaborately organized and coordinated as the other subsectors. Farmers have recently organized themselves for collective price bargaining. Informal trader organizations pool resources, particularly with respect to transport. A group of three to four traders combine to hire a truck to transport bananas or waragi to market. The women craft artisans exhibit the longest-term organizational arrangements. These associations of women craft artisans engage in a variety of economic and social agendas and actively market and promote their products.

Links: Companies and Business Associations/ Farmer Organizations

Support services, such as training and funding for strategic intervention in the respective sectors, are coordinated by umbrella organizations. HPOU solicits support for capacity building and facilitation for services such as laboratory testing from foreign donor agencies. HPOU then directs support to the respective associations for implementation. A good example is the subsidy for tests in a certified laboratory from PIP, a Dutch NGO. The NGO pays 80 percent of the cost of laboratory service, and the local company pays only 20 percent. Tests in a certified private laboratory can otherwise be too expensive for a company to bear on its own.

These organizations also interact with foreign partners for educational purposes and developing strategies that can promote the growth of their related agribusinesses. Box 5.2 describes the HPOU's experience with its Kenyan counterpart, IFPEC.

Learning from the Kenya visit, HPOU has developed a Web site to promote the horticulture industry in Uganda to the rest of the world. This HPOU initiative responded to complaints from the European market partners that there is no information about Uganda. In addition, a technical committee now interprets EuroGAP and advises on the appropriate responses for the Ugandan context. The UgandaGap, which sets out standards and practices, is also under development. The other associations such as HORTEXA, AFPEC, and FAUEX also solicit support and services to benefit their membership. Through such

---

Box 5.2 Institutional Interaction and Learning for Innovation

Under the umbrella of HPOU, we organized a visit to our Kenyan counterpart, IFPEC, to learn how they are organized and how they have managed to comply with the EuroGAP regulations and conditions. We spent two weeks exchanging ideas and experiences and visiting some of their members. What we learned from that visit included the following:

- Use of the Web site to inform partners what is happening in the horticultural industry, but more especially what measures are being taken to respond to EuroGAP
- Documenting whatever they do and making that information available to all stakeholders in and outside the country
- To respond to EuroGAP, the IFPEC organized a meeting of all stakeholders and formed a technical committee, which helped interpret EuroGAP clause by clause and devise appropriate means of responding to each of them. Focus was on improvising to meet the purpose of EuroGAP.
- The relevance of developing the country Gap and clarifying the roles and responsibilities of the various stakeholders as an internal regulatory mechanism.

Source: Rashid Sekandi, publicity secretary, HPOU.

interfaces, the associations bring in knowledge and experiences that can be the springboard for agribusiness innovation.

Similarly UFPEA, in addition to the resources generated by their membership, also solicits for resources from donor agencies to support some of their programs and services such as training. They sometimes facilitate members, participation in exhibitions in and outside the country.

Links: Companies to knowledge/technology generation and training institutions. Training and research institutions are key actors in any innovation system because they control or have access to a huge amount of information/knowledge. Their interaction with other actors in a value chain enhances the level of innovation. The agribusiness firms generate knowledge through their own research and experiences, which would invariably be useful to training and research institutions.

Company links with research and extension institutions. Of the three value chains in Uganda, the fisheries via UFPEA seem to have the closest institutional collaboration, that with the National Fisheries Research Institute (NaFRI). There are indications of collaboration in the generation of information/knowledge through surveys and product development. In the vegetable value chain, the firms occasionally consult research institutes when they experience peculiar problems, but there seem to be few joint undertakings or regular contact. For vegetables,, exporters sometimes access technical services from experts outside their firms. In this way, they may use researchers but more through personal arrangement than institutional collaborations.

NAADS contracts with private firms to deliver services, but is unprepared to provide specialized services to these value chains. NAADS demonstrations provide more general knowledge to a wider group of people rather than focusing on specialized business support for a few entrepreneurs. NAADS addresses needs generated by grassroots farmers, and very specialized services are unlikely to emerge in such a process.

Most firms have access to computers in their Kampala-based offices and use computers mainly to access market-related information. The Internet has yet to be adequately used to access technical information that can enhance innovations for agribusiness firms. Some of the constraints on Internet use include its cost, lack of computer literacy, and lack of electricity in rural areas.

The Kawanda research institute has a banana research program focusing on improvement of plant varieties and pest and disease management. This program has created a supply of disease-resistant germplasm for bananas. Respondents to the survey cite NAADS for supporting multiplication and distribution of hygienic planting materials. Another collaborative banana research program between Makerere University and the NARO emphasizes value addition and product development.

In general, whereas there might be some contact with research institutions, agribusiness firms are not involved in determining the research agenda and are rarely consulted on research priorities for the agribusiness sector.

Some firms also conduct informal research to advance their businesses, but not conventional research characterized by scientific design, rigor, and peer-reviewed publications. The individual fish processing firms conduct routine quality tests and sometimes pay private laboratories for such services. They also experiment with new practices (for example, various ways of skinning and trimming that enable significant gains in fillet yield). Another firm surveyed the local market and found out that in a 25-kilometer stretch between Kampala and Entebbe, there are more than 20 supermarkets and groceries that require a regular vegetable supply, but the company could only satisfactorily supply seven of them. The firms emphasize generating information through informal research for their business, but much of this information is used immediately and not documented.

Links: Companies to training institutions (universities and schools). Training institutions, universities, and colleges that produce professionals should more often collaborate with agribusinesses to train graduates for employment. Many firms sometimes host trainees from various training institutions for internships. Internships are irregular and are neither clearly defined nor share learning objectives with trainees, training institutions, and the businesses. The firms complain of the negative attitude of university trainees towards hands-on field work—many seem to despise work that involves getting dirty. Firms are concerned about extractive behavior by students and university researchers who only seem to be interested in collecting data from the companies but not working together to develop the agribusiness sector. Though some firms benefit from additional labor, the firms have yet to internalize the value of hosting interns. Inevitably, if the agribusiness sector expects to rely on professionals to champion their interests in EuroGAP, private sector firms must participate more in training professionals, including curriculum design. An incentive system is necessary for firms to provide training opportunities for future professionals. But training institutions must negotiate arrangements with the private sector on mutually agreed terms. HPOU has a university representative on its technical team that may bring more active engagement between universities and the agribusiness sector.

Public-Private Sector Interactions

The agribusiness sector interacts with the public sector via their respective umbrella associations. One of the main objectives of the associations is to lobby for appropriate policies for and government support of the agribusiness sector. There are examples of engagement between the associations and the public sector, specifically with ministries and government departments. Many interactions revolve around policy development, implementation, and resource mobilization for investment in infrastructure and services delivery. Associations that represent stakeholders can catch the attention of policy makers and technocrats.

UFPEA, for example, and MAAIF have secured funding from the European Union to support various developments in the fish sector. Part of this fund will be used to develop basic infrastructure at the landing sites for fish handling; some of the fund will be used for capacity building, including quality assurance; and some for mobilization, sensitization, and education of various actors in the fish subsector. UFPEA and MAAIF are currently engaged in an awareness campaign for various stakeholders on the theme, "Fish for the Future." There are also policy dialogues and complementary efforts in the enforcement of rules and regulations. Sanctions for violating UFPEA quality standards and protocols are enforced through the Commissioner for Fisheries, demonstrating collective responsibility between the private and public sector.

HPOU has initiated a policy dialogue with MAAIF to develop specific policies that address the horticultural industry and is also involved in streamlining the food safety bill. HPOU is prepared to play an active role in the implementation of food safety procedures that affect its members. Development of the Uganda Gap is a related activity that will put into place protocols, procedures, and regulations and requires that HPOU and MAAIF work together in a closer partnership. HPOU has MAAIF representation on its technical committee. Other areas of collaboration include capacity building, training and infrastructure development, and resource mobilization.

The agribusiness sector relies on standards from outside, usually from the market, but firms do not always have clear knowledge of the local standards with which they are expected to comply. The National Bureau of Standards is responsible for standards but seems detached from the agribusiness sector. It is for this reason that the UgandaGap, if developed and championed by the private sector, will establish and enforce standards that are relevant to the specific agribusinesses.

POLICY INFLUENCE ON AGRIBUSINESS

Policy is the framework within which innovation takes place. The policy environment therefore could enhance or inhibit agribusiness innovation. Private-sector successes have led agribusiness in international and local markets to depend on the existence of infrastructure and public services that individual private firms cannot undertake. This calls for government investment into basic facilities and services that support agribusinesses, including appropriate policies. It is not enough to have a good policy in place unless mechanisms for effective implementation are also in place. As the subsequent discussion shows, it is more the lack of implementation than the lack of the existence of good public policies that constrain agribusiness innovation. The section will describe a set of conditions and policy-related aspects supporting and constraining agribusiness with specific reference to the fish, banana and vegetable value chains.

Policy-Related Constraints

Lack of public investment in infrastructure. Infrastructure, as referred to here, is public facilities that support the agribusiness sector, but would be too expensive for a private company to invest in. Although under the PMA and related policies, infrastructure issues have been mentioned, these policies have rarely been implemented. The policy-related constraints include specifically:

Sanitary and hygienic fish handling facilities at the landing sites. *(Fish subsector)*: Most landing sites lack the basic facilities for safe fish handling, thereby posing a high risk of contamination at the first point of handling. Sanitary and hygienic facilities, such as toilets, are for public use and are the responsibility of the public sector. As a result, many in the fishing communities live around the lakes, the largest sources of water, but lack access to safe water due to the lack of sanitation and hygienic facilities. Such conditions pose a high risk of contamination of fish at the initial source thereby affecting product quality along the rest of the chain.

Cold-chain facilities. *(Fish and vegetable subsectors)*: Fish and vegetables require maintenance of a cold chain right from harvest to export. The Ugandan government needs to invest in cold houses at the landing sites where traders can temporarily keep their fish for a storage fee before supplying the fish to factories. Not having to keep insulated and iced trucks at the landing sites for several days would considerably reduce the traders' cost of doing business, while ensuring quality of fish. A different cold-chain system for vegetables would be necessary because the facilities for fish are unsuitable for vegetables.

Road network and transportation costs. (*All subsectors*): Because of the lack of electricity in the remote areas where production takes place and the need for proximity to the airport, the processing and packing facilities are conveniently located around Kampala or Entebbe. Products must travel along roads for long distances to the location where they are processed or packaged. In addition to the high transportation costs, the poor state of the road network causes losses from unwarranted delivery delays. With a highly perishable product like fish, trucks have to use more ice and fuel, and the factories would have to pay for workers waiting for delayed supplies. Poor roads constrain all agribusiness, but in the case of fish, poor transportation infrastructure may be the single most constraining factor among fish traders and transporters.

Quality laboratory testing services. *All subsectors*: It is extremely expensive and unnecessary for every firm to establish and adequately equip a laboratory for quality testing. The EuroGAP regulations, for example, require farmers to regularly test the quality of their water sources, procedures that individual farmers cannot afford. Such situations would require leverage by government as part of the infrastructure support to agribusiness. At the moment, fish processing firms carry out their own routine tests and contract with private laboratories to do tests for which they have no capacity. A publicly financed laboratory charging a reasonable user fee would reduce costs and enhance product quality, while providing a mechanism for monitoring of standards.

Lack of public investment in education. In Uganda, a large proportion of farmers is illiterate. Universal primary education only started in the late 1990s, and the recently introduced universal secondary education policies won't have an effect for another generation. Low education levels limit farmers' capacity to access and use existing information and knowledge about agriculture. Use of information and communication technology (ICT) is severely curtailed by low levels of education. Furthermore, the low level of education also inhibits compliance with the EuroGAP/Global Gap requirements for export products, including requirements to keep records of farm management practices and due diligence. As a consequence, Uganda cannot compete with other countries in exporting products that would otherwise contribute to poverty reduction and economic growth for the country and its farmers.

Education is also the key to conscious observance of health and hygiene practices, which are a strict requirement in food handling. A quality assurance manager of a fish processing firm explained the ease with which relatively educated employees, as opposed to uneducated employees, internalize and adhere to hygiene practices.

Lack of government investment in pursuing value addition for local products. The lack of government investment is closely related to the lack of favorable credit facilities, but the emphasis is on the lack of implementation. Several government documents, including the PMA, indicate how important value addition is to agricultural development. If agribusiness is to flourish, it has to be backed by government action to provide incentives, including subsidies for agricultural production and value addition. An example of the lack of government subsidies for value addition is the decline of further waragi purification by distilleries because it is not as profitable as using imported sugar cane alcohol. The brand "Uganda Waragi," once proudly associated with purified waragi brewed from bananas, in reality now can no longer make that claim. Instead, sugarcane alcohol is imported from South Africa, Kenya, and Malawi and simply flavored and packaged or bottled as waragi. Waragi is a clear example of the government's failure to demonstrate its commitment to value addition. It is rational for any business to adopt options with the highest returns or income accumulation, but the government should be more concerned with income distribution and value addition to benefit the entire value chain. In the waragi case, the government would have to deliberately subsidize and assist the distilling companies to acquire the necessary technology to add value to crude waragi brewed from bananas and promote it internationally. Deliberate government action to support value chains guarantees financial flow to the producers and can foster functional poverty alleviation initiatives.

Other market opportunities remain unexploited largely because the private sector alone is unable to invest in such capital-intensive ventures. For instance, banana (matooke) exports to European countries are limited by product bulk and lack of primary processing such as peeling. Overseas buyers prefer ready-to-cook products, but the technology for peeling bananas is not yet available. The much hyped public-private partnership (PPP) could address such needs, but only if the public sector was proactive in collaborating with the private sector.

Lack of favorable credit facilities and "no subsidy" policy for inputs. *Lack of investment capital* is a limiting factor throughout all the value chains. Agribusinesses suffer from lack of access to credit at favorable terms or face the exploitation of commercial banks, which charge unrealistic interest rates for genuine business. In the fish enterprise, some factories have either closed or are under receivership[2] because of the failure to pay back loans obtained from commercial banks. Lack of credit facilities has encouraged the use of cheap illegal fishing gears, which would otherwise be minimized if fishers could receive recommended gears on credit that they could pay back over time. This situation complicates further enforcement regulation.

The *no subsidy policy to agricultural inputs* adopted by the government alongside structural adjustment policies makes inputs too expensive for resource-poor farmers. Microfinance institutions (MFIs) have proliferated to provide credit facilities to small and medium-size businesses, but their conditions, interest rates, and repayment schedules are not favorable to agricultural-related businesses whose markets are not reliable. The government needs to establish a reliable source of favorable credit to agribusinesses to enable the flow of income in the value chain that extends to the producers who happen to be among the poorest workers in the population.

Trade policy: High freight costs and taxes on airlift. Uganda has the highest freight charges among its regional competitors. It is estimated that the freight costs per unit in Uganda are three times as high as those in Kenya, which makes Ugandan products more expensive and business less profitable. The high costs are partly associated with high taxes imposed on airlines, but the lack of a national carrier also makes government intervention very difficult. The 2008 national budget attempted to reduce taxes on airline revenue, which has translated into appreciable reduction in freight charges, but a lot more needs to be done.

Weak enforcement of laws and regulations and political interference in enforcement. The existing laws and regulations are hardly enforced because of weak public sector institutions. A recent newsletter published by UFPEA displays recommended fishing boats compared to those presently used. But the adoption of recommended tools is limited by the lack of credit to purchase them. Government is in a position of double failure, as the same government that fails to facilitate access to recommended tools and facilities cannot effectively penalize the use of illegal ones. Fish is transported in boats with all kinds of merchandise, a practice that is unacceptable. The ministries and National Bureau of Standards (NBS) that should enforce regulations do not have the financial and personnel resources to do monitoring and surveillance. The vegetable subsector faces a similar challenge with the implementation of phytosanitary regulations. Where there are established standards for most practices and products, they are largely unknown to the producers because they are not enforced.

Political announcements that contradict existing laws and regulations complicate enforcement. For example, a presidential announcement to stop apprehending traders transporting immature fish hampered enforcement of size and weight restrictions. Though the announcement was later retracted, it left the enforcement authorities demoralized. Also, some district authorities are more interested in raising revenue than controlling unacceptable practices. Weak enforcement and corruption within the enforcing institutions encourages illegal practices to continue unabated. For example, the Fisheries Act prohibits export of unprocessed fish, but unprocessed and immature undersized fish is exported to neighboring countries. Similarly, even though UFPEA strives to stop processing and exporting immature fish, the fish are openly sold on the local market, rendering futile the concerted effort of the private sector.

Some policies cannot be implemented simply because they are at fault right from the design stage. Such policies are based on wrong premises and are sometimes misunderstood by implementing authorities. The Food Safety Bill, which is marred by confusion as to whether it should be based in MAAIF or in the Ministry of Health is a glaring example. If all relevant stakeholders are not sufficiently involved in the policy development process, the policy may be faulty by design and therefore cannot be implemented.

Open access policy to lake resources. Open lake access is a specific concern to the fisheries enterprise. Unlimited access to lake resources attracts every person interested in fishing and results in exploiting a free resource with nonregulation equipment. Open access makes it difficult to enforce regulations and standards regarding fishing on the lakes. Limited access would ensure that those in the business are compliant with minimum standards and practices.

Stringent and ever-changing international market standards. EuroGAP/ Global Gap sets very tough conditions that demand a huge investment in the value chain to meet the required standards. The regulations are dynamic and frequently change, and some are consumer-initiated at the behest of supermarket chains. Fish and vegetable exports to European markets are severely constrained by these standards and regulations. In the vegetable enterprise, many farmers and exporters have dropped out of business because they are not compliant. Consequently, those exporters who have made huge investments in facilities face huge losses because they can no longer raise sufficient volume to economically run their facilities. The process of certification for the Euro-GAP/Global Gap is too expensive for a typical Ugandan firm. A relevant example is the firm that invested the charcoal cooler but can no longer raise adequate volumes to effectively use the facility, because most outgrowers are not compliant with export regulations. The drive to innovate is suffocated. But high market barriers can also limit competition for the few firms that do meet the requirements. The compliant firms may be rather happy with the stringent market conditions as they keep potential competitors out, but a closed market clearly does not benefit the economy as a whole. Sustaining compliance calls for effective national regulatory and support systems and is a public sector responsibility.

Supporting Policies

Important supportive policies for agribusinesses include nontaxation policy on agricultural exports, liberalization of trade and service delivery, and specific to the fish industry, the burning of illegal fishing gears.

Nontaxation of agricultural exports. Agricultural exports are not taxed as an incentive to agricultural exports and marketing in general. In addition, imported packaging materials for exports and equipment for value addition attract a minimal tax. These policies have been especially beneficial to exporters.

Liberalization of trade and service delivery. Liberalization of trade and service delivery has particularly improved the communication sector, which is very vital to agribusiness. Mobile telephone services are affordable and are accessible countrywide. This has greatly eased information flow and links with markets, service providers, and other actors. Communication is critical especially in value chains of highly perishable products like fish.

Destroying illegal fishing gear to protect immature fish. Though the policy still faces the challenge of effective implementation, inappropriate fishing gear has been burned to protect immature fish and sustain the fish resources. UFPEA was able to put in place a mechanism for enforcing the policy among its members. Here we see how the private sector can support enforcement of a beneficial policy. As a further consequence, fishers will have no incentive to catch undersize fish.

CONCLUSION

Drivers of Innovation

In the context of identifying the roles of the public sector and agribusiness for boosting innovation, a broader discussion on major drivers of innovation is needed. Innovation is usually a reaction to forces and conditions that prevail in a particular environment—in this case the agribusiness environment. There are no universal triggers of innovation but based on the innovations in the fish, banana, and vegetable enterprises described above, drivers that trigger innovations usually include profit orientation; personal and organizational inspiration; compliance with market conditions and regulations; new market opportunities; and access to information and exposure. The most pertinent ones are briefly discussed in the context of the study.

Compliance with market conditions and regulations. Competition, new market conditions like EuroGAP, an unfavorable policy, or failure to implement a beneficial policy are drivers of innovation. Most of the innovations described in the fish subsector are a response to changing market conditions. Improvising and adapting new practices in the vegetable subsector are a response to EuroGAP regulations. If the threat is broad, like that affecting the fish subsector, then it creates motivation for collective action, such as initiatives for comanagement of the lake resources and quality assurance measures within IFPEA, and the resultant organizational innovations are aimed at offsetting a systemwide challenge that requires joint action. Collective action is no substitute for individual/organizational level challenges, but the interorganizational interaction of umbrella associations provides a platform for knowledge exchange about alternative options.

New market opportunities. New markets and opportunities within existing markets continue to emerge. The ability to identify and respond to these opportunities distinguishes innovation. Innovation is very closely linked to demand, which has two dimensions. Demand comes from the market in the form of new specifications or standards, but demand is also proactively created by putting a new product on the market. Processing fish fillets at the landing sides is an example of responding to a demand from supermarkets and hotels, whereas making banana chips is a demand proactively created by putting a new product on the market. The basket packaging of an assortment of vegetables is a demand that responds to a new opportunity within an existing market to target an affluent community, who may wish to be associated with trendy preferences.

Market opportunities can arise for agribusinesses on different levels, including targeting the lowest strata of society and thereby improving the lives of poor consumers. For example, processing cooking oil from Nile perch fat targets the poor communities that cannot afford vegetable oil, while waragi is a commodity for poor communities that cannot afford other kinds of bottled alcohol.

A support system is essential to enhance confidence and reduce the risks of the innovations as profit may not be realized in the short term.

Access and exposure to information. Access to information and exposure induces innovation. The innovation to process hot peppers is linked to exposure and access to information. Factors limiting use of ICT, such as illiteracy or lack of electricity in rural areas, directly limit access to information and knowledge sources and consequently hinder innovation.

Outlook and Recommendations

This study assessed the fish, banana, and vegetable subsectors and their value chains with the AIS framework to gain new insights on the dynamics of innovation and whether public policies impede or encourage innovation. The existing policies demonstrate the government's good intentions to create a conducive environment and to provide support services for the growth of agribusiness in Uganda. Policies on food security and food and nutrition standards are under formulation. Food security policy will address issues including irrigation, publicly held grain reserves, and compulsory retention of farmers' reserve of designated food crops. Through food security policy, the Ugandan government would encourage the private sector to improve markets to increase incentives for farmers and traders to engage in intertemporal crop storage, eventually increasing food exports into regional markets like the upcoming East African Common Market. Policy makers have offered ideas about establishing private sector insurance schemes for the agricultural sector to respond to the risks in agricultural production and agribusiness, such as the adverse impact of droughts and diseases on farm incomes. Such policy is necessary to provide a basis for dialogue and to attract insurance industry interests to the agricultural sector. In addition, a newly formulated land-use policy was launched in 2008. The land-use policy is expected to provide livelihood security through employment or access to land for more intensive use, facilitate appropriate development, deliver land-use services, protect fragile environments, redress historical injustices, and provide more equitable access to land.

The good intentions of policies have not been successfully translated into action. The critical constraints on agribusiness exist despite good policies. The challenge to innovation is policy implementation curtailed by a lack of adequate human resource capacity and facilitation as well as inappropriate institutional arrangements for effective implementation. The PMA provides a comprehensive framework for supporting agriculture in general, and agribusiness in particular, but its implementation is fragmented, uncoordinated, and inadequately funded. In practice, however, bits and pieces of PMA are implemented by a variety of government agencies, thus creating confusion as to who has overall responsibility. Agricultural advisory services and research are implemented by semi-autonomous organizations like NAADS and NARO under the guidance of MAAIF; marketing and agroprocessing (MAP) is under the Ministry of Tourism, Trade, and Industry (MTTI), with some components falling under the Ministry of Finance, Planning, and Economic Development (MFPED) and the Ministry of Foreign Affairs. The president's office and the vice president's office also implement parallel programs under the PMA umbrella.

It takes concerted efforts by the different branches of government to bring about agricultural development, and these efforts have to be well coordinated and rationalized; otherwise the few resources available are simply wasted. But there is a political dimension to the implementation of agriculture-related policies. Because the majority of Uganda's population depends on agriculture, politicians want to implement agricultural programs that increase or strengthen their political support. The technocrats' believe that these policies should be harmonized and their implementation better coordinated to achieve their intended outcomes. These imperatives will put the available resources to better use, notwithstanding the need to increase financial support for implementation of agribusiness support policies.

Innovation is usually an outcome of knowledge interfaces facilitated by institutional interactions that necessitate a reasonable level of organization among the agribusiness actors. There is a trend toward building such organizations, and some of the innovations discussed here are organizational, but an emerging private sector needs government to support and facilitate their efforts. With public sector support, the private sector can establish organizations to interact with public and international agencies as a foundation for innovation. This type of organization is still weak, and opportunities for public-private partnerships to innovate are rather unexploited. Organization of the agribusiness sector creates collective bargaining ability and the recognition to foster public-private interaction, as illustrated by emerging relationships among UFPEA, HPOU, and government departments for program implementation and policy development.

Better information access and learning opportunities can be realized if agribusiness firms and organizations interact with universities, colleges, and research institutions to exchange knowledge and experiences. Both sides need to be proactive in establishing such links based on clearly defined common interests.

Agribusiness firms involved in exports are linked to the external market and other support organizations, but these links have not been fully used for learning and innovation. There is evidence of learning resulting from the interaction between HPOU and its Kenyan counterpart that stimulated creativity. However, agribusinesses still need to effectively use electronic platforms such as the Internet for learning and innovation, but Internet use comes at a cost that many economically constrained firms may not be able to sustain. Currently Internet costs are high, and the Internet is used more for communication than for a learning platform.

Learning within the value chains is facilitated by umbrella organizations, which provide technical support, training, and other support services to the members. But the efforts of umbrella organizations are not adequate to enhance innovation such as training, which is usually supply driven and provides technical aspects rather than being focused on exchanging knowledge and experiences. Competition within the value chain seems to be a barrier to the free flow of knowledge among the members. Some firms hesitate to provide information regarding their business for fear competitors will use it. Open knowledge exchange is a challenge in a competitive environment. Nonbusiness organizations, such as training and research institutions, are best placed to facilitate knowledge exchange, but their involvement in value chains is rather disconnected from the business actors.

Agroprocessing is a trigger for innovation in a value chain because the value-added products have a wider market with an increased shelf life, better packaging, and less bulkiness, and producers are assured of a market for their produce. This is where government needs to deliberately support agribusiness firms involved in processing, because the risk of innovation may be too high for the private firms. An individual private firm will logically take the option that gives it the highest returns, a primary goal that does not necessarily develop the value chain. An example is the situation where distilleries have abandoned further processing of crude banana-based waragi in preference of the easier and more profitable imported sugarcane alcohol because the technology for processing the crude waragi is very expensive. Stimulating innovation in a value chain and guaranteeing the livelihood of those dependent on the chain necessitates government intervention.

International trade policies have placed stringent conditions that exclude poor countries like Uganda from the international markets. The EuroGAP, for example, severely limits export of horticultural products from Uganda due to inappropriate infrastructure and regulatory systems. The export orientation (mainly to Europe) increases the vulnerability of agribusiness in Uganda because the support system does not adequately cushion firms against the high risks associated with innovations. The ever-changing international market regulations not only demand higher investment from agribusiness firms, they also demand governments to invest in infrastructure, regulatory bodies, and agribusiness support services. If the established standards for practices and products were adequately enforced, firms would have an easier time of complying with international market standards, but the enforcement of standards is extremely weak.

NOTES

1. There is a presidential initiative under way to develop such a technology, but it is still in the initial stages.
2. When a factory is under "receivership," the control and management of the firm is taken over by the bank where the entrepreneur borrowed the money. The bank takes over the property to recover the loan.

REFERENCES

Government of Uganda. 1998. "The Local Governments Act, Uganda." *Uganda Gazette* 19 (90).

———. 2001. "The National Agricultural Advisory Services Act, 2001." Acts Supplement No. 9, *Uganda Gazette* 33 (94).

Ministry of Agriculture, Animal Industry, and Fisheries. 2003. *The National Agricultural Research Policy.* Kampala: Government of Uganda.

Ministry of Agriculture, Animal Industry, and Fisheries and Ministry of Finance, Planning, and Economic Development. 2000. "Plan for Modernisation of Agriculture: Government Strategy and operational Framework for Eradicating Poverty." Government of Uganda, Kampala.

Ministry of Finance, Planning, and Economic Development. 2004. "Poverty Eradication Action Plan 2004/5-2007/8." Government of Uganda, Kampala.

Ministry of Tourism, Trade, and Industry. 2005. "The Marketing and Agro-Processing Strategy (MAPS)." Kampala: Goverment of Uganda.

NAADS (National Agricultural Advisory Services). 2000. "National Agricultural Advisory Services Programme (NAADS)." Master Document, Ministry of Agriculture, Animal Industry, and Fisheries (MAAIF), Kampala.

Uganda Fish Processors and Exporters' Association. 2007. *The Fish Newsletter.*

———. 2007. *The Fish Newsletter.*

APPENDIX

Survey Questionnaire

DESIGN

This appendix describes the design of the study and the content of the survey questionnaire used for the interviews of the agribusiness leaders in the six countries surveyed: Ghana, Kenya, Mozambique, Rwanda, Tanzania, and Uganda.

To assess the extent to which prevailing national public policies either enhance or impede the possibilities for growth-stimulating innovation in Africa's agricultural sector, the study comparatively assessed six African nations. The analysis encompassed value chains, institutions, and policies from all sectors that potentially shaped agricultural innovation. The study selected the most relevant subset of policies and evaluated the extent to which the corresponding policy environment created by these policies is conducive to agricultural and especially agribusiness innovation. The review of the literature suggested a framework that focused on policies in six areas: education and human resources; the creation of new knowledge; the transmission and adoption of knowledge; business and enterprise; innovation finance, outputs, and markets; and interactions and linkages. The ultimate research goal was to identify major drivers and impediments within the innovation system for agricultural innovation, and the four or five policies that producers/firms see as placing the greatest constraints on their innovation efforts.

Each of the country studies was conducted by a national researcher familiar with the literature on agricultural innovation systems: George Essegbey (for Ghana), Hannington Odame (for Kenya), Jorge Cardoso de Barros (for Mozambique), Daniel Rukazambuga (for Rwanda), John Mpagalile (for Tanzania), and Paul Kibwika (for Uganda).

Research Questions

The following topics served as a focus for the research undertaking:

- How do agribusiness representatives and other informed observers assess the overall public-policy climate for innovation in the agricultural sector?
- Which policies and/or public institutions are playing a useful role in this regard, and which are not?
- What changes in policies and/or public institutions would be most conducive to improved prospects for agricultural innovation in the country? Are some policies in conflict with others, such as commodity-focused agricultural research policies that are not supported by trade policies?
- What types of technical, financial, and marketing/export services might support this goal?

Scope of Inquiry

To keep the investigation manageable while ensuring comparability and guarding against narrowness, the scope of inquiry focused on the three main subspheres of agricultural production within each country: food staples such as maize, rice, potatoes; high-value products such as flowers, vegetables, fruits; and livestock such as beef, dairy, pork.[1]

Methodology

This study was a labor-intensive undertaking, given that the investigation cut across several policy spheres and was based on a number of personal interviews. Interviewing was required because the topic did not lend itself to statistical analysis or a desk review of existing research publications. In fact, key informant interviewing is useful for assessing the conditions for innovation within countries. Perhaps the best-known example of this methodology is the Global Competitiveness Index generated by the World Economic Forum. To develop appropriate indicators for agricultural innovation system (AIS) performance, "the value of expert surveys as a method to collect data should not be underestimated" (Spielman and Birner 2008: 23).

Prior to the start of the research, the six country researchers received an orientation and were asked to develop a common research framework and agree on the specifics of the investigational approach. This exercise sought to adjust the research design to what was feasible for the region, to ensure comparability of the country cases, and to flesh out the research methodology. An experienced senior agricultural researcher, John Lynam (the research coordinator) led the two-day workshop in December 2007 in Nairobi, Kenya. The research coordinator was familiar with the AIS concept and provided methodological support to the researchers during the conduct of their investigations.

Each case study included interviews with 25 to 30 senior managers from a cross-section of domestic and international agribusiness firms and cooperatives operating in the country. The interviewees were distributed among the three categories identified in the scope of inquiry above (that is, food staples, high-value products, and livestock). The purpose of the interviews was to identify major dynamics, drivers, and impediments for agribusiness innovation within value chains and the innovation system; to determine and evaluate the effects of the *main* public policies and institutional cultures of public organizations that generate positive or negative incentives for innovation in agribusiness; and to suggest ways in which each identified policy might be either reinforced (positive) or rectified (negative). Because agribusiness representatives were generally unaccustomed to thinking in terms of innovation policies and systems, the interview questions focused on practical issues and were problem oriented. The list of interview questions is presented below.

Next, each researcher cross-checked this initial list of identified drivers, impediments, and policies by asking 8 to 10 representatives of nongovernmental organizations (NGOs), business associations, and applied research centers for their opinions on this matter. The results of the two sets of interviews were combined to assess the overall policy environment for supporting agricultural innovation and to identify policy improvements that would enhance the prospects for innovation. The researcher then selected a final list of key policies and analyzed available documentation for each (for example, legislative acts and government regulations).

The third step required the researcher to interview at least three persons from each ministry or public agency with primary responsibility for the area covered by each selected policy. These interviews sought to ascertain the extent to which the institutional culture of the agency supports or constrains innovation, and to identify possible discrepancies between the written policy and public officials' verbal interpretation of it (that is, "theory versus practice"). This step incorporated an institutional assessment that characterized the agency's organizational culture, its understanding of innovation processes, staff attitudes towards innovation, and its existing capacity to support innovation within the country.

Quality Control

Two additional activities enriched interpretations and provided quality control. On the one hand, the researchers discussed the country case studies on agricultural innovation and shared common insights and conclusions across the country reports at a seminar in Addis Ababa. On the other hand, the main conclusions of the synthesis chapter prepared by John Lynam as well as the country case studies were presented for comment, suggestion, and validation to policy makers, agribusiness leaders, academics, NGOs, and farmer organizations at the Forum on Practicing Agricultural Innovation: A Platform for Action in May 2008 in Dar es Salaam.

THE LIST OF INTERVIEW QUESTIONS

The interview guide covered six areas of government agricultural policy, as identified in the relevant research. The guide focused on the main issues identified under each:

- Education and human resources
  - Supply and relevance of skilled human resources
  - Government incentives for individuals to study and firms to train
  - Quality of secondary and technical education

- Creation of new knowledge
  - Research and development (R&D) funding and priorities
  - Competitive remuneration for public researchers
  - Performance incentives for public researchers

- Transmission and application of knowledge
  - Extension and technical support services
  - Intellectual property rights protection
  - Media/communications policies on information access

- Business and enterprise
  - Specific trade promotion policies
  - Legal guarantees for contracts and property
  - Consistent enforcement of standards and regulations
  - Innovations recently tried and adopted

- Innovation finance, outputs, and markets
  - Tax incentives for technology upgrading
  - Risk sharing on experimental approaches
  - Investment incentives

- Interactions and linkages
  - Government-sponsored platforms, conferences, associations
  - Government incentives for collaborative efforts
  - Government facilitation of interactions, linkages, and networks
  - Membership in national, regional, or international associations.

The interview questions, organized under these six areas, are provided below.

Education and Human Resources

1. How would you assess the "preparedness for work" among recent university graduates? Among polytechnic or technical college graduates?
2. Do you find that the education system fails to impart to graduates certain skills or abilities that are required by your firm? If so, please give examples.
3. Do you find that the university system is remiss in providing certain types of graduates that would be useful for your firm? If so, please give examples.
4. Does the government provide any incentives to firms like yours to accept student work placements? What incentives?
5. Does the government provide any incentives to firms like yours to upgrade worker skills through training or other investments in skills development?
6. To what extent do universities or technical institutes consult firms like yours in setting their strategic priorities, or incorporate representatives from private enterprise into their institutional governance bodies such as university councils?
7. What is the most common shortcoming characterizing new graduates hired by your firm?

Creation of New Knowledge

1. Do government research institutes consult firms such as yours in setting their research priorities, or incorporate representatives from the private sector into their governing boards?
2. Does your firm conduct any research "in-house?" If so, what type(s)?
3. Does your firm seek to innovate in any aspect of production or marketing? How does it seek to do this? Does it invest in research?
4. What do you see as the main impediment to research activities within your firm?
5. Does the government provide any incentive or support for private sector research?
6. To what extent does government science and technology policy support the efforts of private firms in the agricultural sector?

Transmission and Application of Knowledge

1. From where does your firm obtain new knowledge relevant to your business operation and information on the market conditions that affect your firm's competitive performance? Are you satisfied with the availability of such resources?
2. What is your working relationship with public agricultural research centers in terms of access to knowledge and information? What do you find to be the most useful aspects of these relationships?
3. What is your working relationship with local or national universities in terms of access to knowledge and information? What do you find to be the most useful aspects of these relationships?

4. What is your working relationship with input suppliers in terms of access to knowledge and information? What do you find to be the most useful aspects of these relationships?
5. How do you find the advisory expertise necessary to diagnose problems that lie beyond the technical capacities of your firm's staff? Which organizations do you find particularly helpful in this regard?
6. Does the government sponsor or facilitate agricultural expositions or other encounters among representatives of the agricultural value chain at which information can be shared and new ideas disseminated?
7. To what extent does your firm make use of information and communications technologies (e.g., computers, cellular telephones, Internet access)? For what purposes?
8. How does your firm organize itself to identify and learn from relevant experiences elsewhere in the country, the region, or the world?

Business and Enterprise

1. Has your firm experimented with new ideas or the use of new knowledge during the past year, for example, new crop variety or shipping techniques? How did it experiment?
2. Has your firm experimented with new forms of organizing activities or procedures during the past year, for example, new marketing arrangements or more efficient product processing? How did it experiment?
3. What do you see at present as the main impediments to improved productivity and/or sales by your firm?
4. Does your firm feel that current legal guarantees provided for contracts, intellectual property, and physical assets are adequate? If not, what changes would be beneficial?
5. Do you feel that existing standards and the enforcement of them for weights, quality, or environmental safety are consistent and fairly enforced?
6. Do government trade policies and procedures help or hinder the business prospects for your firm? Please explain.
7. How would you characterize the attitude of Ministry of Agriculture officials towards the challenge of promoting technological change in agriculture? Is it resistant, indifferent, or supportive? What is your evidence for this conclusion?

Innovation Finance, Outputs, and Markets

1. Do you feel that your country contains adequate mechanisms for the provision of venture capital? If not, what might be done to improve this situation?
2. Does the government offer any particular incentives for firms like yours to update or expand their use of technology (for example, loan guarantees, fertilizer subsidies, equipment subsidies, seed subsidies)?

3. Does government share the risks of new investments with firms in any way? How so?
4. Does government financing for agricultural R&D encourage institutional collaborations or partnerships of any kind? If so, please explain.
5. Does the tax system encourage or penalize experimentation and calculated risk taking by firms? How so?
6. Does your firm cooperate with other firms or organizations in financing the development and testing of new products, processes or technologies? If so, please explain how this occurs.
7. How does your firm find the resources it needs to test and evaluate new ideas? Can you give an example?
8. Does your firm invest in information technology and Internet access? Do you think this technology provides your firm with any particular competitive advantage?

Interactions and Linkages

1. Who are the main external actors that affect your firm's performance and influence its decision making? Public sector? Other firms? Collective or business associations?
2. For each identified actor, (i) characterize its main role from the perspective of your firm, (ii) assess its facilitating/impeding relationship to your business activities, and (iii) evaluate its performance in supporting technical change and innovation.
3. Do you work in partnership with any other firms or agencies? Which ones? What kinds of partnerships? Are these partnerships facilitated by any government incentives or public agencies?
4. What is the frequency of your firm's contacts with local government, national parliament, and the Ministry of Agriculture? Who initiates these contacts? What is their main purpose?
5. Do you participate in networks or maintain occasional communications with any firms or organizations outside the country? If so, what is the main purpose of these communications?
6. Does your firm participate in any business or collective associations? If so, what is the main motivation for doing so?
7. Has the government established any new public agencies within the past year or so whose mandate is to facilitate coordination and collaboration among various types of organizations/firms engaged in the agricultural sector? If so, why were they created and what is their purpose?

NOTE

1. These categories are used frequently by the International Food Policy Research Institute in its analyses (for example, Spielman and Birner 2008).

REFERENCE

Spielman, David J., and Rejina Birner. 2008. "How Innovative Is Your Agriculture? Using Innovation Indicators and Benchmarks to Strengthen National Agricultural Innovation Systems." ARD Discussion Paper 41, World Bank, Washington, DC.

INDEX

Boxes, figures, notes, and tables are denoted by *b*, *f*, *n*, and *t*, following the page numbers.

transport networks
  agricultural innovation and, 43
  as constraint, 180
  in Ghana, 83
  infrastructure for, 41–42, 51
  in Tanzania, 147–48
Trufoods, 104, 118, 119

Uchumi supermarket, 107*b*
UDAMACO (Umutara Dairy
    Marketing Cooperative Union,
    Rwanda), 31
UDSM. *See* University of Dar es Salaam
UFPEA. *See* Uganda Fish Processors
    and Exporters' Association
Uganda, 163–89
  agricultural innovation context, 16*t*,
      16–17
  agricultural policy context, 165–67
  banana subsector and value chain,
      164–65, 170*f*, 170–71, 175
  coordination within innovation
      system, 173–79
    business associations, 175–78
    educational institutions, 178
    farmers' associations, 175–78
    knowledge/technology generation
        and training institutions,
        177
    public-private interactions and
        partnerships, 178–79
    research institutions, 177–78
    universities, 177–78
  distribution networks, 42
  fish subsector and value chain, 167*f*,
      167–70
    coordination within innovation
        system, 28–31, 173–75
    intermediary domain and, 45–46
  high-value horticulture value chains
      in, 25–28
  income and price elasticities in, 25
  innovation drivers in, 184–85
  policy influence on innovation,
      179–84
  public investment in, 51–52
  public-private interactions in, 47
  recommendations, 185–88

research methodology, 191–98
vegetable subsector and value chain,
    25–28, 171–73, 174*b*, 175
Uganda Fish Processors and Exporters'
    Association (UFPEA), 29, 44,
    163–64, 165, 169–70, 174–75, 179
UgandaGap, 176, 179
Ultra Heat Treated (UHT) packaging,
    114*b*
Umuchi supermarket, 107*b*
Umutara Dairy Marketing Cooperative
    Union (UDAMACO,
    Rwanda), 31
Undugu SACCO Society, 112*b*
universities
  See also specific universities
  coordination within innovation
      system, 80–81, 152–53,
      177–78
  private sector employment of
      graduates, 48–49
University of Dar es Salaam (UDSM),
    43, 152, 153–54
University of Florida, 81

value chains
  See also specific value chains
  agribusiness and, 6–9
  agricultural innovation and, 20–37
    fish and livestock, 28–34
    high-value cash crops, 20–23
    high-value horticulture, 25–28
    staple foods, 23–25
  links and organization, 77*f*, 77–82,
      119–20, 154–55
  vertically integrated, 19, 56*n*3
vegetable subsector and value chain,
    25–28, 171–73, 175
vertically integrated value chains, 19,
    56*n*3, 109
veterinary services, 109–10, 127
village banks, 116, 124
Vision 2025 (Tanzania Development
    Vision, Tanzania), 137

Wad African Foods (Ghana), 75
WAMCO (West African Mills
    Company, Ghana), 73, 74*b*, 81